WORSHIP SERVICES
FOR
TEEN-AGERS

WORSHIP SERVICES

FOR

TEEN-AGERS

By
ALICE ANDERSON BAYS

264
B34wo

ABINGDON PRESS

NEW YORK · NASHVILLE

WORSHIP SERVICES FOR TEEN-AGERS

Library of Congress Catalog Card Number: 54-9195

The story "Narcissa and Marcus Whitman," in Service 17, is from *Ted Malone's Favorite Stories,* by Ted Malone. Copyright 1950 by Doubleday & Co., Inc.

The story "The Shepherd Who Was Not in the Field," in Service 24, is taken from *The Book of Three Festivals,* by Amy Morris Lillie, published by E. P. Dutton & Co., Inc., New York. Copyright, 1948, by Amy Morris Lillie.

SET UP, PRINTED, AND BOUND BY THE
PARTHENON PRESS, AT NASHVILLE,
TENNESSEE, UNITED STATES OF AMERICA

To
MARGARET AND CLAUDE MADISON
whose friendship and unselfish service
have brought happiness to many people

855658

FOREWORD

This is the seventh book in a series of planned worship services written that young people may be led into an enriching experience with God and discover his will for their lives. These services should be adapted to local situations and used to supplement the worship suggestions of the various denominational boards. They are prepared for the worship section of the Sunday-school program, for the Sunday evening and week-night sessions of youth groups, for camps and summer assemblies. They may be shortened by leaving out certain parts, or used as an anthology by lifting out a story, poem, or some other selection to use in another service. The leader may offer his own prayer instead of using prayers suggested, and other hymns and poems may be substituted.

This book has grown out of actual experiences with youth in local churches, camps, and summer conferences. The entire youth group has been considered; however, the first four series are planned for high school and older youth, while the last two series are for intermediates, or the junior high school group. Many of the stories and entire services may easily be adapted to the entire age group.

In each service the stories included shed light on choices young people make. The characters often are young people facing present-day problems and learning how to apply the teachings of Jesus to complex situations. It is hoped that these services will lead to a deeper experience with God, discover his will, and thus find a richer, fuller life.

I wish to acknowledge indebtedness and to express appreciation to all who helped in the preparation of this volume—to young people themselves and youth leaders of various churches for their helpful suggestions. Grateful acknowledgment is made to authors and publishers for the use of their material. Every effort has been made to trace ownership of all copyright material and to give proper credit.

ALICE ANDERSON BAYS

Oak Ridge, Tennessee

CONTENTS

SERIES THREE

MESSENGERS OF HOPE

SERIES FOUR

SPECIAL OCCASIONS

Part II. For Intermediates

SERIES FIVE

FINDING GOD

CONTENTS

SERIES SIX

SPECIAL OCCASIONS

Part I. For Seniors and Older Youth

SERIES ONE
COURAGEOUS LEADERS

SERVICE 1

ATTAINING THE BEST

PRELUDE: Hymn tune *"Vox dilecti"*

CALL TO WORSHIP:

> They that wait upon the Lord shall renew their strength;
> They shall mount up with wings as eagles;
> They shall run, and not be weary;
> And they shall walk, and not faint. . . .
> Wait on the Lord: be of good courage,
> And he shall strengthen thine heart:
> Wait, I say, on the Lord.[1]

SCRIPTURE:

Grace and peace be multipled unto you through the knowledge of God, and of Jesus our Lord, according as his divine power hath given unto us all things that pertain unto life and godliness, through the knowledge of him that hath called us to glory and virtue: whereby are given unto us exceeding great and precious promises; that by these ye might be partakers of the divine nature, having escaped the corruption that is in the world through lust. And besides this, giving all diligence, add to your faith virtue; and to virtue, knowledge; and to knowledge, temperance; and to temperance, patience; and to patience, godliness; and to godliness, brotherly kindness; and to brotherly kindness, charity. . . .

Finally, brethren, whatsoever things are true, whatsoever things are honest, whatsoever things are just, whatsoever things are pure, whatsoever things are lovely, whatsoever things are of good report; if there be any virtue, and if there be any praise, think on these things.[2]

PRAYER:

Grant, we beseech thee, Almighty God, that the words which we have heard this day with our outward ears may, through thy grace, be so grafted inwardly in our hearts that they may bring forth in us the fruit of good living, to the honor and praise of thy Name; through Jesus Christ our Lord. AMEN.

HYMN: "Go Forth to Life" or
"Now in the Days of Youth"

POEM:

Ah, my God,
What might I not have made of thy fair world,
Had I but loved thy highest creature here?
It was my duty to have loved the highest:
It surely was my profit had I known;
It would have been my pleasure had I seen.
We needs must love the highest when we see it.[3]

—ALFRED TENNYSON

LEADER:

We will hear the story of a man who accomplished a great deal because he loved the highest.

STORY:

THE UGLY DUCKLING OF BURSLEM

"I met a young man by the name of J. Wedgwood, who had planted a flower garden adjacent to his pottery. He also had his men wash their hands and faces and change their clothes after working in the clay. He is small and lame, but his soul is near to God."

So wrote John Wesley after a visit to Burslem, in the heart of England's pottery district. The potters were a rough set who did their best to discourage Mr. Wesley—a man not easily discouraged. But he was favorably impressed with at least one acquaintance—Wedgwood.

If adversity brings men closer to heaven, Josiah Wedgwood must have been very near the gates of pearl. Born in 1730, he was the seventh son and the thirteenth child of a poor, hard-working, unimaginative potter who was following the trade of his father and grandfather. What little formal education young Josiah received he got from a Mr. Blount who taught a day school at Newcastle-under-Lyme, about two miles from Burslem.

Even that scanty instruction came to an end when the boy's father died in 1739. By this time, child though he was, Josiah was working in the family shop, "throwing" clay on the potter's wheel. His chores became no easier under his eldest brother, Tom, who took their father's place as master of the shop.

Two years later smallpox, the scourge of the eighteenth century, struck in the humble Wedgwood home. For days the eleven-year-old Josiah hovered between life and death. Then the doctor's skill and his mother's prayers bore fruit. He passed the crisis. He would live.

But his face was a mass of repulsive scars, and his right leg would hardly bear his weight. How could he ever become a potter without a strong right leg to work the treadle that turned the wheel?

The sensitive boy shrank from the stares of the Burslemites. But there were many mouths to feed in the Wedgwood home, and at last Josiah limped to the shop. He became general flunky and errand boy for the workers. During his leisure moments he found a refuge in books and beauty, two scarce commodities in poverty-stricken Burslem.

At fourteen he was apprenticed to his brother Thomas. For five years Josiah was to receive instruction in the "mystery, trade, occupation and secrets of throwing and handling clay, and also burning it." He received no wages whatever, merely the means of subsistence.

Then his mother died. His world became bleaker still. But the darkest hour can grow no darker. And his life was about to brighten.

One day Richard Wedgwood, a second cousin, came by the pottery with his little daughter Sarah on a visit to the poor relations. The other members of the family were agog with excitement over the occasion, but Josiah resented his visit. That is, until eleven-year-old Sarah stopped and made his acquaintance in the friendliest manner possible. They were too young for love, these children, but something happened in the Burslem pottery that day. When Squire Wedgwood and his daughter rode away, they left a slightly dazed Josiah with the memory of a pair of dancing brown eyes in his heart, a copy of Thomson's *Seasons* in his hands, and a renewed interest in living throughout his being.

In spite of his lame leg, the boy set himself to an almost impossible task—that of working the treadle with his good leg. He failed. He tried again. He failed. He tried again and again and again. At last he became the most successful potter in the shop. But still he was not satisfied.

They said—his family and his neighbors—that he was given to

17

"flights of fancy." A manufacturing town of eighteenth-century England was a sorry spot. Hard labor from dawn to dark. Scanty wages. Ill-fed bodies. Relaxation only at the corner grogshop. Wasted lives that ended all too soon in the village churchyard. Life was a grim business, and a man must face it.

Yet here was this potter's son wasting his time with books. Oh, he was a good enough potter—one of the best—but he was a dreamer. He wasted time in making the shop tidy, in planting flowers outside, and even in experimenting with shapes and forms that honest Englishmen would never favor.

Seven years went by. After work hours Josiah was making a gift for Sarah, no longer a little girl. All the dreams of his beauty-loving young heart went into the workbox he was fashioning. By day he molded sturdy earthen pots and jugs, but at night he became his own master. And the result was an exquisite little porcelain box, lovelier than anything that had ever been made in Burslem.

With many doubts and fears he sent the box to Sarah. Did she like it? "Lovely," she wrote him. "Beautiful. I have never had anything quite so exquisite."

The reply was heady wine for the boy, who by now knew himself helplessly, hopelessly in love. He even experimented in the daytime with new glazes, different porcelains, and various tints before the eyes of the outraged Thomas.

Thomas told Josiah that such foolishness must cease. Josiah reminded his brother that the years of his apprenticeship were drawing to a close. When the verbal battle died down, Josiah collected the twenty pounds left him in his father's will and left the family shop forever.

Furthermore, he, an almost penniless potter, had the temerity to go to Squire Wedgwood's handsome home in nearby Cheshire and woo the lovely Sarah. The evidence says that the young woman was very willing, but her father looked down his nose at his impecunious young kinsman.

"Have you any money?" he asked Josiah.

"No, sir."

"My daughter has a dowry of ten thousand pounds. No man except one who matches it shall ever marry her."

Josiah went away heavyhearted. Sarah and the moon were equally beyond his reach.

But he was young. He was in love. And he believed in himself.

"I will get the ten thousand pounds!" he vowed between his teeth.
He went back to his potter's wheel and set to work. He worked as
he had never worked before while Sarah's letters and the memory of
her loving brown eyes spurred him on. He saw her only at long intervals; they exchanged letters three times a week.

Josiah worked, studied, and experimented. He created honest, sturdy
pieces which were also beautiful. He made the fortunate acquaintance
of a man named Thomas Bentley, who recognized Josiah for the
genius that he was. This new friend had been to Italy. He had seen
the excavations at Pompeii and Herculaneum. He was an ardent disciple of the classic revival that was sweeping Europe. He inspired Josiah
to greater heights in creating beautiful pottery.

The two set up a partnership. Bentley took some of their wares up to
London. The name of Wedgwood began to be known in fashionable
circles.

Four years passed. Josiah Wedgwood was twenty-five. He was
worth two thousand pounds, a fortune in the eyes of Burslem inhabitants. But Josiah had only begun. In five more years he had amassed
ten thousand pounds.

But the end was not yet. The eager young man asked Squire Wedgwood to inspect the pottery works and his books. His prospective
father-in-law informed him that wise investments had increased Sarah's
dowry from ten thousand to fifteen thousand pounds.

Josiah was inconsolable. But Bentley only laughed at his fears and
told him that he would match the dowry within a year. In scarcely
twelve months Josiah claimed his bride.

And a happy marriage it was. The two lovers had planned together
an ideal village which they would name Etruria for the ancient
Etrurians, who fashioned some of the earliest and loveliest pottery that
the world has ever known.

The dream came true. Josiah kept on working and planning with
Sarah, "who had a head for figures," beside him.

His medallions, which were really large-sized cameos, were sometimes
used as insets in boxes, cabinets, bookcases, pianofortes, tables, trays,
and tea caddies. Others were wall decorations. In the latter class is
the series "Heads of Illustrious Moderns." Some of the subjects are
King George III, Queen Charlotte, his wife, Isaac Newton, and William
Pitt.

Josiah and Sarah spent their fortune wisely. Their workmen were
better housed at home and in the factory than any in all England. They

were active in improving the roads of the period and in founding schools and chapels.

At beautiful Etruria Hall, Josiah and Sarah Wedgwood lived happy, useful, almost idyllic lives.

Josiah never gave up. He never compromised. He held high his ideals. He loved his fellow men. He gave his best to his generation, and lovers of beauty still revere his name.

And so the "Ugly Duckling of Burslem" became at last the admired and loved "Swan of England." [4]

POEM:

> Keep me from bitterness. It is so easy
> To nurse sharp bitter thoughts each dull dark hour.
> Against self-pity, Man of sorrows, defend me,
> With thy deep sweetness and thy gentle power.
> And out of all this hurt of pain and heartbreak
> Help me to harvest a new sympathy
> For suffering human kind, a wiser pity
> For those who lift a heavier cross with thee.
>
> —VIOLET ALLEYN STOREY

PRAYER:

O God, whom to know is life eternal, incline our hearts to do thy will; open our eyes to see thee in the beauty which thou hast created. We are grateful for the beauty which thou hast provided for the enrichment of our lives. We thank thee for the inspiration coming from gifted persons such as Josiah Wedgwood. Grant us the same strength and courage which sustained him and gave him power to overcome handicaps, face obstacles fearlessly, and see clearly the course he should follow. Help us to so live and labor that we may be conscious of thy presence at all times and have the stamp of thy approval upon our lives. In Jesus' name, we pray. AMEN.

HYMN: "Courage, Brother! Do not Stumble" or
"Father in Heaven, Who Lovest All"

BENEDICTION:

May the blessing of God our Father be with you and abide with you now and evermore. AMEN.

SERVICE 2

BRINGING LIGHT

PRELUDE: Hymn tune "Sicilian Mariners' Hymn"

CALL TO WORSHIP:
Serve the Lord with gladness. . . .
Enter into his gates with thanksgiving, and into his courts with
    praise. . . .
O come, let us worship and bow down:
Let us kneel before the Lord our Maker.
He is our God; and we are the people of his pasture, and the sheep of
    his hand.[1]

HYMN: "How Beauteous Were the Marks Divine" or
        "O Son of Man, Thou Madest Known"

INVOCATION:
    O God, by whom the meek are guided in judgment, and light riseth
up in darkness for the godly, grant us, in all doubts and uncertainties,
the grace to ask what thou wouldst have us to do, that the spirit of
wisdom may save us from all false choices, and that in thy light we
may see light and in thy straight path may not stumble; through Jesus
Christ our Lord. AMEN.

SCRIPTURE:
    The Lord is my strength and my shield; my heart trusteth in him,
and I am helped:
    Therefore my heart greatly rejoiceth; and with my song will I praise
him.
    The Lord is their strength, and he is the saving strength of his
anointed.
    Save thy people, and bless thine inheritance: feed them also, and
lift them up for ever. . . .

Thy mercy, O Lord, is in the heavens; and thy faithfulness reacheth unto the clouds.

Thy righteousness is like the great mountains; thy judgments are a great deep: O Lord, thou preservest man and beast.

How excellent is thy lovingkindness, O God! therefore the children of men put their trust under the shadow of thy wings.

They shall be abundantly satisfied with the goodness of thy house; and thou shalt make them drink of the river of thy pleasures.

For with thee is the fountain of life: in thy light shall we see light.

O continue thy lovingkindness unto them that know thee; and thy righteousness to the upright in heart.[2]

POEM:

I count this thing to be grandly true,
That a noble deed is a step toward God,
Lifting the soul from the common sod
To a purer air and a broader view.

We rise by things that are 'neath our feet;
By what we have mastered of good and gain,
By the pride deposed and the passion slain,
And the vanquished ills that we hourly meet.

We hope, we aspire, we resolve, we trust,
When the morning calls us to life and light;
But our hearts grow weary, and ere the night,
Our lives are trailing the sordid dust.

. . . .

Heaven is not reached at a single bound:
But we build the ladder by which we rise
From the lowly earth to the vaulted skies,
And we mount to its summit round by round.[3]
—JOSIAH GILBERT HOLLAND

LEADER:

We will hear the story of one who used a handicap as a stepping-stone to a great achievement.

STORY:

NILS GUSTAF DALÉN

Today when our ships and airplanes are traveling the wide world over, we shall do well to remember gratefully the great Swedish inventor, Nils Gustaf Dalén, who has made both sea lanes and airways safer for all who use them. Known as the Aga Lamp, Dalén's supreme invention shines on the wildest coasts, in the remotest places, even on high mountain peaks.

Dalén was born on a little farm in southern Sweden on November 30, 1869, and he began to work hard very early in life. But he did not like the many chores that fell to his lot, and most of all he hated to get up on a cold winter morning. His first invention was a "bean-sheller," and for this he used an old threshing machine, powered with a still more ancient spinning wheel. It worked with treadles, and in some way known only to himself he managed to persuade his small brother that pumping treadles was the best kind of fun.

Next he decided to make early winter mornings a little less painful. For his fantastic "sleep-prolonger" Dalén used an old wall clock, a spool, an oil lamp, a match, a bewildering array of cords and levers. It probably looked like nothing else on earth but it actually worked. At a set time the spool rubbed the match, the cords and levers swung the match over the oil lamp wick and lighted it. Over that was swung a coffee pot. Within fifteen minutes the clock started a hammer beating against an old iron plate. And by that time the coffee was hot.

His parents were probably much amused at the quaint inventions of their young son who so hated getting up in the morning, but little did they dream to what a wonderful use he would one day put his inventive genius.

The crowning work of Dalén's busy and heroic life was his acetyl lamp or Aga Lamp—the world's most perfect beacon, needing neither electricity nor clockwork. Automatically it sends out its brilliant, life-saving beam when darkness falls. It is probably the world's simplest and most efficient lifesaving light.

When Dalén first brought out his acetyl lamp, even Thomas Edison said it would not work, and the German Patent Office snorted that it was "impossible." But Dalén was made of stern stuff and he went on working until he was positive his acetyl lamp would work. In May, 1905, he found his own faith justified for the lamp worked perfectly—to his own joy and the pride of his young wife who had stood loyally by him during all his struggles.

The core of this invention is the sun valve that contracts in darkness, letting acetylene gas pass to the burner, expanding when daylight comes and shutting off the flow of gas. An automatic device controls the length of the flash. Later an incandescent gas mantle was added to brighten the beam. A remarkable mechanism actually replaces a burnt out mantle with a new one and the lamp is supplied with mantles for a year. The Aga Lamp is a great deal more magical than Aladdin's famous lamp.

This remarkable beacon will run perfectly for a year without any human help. It has saved Sweden an immense amount of money in guarding her own rugged coast that used to need a whole string of lighthouses. In London the lamp has been used in traffic signals and many railroads have adopted it. Our own Lighthouse Service today is using five thousand Aga Lamps. And the lamp also shines from the great towers that guard the Panama and Suez canals. It is used in Austria, South America, and many other faraway places. It is on lighthouses, lightships, and buoys in all the waters of the world.

Another of Dalén's benevolent inventions is a stove that maintains cooking heat for twenty-four hours with only eight pounds of coal. It has proved a boon and a blessing to many who had neither gas nor electricity. The United States Coast Guard has installed large numbers of these stoves in their remote stations, and many a gallant coastguardsman has come in cold and hungry to find a good hot meal awaiting him, thanks to this Dalén stove.

In 1912 Dalén won the Nobel Prize for physics for his inventive genius and his inestimable service to humanity. A year later, during an experiment in which he was trying to render this hottest of all the gases safe to handle, he was blinded. In spite of the pain he was suffering his first thought was for the men who had been working with him when the terrific explosion happened. By some strange coincidence all of them were only very slightly injured.

Dalén never regained his sight. An ordinary man must surely have died of those terrible burns, but his will to live saved him and he worked on, conducting the business that had expanded from a group of fifteen to a great company with hundreds of employees and many branch offices. He carried on at his office with an army of telephones. He traveled abroad and went on even with his designing. So amazing was his memory and power of concentration that his assistants had only to describe a drawing and he would immediately discover a weak point or think of some necessary addition.

Those who met him for the first time wearing those dark glasses never dreamed that this dapper, kindly man with the gay boutonniere was blind. Dalén never let his loss of vision depress him, but remained for the rest of his life a tireless, enthusiastic worker who still loved life even if he could no longer see it. He became a good statesman, able often to help his government.

On December 9, 1937, Nils Gustaf Dalén died in his own beloved city of Stockholm, whose streets were lit at night with his own lamps. Every ship, as it made its way safely into Sweden's harbor on that cold winter morning, reduced speed and lowered its flag in honor of the man who had proved himself the friend of all those who "go down to the sea in ships." [4]

POEM:

Walk in the light! and thou shalt find
  Thy heart made truly his,
Who dwells in cloudless light enshrined,
  In whom no darkness is.

. . . .

Walk in the light! and thine shall be
  A path, though thorny, bright:
For God, by grace, shall dwell in thee,
  And God himself is light.

—BERNARD BARTON

PRAYER:

Our Father, we thank thee for men like Dalén, who in spite of handicaps have made great contributions to mankind. Help us also to use handicaps, not as a crutch upon which to lean, but as an incentive to greater achievement. We thank thee for inventors, scientists, and others who with their skill have made modern conveniences available for use. We are grateful that they put self into the background and worked tirelessly to make this world a better place in which to live. Grant that their example may be an inspiration to us to use whatever skill or ability we may have to render service to others. As we have benefited from their labors, may we feel a responsibility for making our own contribution according to our ability. In Jesus' name we pray. AMEN.

HYMN: "O Young and Fearless Prophet" or
      "O Jesus, Master, When Today"

BENEDICTION:

May the peace of God which passeth all understanding be with you always. AMEN.

SERVICE 3

GIVING OPPORTUNITIES

Prelude: Hymn tune "Vesper Hymn"

Call to Worship:
> The Lord is nigh unto all them that call upon him,
> To all that call upon him in truth.
> He will fulfil the desire of them that fear him:
> He also will hear their cry, and will save them.[1]

Hymn: "Shepherd of Tender Youth" or
> "Come, My Soul, Thou Must Be Waking"

Scripture:
My son, if thou wilt receive my words, and hide my commandments with thee; so that thou incline thine ear unto wisdom, and apply thine heart to understanding; yea, if thou criest after knowledge, and liftest up thy voice for understanding; if thou seekest her as silver, and searchest for her as for hid treasures; then shalt thou understand the fear of the Lord, and find the knowledge of God. For the Lord giveth wisdom: out of his mouth cometh knowledge and understanding. He layeth up sound wisdom for the righteous: he is a buckler to them that walk uprightly. He keepeth the paths of judgment, and preserveth the way of his saints. Then shalt thou understand righteousness, and judgment, and equity; yea, every good path. . . .

Happy is the man that findeth wisdom, and the man that getteth understanding. For the merchandise of it is better than the merchandise of silver, and the gain thereof than fine gold.[2]

Prayer-Poem:
> Lord Christ, who came from God to make men free,
> Come Thou into my heart, lift even me.

26

Lord Christ, our Saviour in this world of strife,
Help me to do Thy will: purge Thou my life.

Lord Christ, our Beacon in the darkest night,
Guide Thou my steps, my Leader and my Light.

Lord Christ, our Comrade of the daily task,
Walk with me in the way: no more I ask.[3]

—GEORGIA HARKNESS

HYMN: "Let Us With a Gladsome Mind" or
"Awake, My Soul, Stretch Every Nerve"

LEADER:

We will hear the story of Sophie Wright's effort to provide educational opportunities to many who had for various reasons missed an education.

STORY:

SOPHIE WRIGHT OF NEW ORLEANS

For every fifty persons who have heard about Andrew Jackson's smashing victory at New Orleans, there probably are not five who know about Sophie Wright's triumph in the same city.

Even her most loyal friends would have been forced to admit that Sophie Wright never looked like a heroine. She was a struggling schoolteacher, humble and obscure. A cripple from childhood, she was small in both size and strength. The only big thing about her was her heart.

One night over seventy years ago there came a knock at the small private school for girls which Sophie Wright conducted in New Orleans. When she answered, she found a stalwart young fellow at the door. He had been connected with a circus, but it had just broken up in the city.

Thrown on his own, the youth had to find work in a hurry. Now at last he realized his mistake in never bothering about an education.

The frail-looking young woman listened sympathetically as this boy poured out his story. He wound up with this plea: Would she be willing to teach him to read and write?

Without a moment's hesitation Sophie said, "Yes."

It may sound incredible, but in that same instant the first American night school was born.

Sophie Wright began it all alone. No school board voted her a single dollar. Her first pupil was too poor to pay for even his books. Yet Sophie was happy in the undertaking. After a long day of teaching the daughters of New Orleans' best families, she stayed till late in the evening to make the circus athlete perfect in his three R's.

There seems to be a law of nature that when you have done one good deed you are bound to do more. That happened in Sophie's case.

From her first pupil other New Orleans boys heard about the "night school," and one by one they asked if they might attend. Soon they were coming in a steady stream, all hopeful seekers after an education. And Sophie welcomed every one.

If the same experiment had been carried out in other cities, it might not have worked. This teacher of a "select school for girls" certainly had courage. One almost can see the disdain with which proud fathers in some communities would have snatched their daughters away from a teacher who taught the city's riffraff by night.

Fortunately New Orleans was not like that. The spirit of snobbery never showed itself. Sophie's "select school," the Home Institute, had never been more prosperous. It was crowded with well-to-do young misses to whom their beloved teacher would be a lifelong inspiration.

At night Sophie taught an entirely different crowd. They came in never-ending procession—grown men to learn their ABC's, boys to improve their arithmetic, and young men to take up mechanical drawing. Frail, crippled, with no rich patrons, with not a cent of public money, Sophie Wright enrolled all who came, turning nobody away.

The financial outlay was no easy load. To maintain the night school Sophie was forced to borrow money at 8 per cent compound interest. She even bought a larger building. Everything seemed to be going fine, the day school had a record enrollment, and with the profits she was able to buy needed books and maps for her "boys."

Then overnight yellow fever invaded New Orleans. Swiftly Sophie turned the schoolhouse into a dispensary, from which went out a continuous flow of medicine, linen, food, and clothes to victims. Supervising a large staff of helpers, the teacher stayed on duty till the most wearying hours in that time of horror.

When the epidemic was over and Sophie took stock, she saw she was ruined. She had not enough money left to reopen either the Home Institute or the night school. But New Orleans had not forgotten. Unsolicited, a leading banker came forward to take over her mortgage and lend her $10,000. Two other businessmen guaranteed her $2,000 a year income. They were only three in a crowd, for the whole city wanted to help.

Sophie's "come back" was a dazzling triumph. Before the epidemic she never had more than three hundred in the night school, but now the enrollment was over a thousand.

Also, after the epidemic she not only had plenty of room, but she was able to furnish up-to-date texts, new desks, and the latest maps.

In the teaching staff of forty, Sophie had expert European linguists who could help immigrant pupils find their bearings. There never had been so many young people eager for an education. They came from every occupation imaginable—clerks, machinists, typesetters, newsboys, even bootblacks.

Sophie Wright was never asked to pay back that $10,000. There came a day which many besides herself never forgot. At a special ceremony where she was guest of the city, a check for the full amount, raised by popular subscription, was placed in her hands. Then as a climax the mayor presented her with a huge loving cup—the tribute of all New Orleans to its "Best Citizen."

Doubtless in that moment Sophie must have found it hard to believe that all this could have happened to the little girl who, born in 1866, in the South's darkest hour, and crippled by a fall in infancy, had been forced to spend six years of her childhood hopelessly strapped in a chair. It did not seem possible for one whose outlook had once been so cheerless. Yet it had all come to pass.

New Orleans has never forgotten Sophie Wright. When age forced her at last to hand over her great enterprise to the city, there were over fifteen hundred pupils in the night school.

It was logical that not long ago when a new girls' high school was built, it took no time at all to decide upon its name. There, blazoned high, bringing back a shining memory to a new generation of pupils, the name of Sophie Wright is permanently inscribed.[4]

POEM:

> A builder builded a temple,
> He wrought it with grace and skill;
> Pillars and groins and arches
> All fashioned to work his will.
> Men said, as they saw its beauty,
> "It shall never know decay;

Great is thy skill, O Builder!
Thy fame shall endure for aye."

A teacher builded a temple
With loving and infinite care,
Planning each arch with patience,
Laying each stone with prayer.
None praised her unceasing efforts,
None knew of her wondrous plan,
For the temple the teacher builded
Was unseen by the eyes of man.

Gone is the builder's temple,
Crumpled into the dust;
Low lies each stately pillar,
Food for consuming rust.
But the temple the teacher builded
Will last while the ages roll,
For that beautiful unseen temple
Was a child's immortal soul.

—AUTHOR UNKNOWN

PRAYER:

Thou, O God, the Father of us all, art concerned that we come to our best development. We are grateful that we live in a country where it is possible for everyone to have an education. We thank thee for the vision, courage, and zeal of such educators as Sophie Wright, who made possible an education for the underprivileged. For the unselfish service of godly parents and teachers, for their efforts to open up opportunities for our education, we are truly grateful. Help us to value this heritage and to strive to pass it on to others. Reveal thy purposes to us and grant that we may fulfill thy hopes for us; through Jesus Christ our Lord. AMEN.

HYMN: "Teach Me, My God and King" or
       "Dear Master, in Whose Life I See"

BENEDICTION:

Now unto him who is able to lead you into the way of love and service, be glory and honor, now and evermore. AMEN.

SERVICE 4

GOD'S WORKMAN

PRELUDE: Hymn tune "Kremser"

CALL TO WORSHIP:

> Holy Spirit, Truth divine,
> Dawn upon this soul of mine;
> Word of God, and inward Light,
> Wake my spirit, clear my sight.
>
> Holy Spirit, Love divine,
> Glow within this heart of mine;
> Kindle every high desire;
> Perish self in thy pure fire.
> —SAMUEL LONGFELLOW

HYMN: "O for a Thousand Tongues to Sing" or
"Ye Servants of God"

SCRIPTURE:

Be strong and of a good courage, fear not, nor be afraid of them: for the Lord thy God, he it is that doth go with thee; he will not fail thee, nor forsake thee. . . .

The Lord is my strength and my shield. . . .

Watch ye, stand fast in the faith, quit you like men, be strong. . . .

Sing unto the Lord; for he hath done excellent things: this is known in all the earth.

Cry out and shout, thou inhabitant of Zion: for great is the Holy One of Israel in the midst of thee. . . .

Behold, a King shall reign in righteousness, and princes shall rule in judgment. . . .

Blessed be the Lord God of Israel; for he hath visited and redeemed his people. . . .

31

To give light to them that sit in darkness and in the shadow of death, to guide our feet into the way of peace.[1]

PRAYER:

Thou madest light for our comfort and broughtest forth darkness out of thy treasures to overshadow the earth, that the living creatures of it might take their rest. Fire and hail, snow and vapor, wind and storm, fulfill thy word and manifest thy glory. Suffer not the sons of men to be silent, but let the noblest work of thy creation pay thee the noblest sacrifice of praise.[2] AMEN.

LEADER:

When Augustine Birrell visited Cornwall he said to a miner: "You seem a very temperate people here. How did it happen?" The miner replied: "There came a man amongst us, and his name was John Wesley."

Birrell says of him: "No man lived nearer the center than John Wesley. . . . You cannot cut him out of our national life. No single figure influenced so many minds, no single voice touched so many hearts. No other man did such a life's work for England."[3]

We will hear the story of the man who by calling the people back to God saved England from a bloody revolution.

STORY:

HE CARRIED A WORLD OF HOPE IN HIS SADDLEBAGS

On June 17, 1953, fourteen million persons celebrated the 250th anniversary of the birth of John Wesley. This circuit rider spent fifty-two years in the saddle, sloughing through thousands of miles of muck and mire to preach from tree stumps in open fields, from slag piles near mouths of mines, from boxes on street corners. Tuberculosis threatened him, mobs stoned him, churchmen denounced him, and his own sensitive nature cringed from the roughness of the life he led. But with faith aflame he rode on to accomplish his purposes.

The historian Lecky says that the Methodist revival saved England from bloody revolution, that Wesley influenced practical Christianity more than any other man since the sixteenth century. Be that as it may, his shadow has lengthened into one of the largest Protestant denominations; scores of hospitals, schools, colleges, churches, and missions today bear the name that England once scorned.

There was little reason to suppose, during his early life, that his name would be widely known at all. At ten John Wesley was sent

32

from Epworth, where he was born in 1703, to the famous Charterhouse school in London. He mastered Greek and Hebrew, and at seventeen he entered Oxford. There he remained for most of fifteen years as student and teacher. In 1728 he was ordained a priest of the Church of England.

Serious-minded individuals like John and his brother Charles found themselves out of step with other students of the day. They with a small group banded themselves together to seek refuge in religion and asceticism. They gave all but their barest necessities to the needy, visited the sick and the imprisoned, and spent long hours in prayer.

When missionaries were called to go to America to serve the colonists in Georgia, John Wesley responded enthusiastically. But life on the rough frontier did not live up to his exalted expectations, and presently he returned to England, frustrated and somewhat embittered.

Yet one bright thing stood out in Wesley's memory—association with the Moravians, people of tranquil faith, whom he had seen aboard ship. In a storm that threatened disaster they alone were calm. "Why be disturbed by the waves and the wind?" they had said, "God will take care of us all." That was the sort of peace he craved—and could not find.

One night in May, 1738 the despairing clergyman made his way to a little room in London where the Moravians gathered for prayer. Someone was reading from the works of Luther about the change God works in the human heart through Christ. Suddenly something came alive in the soul of Wesley. "I felt my heart strangely warmed," he later wrote. It was to set off his career.

George Whitfield, who was preaching to multitudes with the fire of a crusader, invited Wesley to share his "ministry of the open air." Wesley shrank from it. Preach outdoors? He was aghast. Yet there was something about the "untouchable" miners of Kingswood that stirred him. They considered themselves outcasts—men completely without religion, desperate men who cursed life itself. Wesley took the plunge.

It was a motley crew of grimy-faced men who crowded about the little man, only five feet four, but he seemed to tower above them. Something in that voice gripped his listeners. With deadly earnestness Wesley drove deep into their hearts his message: "You are the sons of God, the heirs of eternal life. Lift up your heads as free men, and let your hearts overflow with joy." He pleaded with them to forsake their erring ways, he spoke of "forgiveness," "redemption," and "hope," and pointed to the road of glory ahead. He so pictured the love of God for lost men that they were transfixed as by a heavenly Presence. For weeks the crusader preached with all the flame within him. He told an inquirer: "The scene is already changed. Kingswood is no more filled with drunkenness and uncleanness, with fights and bitterness. Peace and love are there."

To expand his work Wesley came to London, where he ignored the fine points of theology and stressed a rigid, "methodical" routine of prayer and good works. Regular societies were formed to carry on his work, with "preaching houses" manned by "Methodist" lay preachers. An abandoned cannon factory was turned into a tabernacle, and the first service drew five thousand people.

When spiritually starved people of other cities besought Wesley, he began his incredible career as a parson of the saddlebags. He set for himself a strict regimen: he rose daily at four o'clock, preached his first sermon at five, and was on the road by six. He often made sixty to seventy miles a day and usually preached at least three times. And he demanded as much Spartan labor of his preachers as he did of himself. Any man who would not gladly get up at four in the morning and be ready at five with a fresh sermon was no worker of his.

Wesley's ruthless denunciation of the evils of the day aroused fierce hostility. Slowly, irresistibly, sympathizers were won to his crusade for decency, honesty, and goodness. Though slavery was protected by the law, he did not hesitate to fight it. He also fought the horrible prison system, exposing conditions of filth, starvation, and degradation. He visited some of the vilest of the jails to minister to the unfortunates. In 1761 he was able to say of Newgate Prison that it had changed from "filth, stench and wickedness" to a place that was "clean and sweet," where prisoners were paid for their work, where free medical care was given the sick. The key to the improvement lay in the fact that the keeper of the prison was a convert of Wesley's.

The rough-and-tumble world in which John Wesley lived never compromised his fierce devotion to learning. In the saddle he read the classics or made shorthand notes for his daily journal. He mastered six languages and studied their best literature. His writings were prodigious in range as well as volume. He compiled a *Christian Library,* comprising a wide range of devotional literature culled from the history of the Christian church.

His best-seller was a primitive "medical" booklet called *An Easy and Natural Method of Curing Most Diseases.* It stressed plain food, fresh

34

air, abundant exercise, and a contented spirit. Its sale netted Wesley $150,000, which he plowed back into publishing the book for free distribution. In all, some four hundred publications flowed from Wesley's pen. Says the *Encyclopaedia Britannica:* "No man in the 18th century did so much to create a taste for good reading and to supply it with books at the lowest prices."

John Wesley was the founder of England's first free medical dispensary. He set up spinning and knitting shops to give employment to the poor, and he established a loan fund to help finance new business enterprises and to give relief to "poor, sick, friendless strangers." He gave away $200,000—royalties from his books—but limited himself to $150 a year for personal expenses.

Wesley lived to be eighty-eight. Even to his last he was preaching and writing daily. On his deathbed he called out: "Where is my sermon on the love of God? Take it and spread it abroad. Give it to everyone."

His burial was in keeping with his convictions about service to others. His instructions were followed to the letter—burial in nothing more costly than wool; whatever remained in his dresser and pockets to be given to the poor. In keeping with his modesty, Wesley was borne by his own orders to his grave in secret—he was buried one March morning in 1791 before the day dawned, with flickering torches affording the only light.[4] 855658

POEM:

> Arise, O church of God, arise,
>   And face the urgent hour;
> Dare strenuous life in holy strife
>   With vision, courage, power;
> Oppose the wrong with righteousness,
>   With eagerness and good;
> And build through grace for every race
>   Eternal brotherhood.
>
> Arise, O church of God, arise
>   And serve the human need;
> Make truth your light and love your might,
>   And prove them by your deed;
> Go forth and preach the saving word
>   Where toiling masses plod;

For he has willed, go forth and build
The Kingdom of our God.
—CHAUNCEY R. PIETY [5]

PRAYER:

Almighty and most merciful Father, in whom we live, move, and have our being; to whose tender compassion we owe our safety the day that is past, together with all the comforts of this life and the hopes of that which is to come; we praise thee, O Lord. We bow ourselves before thee, acknowledging we have nothing but what we receive from thee. Unto thee do we give thanks, O God, who daily pourest thy benefits upon us. . . .

We implore thy tender mercies in the forgiveness of all our sins whereby we have offended either in thought, word, or deed. We desire to be truly sorry for all our misdoings and utterly to renounce whatsoever is contrary to thy will. . . .

Gracious Father, keep us, we pray thee, this day in thy fear and favor, and teach us in all our thoughts, words, and works to live to thy glory. If thou guide us not, we go astray; if thou uphold us not, we fall. Let thy good providence be our defense and thy good Spirit our guide and counselor, and supporter in all our ways. And grant that we may do always what is acceptable in thy sight, through Jesus Christ our Lord. AMEN. [6]

HYMN: "O for a Heart to Praise my God" or
"O Thou Who Camest from Above"

BENEDICTION:

Dismiss us with thy blessing. AMEN.

SERVICE 5

A WOMAN PIONEERS IN AVIATION

PRELUDE: "O Rest in the Lord" from *Elijah* by Mendelssohn

CALL TO WORSHIP:

> Give thanks, O heart, for the high souls
> That point us to the deathless goals—
> For all the courage of their cry
> That echoes down from sky to sky;
> Thanksgiving for the armed seers,
> And heroes call to immortal years—
> Souls that have built our faith in man
> And lit the ages as they ran.
>
> —AUTHOR UNKNOWN

HYMN: "Fight the Good Fight" or
"Be Strong!"

SCRIPTURE:

Have I not commanded thee? Be strong and of a good courage; be not afraid, neither be thou dismayed: for the Lord thy God is with thee withersoever thou goest. . . .

Wait on the Lord: be of good courage, and he shall strengthen thine heart: wait, I say, on the Lord. . . .

And from thence, when the brethren heard of us, they came to meet us as far as Appii Forum, and the Three Taverns: whom when Paul saw, he thanked God, and took courage. . . . And Paul dwelt two whole years in his own hired house, and received all that came in unto him, preaching the kingdom of God, and teaching those things which concern the Lord Jesus Christ, with all confidence, no man forbidding. . . .

Trust ye in the Lord for ever: for in the Lord Jehovah is everlasting strength.[1]

PRAYER:

Our Heavenly Father, we adore thee, whose name is love, whose nature is compassion, whose presence is joy, whose word is truth, whose spirit is goodness, whose holiness is beauty, whose will is peace, whose service is perfect freedom, and in knowledge of whom standeth our eternal life. AMEN.

LEADER:

We will hear the story of a courageous woman who pioneered in the field of aviation.

STORY:

AMELIA EARHART

Even as a small girl Amelia Earhart demonstrated originality and independence of spirit. She was never afraid to do a thing just because it was not done by other little girls. Once she and her sister shocked the neighborhood by appearing for play in their gym suits. They felt happy and free in this attire and actually pitied the other girls who had to play demurely in their pretty ruffled dresses. The fact that they themselves were a shocking sight to their decorous friends bothered them not at all.

Another practice of Amelia's which shocked her friends probably saved her life. She loved to lie flat on her stomach on her sled when she went coasting. One day on her way down a steep hill she saw a junkman's wagon move into her path. She was traveling too fast to stop, and the hill was too icy for her to change her course. So she clung tight to her sled and prepared for a crash. By some miracle she shot under the horse between his front and hind feet and never got a scratch. Had she been sitting up like a prim little lady was supposed to do, she probably would have been killed.

Amelia's father was a railroad man and the family moved often. Amelia was born in Atchison, Kansas, but she attended school in many places. She graduated from high school in Hyde Park, Chicago, in 1915. She was considered a quiet, unassuming student and at that time no one would predict an unusual career for her. She attended Columbia University for a time, and here again she often did things which shocked and surprised her friends. Once she climbed into the lap of a statue in front of the library to study. Another time she climbed on top of the library building for an unobstructed view of an eclipse of the sun. It was her interest in what she was doing and her lack of inhibition which prompted these unusual actions rather than any desire on her part to be different. What people might think just failed to impress her.

Her interest in aviation began when a friend invited her to visit a flying field near Philadelphia. The airplanes were army training ones. Her challenge came when the propellers of a large biplane spattered snow in her face as it took off. Then and there she decided that some day she would "ride one of those things." Since no civilian was allowed to ride in army planes, she hung around the field watching and learning all she could. Already she was determined to fly. Then the family moved to California. As if fate had a hand in this move, their home was located near an airfield. Amelia attended an airmeet with her father, and on that day she told him of her desire to fly. He knew from the tone of her voice that she meant what she said. He was frightened. In his mind flying was a dangerous thing. In order to discourage her he sent her up on a trial flight but he refused to accompany her. By previous arrangement she was supposed to get a good stout view of the hazards of flying. She was required to sit in the rear cockpit with a copilot who had instructions to prevent her from interfering with the controls, by force if necessary, when she became panicky. They took her up some five thousand feet, sailed and dipped, and kept up the "ordeal" for some time. When they finally landed, her father was to learn that Amelia was thrilled rather than dismayed. Now there was no doubt in her mind. She would be a pilot.

Since she suspected that a man would assume a superior air toward her and arouse her anger, she secured a woman instructor at first. Later she studied under men without reservation. She insisted on stunt flying early in her career, not because she wanted to show off, but because she believed that the best way to learn complete mastery of her airplane. She bought her first one on credit, and in order to meet the payments she worked as a telephone operator, a commercial photographer, and even a truck driver. Finally her mother paid off the balance just to keep Amelia at home.

Amelia loved to fly alone and she loved to try out her plane. On one of these "trying out sprees" she accidentally broke the women's altitude record. Already she was on her way toward her future record-breaking career. In order to finance her work in aviation she took up social work in Boston as a part-time job. She did well in her work and enjoyed it, but destiny had other things in store for her. One day while on duty a man telephoned her and asked if she would be interested in a flying job which involved danger. Amelia did not fear the danger connected with flying, but she distrusted the man who called her. She asked for references and was surprised to learn upon checking that they were good. Finally she arranged for an interview. The question asked her was, "Would you like to fly the Atlantic?"

Naturally Amelia's answer was in the affirmative. With a copilot and a mechanic she left New York for Halifax, Nova Scotia, and flew to Tuspassy, Laborador, to wait for favorable weather. On June 17, 1927, they headed out over the Atlantic. They landed on the western coast of Wales in twenty hours and forty minutes. For two weeks they were showered with honors in London. When they returned to the United States, they were given a great welcome. Incidentally, the man who had called Amelia about this flight was George Palmer Putnam, whom she later married.

Back home again Amelia began thinking about a solo flight. She wrote a book about her trip, calling it *20 Hours, 40 Minutes*. She toured the country in a new plane she had bought in England and finally flew to California for the National Air Races. This trip proved to be the first solo flight ever made by a woman.

Even after her marriage, Amelia remained active in aviation— lecturing, acting as air editor of a magazine, and serving as publicity agent for one of the passenger air lines. She also experimented with autogiroes and wrote another book entitled *The Fun of It*. Although her transatlantic flight had brought her fame and fortune, she still wanted to fly it alone.

She engaged an experienced aviator to groom her for this flight. She spent months in preparation. When she felt she was ready, she decided to go to Harbor Grace, Newfoundland, for her takeoff. It was at seven o'clock in the evening on May 20, 1932, that she set out on this trip alone. She expected to fly mostly by instruments. At first all went well and she, no doubt, felt that sense of freedom she had loved all her life as she flew far above the waters in an open sky. And then her altimeter ceased to register. She had no way of telling how high she was except by sight, and she knew if she hit fog, disaster might follow. All night the sky remained clear, but at daylight she found herself between two layers of clouds. She could no longer see the water below. When the sun came up, the reflection on the clouds was so great it almost blinded her. She dropped lower to try to see ships and finally located a small fishing boat. By blinking her lights, she attracted the attention of the crew. They were able to communicate with her sufficiently for her to learn that she was approaching the coast of Ireland.

But the relief which came with getting her bearings was short-lived. Her engine began to falter because of a defective manifold and her reserve gas tank began to leak. She knew then she could not stay aloft long enough to get to England. She headed for the coast of Ireland and managed to land without mishap in a pasture. Two Irish peasant women were near, but they were too amazed to give her much information. She finally obtained help and went on to London, where she was received with much more acclaim than on her initial flight.

She returned home perhaps one of the greatest heroines of all time. But she did not retire to rest on her laurels. Later she flew from Hawaii to Oakland, California, being not only the first woman but the first person to make this flight over the longer and more hazardous route. This flight was one and one-half times the distance of her Atlantic flight and the course was filled with danger. The flight was made in 1935, and during the next two years she received much recognition for her work. She was the first woman to receive the Distinguished Flying Cross and the gold medal of the National Geographic Society. But her pioneer spirit would not let her retire. In 1937 she attempted a flight around the world, alone except for a navigator. All was going well until they left New Guinea for a small island in the Pacific on what was to be the last lap of the journey. They were lost somewhere in the Pacific and never heard from again.

During the days of her popularity Amelia Earhart was often mistaken for a society woman whose picture was frequently in the newspapers. She attributed this to what she called her "funny face" and a "smear of features." Although Amelia was not beautiful in the usual sense of the word, her quaint sense of humor, her modest manner, her happy disposition, and her ready smile more than compensated for anything she might have lacked in physical perfection. She was a good sport and unafraid.[2]

POEM:

> Courage is the price that Life exacts for
>   granting peace.
> The soul that knows it not
> Knows no release from little things:
> Knows not the livid loneliness of fear,

Nor mountain height where bitter joy can hear
The sound of wings.

How can Life grant us boon of living,
  compensate
For dull gray ugliness and pregnant hate
Unless we dare
The soul's dominion? Each time we make a
  choice, we pay
With courage to behold resistless day,
And count it fair.[3]

—AMELIA EARHART

POEM:

Lament not that her time on earth was brief,
But rather magnify her spirit's keen
Enthusiasm—there can be no grief
For one so valiant; thus her life should mean
A quickening power for the ones who plod—
A force to spur the tired, discouraged mind
To new endeavor—an invisible rod
Of strength for travelers who have lagged behind.

Se we must never think of her as dead,
But joyous and alive with eager face;
Seeking new truths, some goal that lies ahead,
Whose bright, brave spirit glories in the race,
With faith and courage radiant as the dawn,
Who still is ever flying, on and on.[4]

—MARGARET E. BRUNER

PRAYER:

O God, thou art the strength of our life and a help in time of trouble. We thank thee for the valiant men and women of the past whose faith and courage have won great victories for mankind. At times when we face problems too great for our intelligence, or tasks which test our endurance, we are encouraged by their example. May we not shirk our tasks, or evade our responsibilities, but face the situation fearlessly with faith and confidence, regardless of the problems involved. Strengthen us and grant us the ability to meet whatever the day sends; through Jesus Christ our Lord. Amen.

HYMN: "He Who Would Valiant Be" or
       "O Thou Who Camest from Above"

BENEDICTION:

Now unto him who is able to keep you from falling, and to present you faultless before his presence, be glory and power, both now and forever. AMEN.

MASTERING HANDICAPS

PRELUDE: "Intermezzo" by Bizet

CALL TO WORSHIP:
I was glad when they said unto me, Let us go into the house of the Lord. . . .
A day in thy courts is better than a thousand. I had rather be a doorkeeper in the house of my God, than to dwell in the tents of wickedness.[1]

HYMN: "My Times Are in Thy Hand" or
   "My God, I Thank Thee, Who Hast Made"

SCRIPTURE:
Out of the depths have I cried unto thee, O Lord.
Lord, hear my voice: let thine ears be attentive to the voice of my supplications. . . .
I wait for the Lord, my soul doth wait, and in his word do I hope.
My soul waiteth for the Lord more than they that watch for the morning: I say, more than they that watch for the morning. . . .
The Lord upholdeth all that fall, and raiseth up all those that be bowed down. . . .
The Lord is nigh unto all them that call upon him, to all that call upon him in truth. . . .
Wherefore, seeing we also are compassed about with so great a cloud of witnesses, let us lay aside every weight, and the sin which doth so easily beset us, and let us run with patience the race that is set before us, looking unto Jesus the author and finisher of our faith; who for the joy that was set before him endured the cross, despising the shame, and is set down at the right hand of the throne of God. . . .
Behold, I have set before thee an open door, and no man can shut it.[2]

MASTERING HANDICAPS

LEADER:

William Lyon Phelps said, "One man finds an obstacle a stumbling block; another finds it a steppingstone."

An oyster takes that which is at first an irritation of which it cannot be rid, and by some mystic alchemy changes it into a thing of irridescent beauty, a pearl.

Pasteur's poor health and his early paralysis did not disqualify him for the monumental service he was to render to suffering humanity. Brother is he of all those who by rugged determination have not been mastered by handicaps, but have become masters of them.

Henry Fawcett, when both eyes were rendered sightless by a hunting trip accident, declared within ten minutes after that terrible happening that he was resolved not to allow it to make any difference to his life. Without eyes he worked his way through Cambridge, was made professor of political economy at his alma mater.

What would the world be without handicaps harnessed to its most inspiring tasks? By sheer ability and capability the handicapped have hired themselves to the ages. They have been ever among the immortal legion who have served best.

There are just two things any of us can do with limitations which narrow the scope of our activities. We can submit supinely to them or we can superbly surmount them. Handicaps can prove stumbling blocks or steppingstones. Limitations in one direction often but open the gateway to even wider fields.[3]

POEM:

> What a piece of work is man!
> How noble in reason!
> How infinite in faculty!
> In form and moving
>   How express and admirable!
> In action how like an angel!
> In apprehension how like a god![4]

—Shakespeare

HYMN: "O Jesus, Prince of Life and Truth" or
      "Jesus, Thou Divine Companion"

LEADER:

We will hear the story of a young man who used a handicap to reach greater heights than otherwise would have been reached.

STORY:

BEATING HIS HANDICAP

All-American! Climaxing one of the strangest stories in the realm of football, Ellis Jones rose to the heights of football in 1944. He was rough and ready on the field just as any other great guard, but all the same, his case was different.

For, you see, Ellis Jones had only one arm!

Yet this stalwart young man went to the University of Tulsa, not only earning a first-string position, but eventually All-Missouri Valley, All-Sectional and finally All-American!

Jones reached his peak in 1944, but he had long before been playing the sport he enjoyed best. He was a three-year man for Tulsa, for he was in the Hurricanes' line-up also in 1942-43.

Twice this one-armed gridiron wonder played in the Sugar Bowl game at New Orleans before crowds of some 75,000, and another year he proved a star in the Orange Bowl contest on New Year's Day at Miami, Florida.

The real story of Jones's unique football career goes back to 1932— to Abilene, Texas, where he lived. Jones was in the fifth grade of his school. He had already decided to become a football player.

But one day, playing in a tree in the front yard of his home, he came tumbling down. The ground seemed to leap up and crash into his arm.

"My arm, my arm!" he called.

His mother raced out of the house to him. She rushed him to a hospital. The news was not good. "It is a compound fracture of the arm," she was told.

Little did either of them realize that the worst was yet to come. The lad had suffered a bad break. But the arm was placed in a cast. That should be sufficient, with healing certain in due time. However, the arm began swelling badly. Physicians had another look at the injury.

"Gangrene!"

This terrible poisoning had set in—and the youth would have to lose his arm! Amputation to the shoulder would be necessary, and in a hurry.

Ellis Jones lost his right arm, and anyone except a truly stout-hearted boy would have given up all ideas of sports. Forget about football? Certainly not! When his wound was completely healed, Ellis began working hard—learning how to use his left arm. He had

46

to make the football team somehow. His left arm began to do things it had never done before.

When football season arrived at his junior high school that fall, Ellis went out for the team. And made the grade! A year later he toiled with the scrubs as they practiced with the high-school regulars. But Ellis was different from the other boys—and not just because he was minus an arm. For he was the hardest worker out there! Not simply content to go through the usual practice routine, Ellis worked independently many hours.

The next year Ellis returned to the squad. Once more he was assigned to the scrubs. He watched the brilliant performances of a couple of Abilene regulars named John Kimbrough and Odell Herman. He could not guess that they were to become top stars for Texas A. and M., and that subsequently Kimbrough was to rate as one of the best professional backfield men in the country. But Jones's admiration of their play stimulated his desire to make good. Could he do it under so great a disadvantage?

Well, the answer is yes—for in the third year the coach no longer could use him with the scrubs. Ellis Jones was too good. They needed him in the regular line-up. He went on to play remarkably well that year. Then came his senior season. Once again Jones was a standout guard for Abilene High School.

Following in the footsteps of Kimbrough and Herman, Jones enrolled at Texas A. and M. He wanted to trail his teammates there for football action. But something happened. One day his side began to pain him so much he could hardly stand it. The physician lost little time diagnosing his case as appendicitis. He underwent an emergency operation. That knocked his football out for the time.

Since he had dropped so far behind, Jones figured it was useless to try at Texas A. and M. He went to San Angelo, Texas, where his father had entered the insurance business. Then Ellis decided to enroll at San Angelo Junior College and try out for the football team.

Instantly Jones became a sensation at San Angelo. The big, red-haired youngster of six feet, a hundred and eighty-five pounds, quickly made the first team. Furthermore, he proved to be a mainspring in the machine to the Texas junior college championship.

The next year Jones was back with San Angelo. This time they could finish only fourth in the state. But Jones was elected captain, a signal honor for a one-armed player. Thus he gained renown that sent him on to Tulsa—and All-America honors.

One of his Tulsa teammates gave Ellis a great compliment too. Sax Judd, a member of the Hurricane coaching staff, grinned as he said: "Why, we didn't even know Ellis had only one arm until we read about it in the papers!" [5]

PRAYER:

O God, who didst give thy Son to be our Saviour, we pray thee help us to overcome our fears, indifference, selfishness, and indolence. Enable us to accept our limitations and handicaps and endeavor to make them assets whenever possible. We seek purity of heart, strength of purpose, and steadfast devotion to thee that we may perform faithfully the tasks which thou hast committed to us. Give us courage to meet emergencies as well as the demands made upon us daily. Endue us with thy Spirit, and forbid that we should ever compromise our principles in order to gain an immediate advantage. Guide and direct us as we strive to develop our talents that they may be used in building thy kingdom. In Jesus name, we pray. AMEN.

HYMN: "March on, O Soul with Strength" or
        "Soldiers of Christ, Arise"

BENEDICTION:

The Lord bless you and keep you and be gracious unto you. AMEN.

SERVICE 7

GREAT, WITHOUT SEEKING TO BE GREAT

PRELUDE: Hymn tune "Dix"

CALL TO WORSHIP:
> O come, let us sing unto the Lord;
> Let us make a joyful noise to the rock of our
>   salvation.
> Let us come before his presence with thanksgiving,
> And make a joyful noise unto him with psalms.[1]

HYMN: "Fairest Lord Jesus" or
"Father, in Heaven, Who Lovest All"

SCRIPTURE:

And he began again to teach by the sea side: and there was gathered unto him a great multitude, so that he entered into a ship, and sat in the sea; and the whole multitude was by the sea on the land. And he taught them many things by parables, and said unto them in his doctrine, Hearken; Behold, there went out a sower to sow: and it came to pass, as he sowed, some fell by the wayside, and the fowls of the air came and devoured it up. And some fell on stony ground, where it had not much earth; and immediately it sprang up, because it had no depth of earth: but when the sun was up, it was scorched; and because it had no root, it withered away. And some fell among thorns, and the thorns grew up, and choked it, and it yielded no fruit. And other fell on good ground, and did yield fruit that sprang up and increased, and brought forth, some thirty, and some sixty, and some a hundred. And he said unto them, He that hath ears to hear, let him hear. . . .

When Jesus heard of it, he departed thence by ship into a desert place apart: and when the people had heard thereof, they followed him on foot out of the cities. And Jesus went forth, and saw a great multitude, and was moved with compassion toward them, and he healed their sick.[2]

POEM:

> Tried as by furnace fires, and yet
>   By God's grace only stronger made;
> In future tasks before thee set
>   Thou shalt not lack the old-time aid.
>
> Great, without seeking to be great
>   By fraud or conquest; rich in gold,
> But richer in the large estate
>   Of virtue which thy children hold.
>
> With peace that comes of purity,
>   And strength to simple justice due,
> So runs our loyal dream of thee,
>   God of our fathers! make it true.[3]
>
> —JOHN GREENLEAF WHITTIER

PRAYER:

O Holy Father, lift us from the sordid depths of selfishness and unworthy motives to the higher levels of truth and righteousness. Let the mountain breezes sweep through our minds and souls and cleanse us from all that is unlovely and impure, and may the healing rays of the sunshine of thy love permeate our being until it glows with spiritual warmth and a vigorous faith. AMEN.[4]

LEADER:

We will hear the story of a man who spent his energy to make the world a happier and better place in which to live.

STORY:

JOHNNY APPLESEED

It is a little over a hundred years since the death of Johnny Appleseed, a man so unusual that many people have the idea he was a legendary character. To the early settlers in the Middle West, however, John Chapman, whom they called "The Appleseed Man," was a very real person. Not only did he give them the precious seeds and help them start nurseries, but he often aided them in times of trouble. Many facts concerning the life and peculiarities of this extraordinary man have been recorded by his contemporaries.

GREAT, WITHOUT SEEKING TO BE GREAT

Johnny Appleseed was born in Massachusetts in 1776. When he was eighteen years old, he persuaded his half brother to go on a walking trip to the West. Near Fort Duquesne, Pennsylvania, where later the city of Pittsburgh was founded, he built a four-room house of logs and stone. He lived here twelve years and during that time he developed an apple orchard that was said to be the wonder of the wilderness. He often walked great distances to Pennsylvania Dutch settlements to obtain seeds from the refuse of cider presses.

To many of the pioneers who migrated from New York and eastern Pennsylvania, his home was a great refuge. Not only did he permit people to stay there without charge, but he provided free food. Regardless of the season of the year, he always had a large supply of apples. These he kept in a cave he had dug. When the travelers continued on their way, he gave them deerskin bags containing apple seeds to plant in their new settlements.

As this method of establishing orchards seemed too uncertain, Johnny decided to travel about and plant orchards. He easily disposed of his home by giving it to a poor widow who had a number of children. The house was to be hers as long as she lived, the only stipulation being that she must be kind to the traveling settlers.

On his first journey Johnny went down the Ohio River. His craft consisted of two canoes lashed together, each containing a load of appleseed. Whenever he found a favorable spot he stopped to plant seeds.

His first winter was spent in Marietta, Ohio, where he made many friends. In the spring he began his wanderings which extended over a period of forty years. During this time he established numerous nurseries and gave personal assistance to countless settlers in Ohio, Illinois, Indiana, Michigan, and Wisconsin.

When we consider that all his traveling, except his one trip down the Ohio River, was done on foot through uncleared land, or at best over Indian trails, we marvel at the distance he covered. Going through the woods he carried an ax and a hoe. With these tools he was able to make a clearing and to prepare the soil for his seeds. He generally located his nurseries along streams and surrounded them with brush fences.

As he was entirely without fear, he never carried firearms. The wild animals seemed to feel instinctively his friendly regard for them and never molested him. His diet was vegetarian, for he believed it a sin to kill any creature for food. His meals consisted chiefly of fruits,

51

nuts, and mush which he made in a mush pot that also did duty as a hat.

Sometimes in payment for his trees or seeds he would accept castoff clothing, but he seldom kept it long, for he found someone he thought needed it more than he. In his later years his principal garment was a burlap sack in which he cut holes for his head and arms. Even in the coldest weather he went barefoot.

Interested as he was in establishing orchards, Johnny Appleseed had another mission in life. An inscription on the monument at Ashland, Ohio, erected in his memory, contains these words, "He went about doing good." At all times he carried a copy of the New Testament. As he could not afford to give away whole Bibles, he often tore out pages and left them in the cabins where he had been invited to stay all night. He liked nothing better than to lie on the floor and read the Scriptures to the settlers.

Miss Rosella Rice of Perryville, Ohio, recorded the following concerning Johnny Appleseed's visit to her home. "I can hear him read now just as he did that summer day when we were busy quilting. He lay near the door, his voice now rising, denunciatory and thrilling, strong and loud as the roar of the waves and the wind, then soft and soothing as the balmy airs that stirred and quivered the morning-glory leaves about his gray head. His was a strange, deep eloquence."

When he came upon people who were ill or hungry, he tarried with them as long as he could be of service. He cared for the invalids, planted the crops, and in one particular case, dug a grave and preached a funeral sermon that amazed his audience.

A number of monuments have been erected to his memory. In two Ohio towns, Mansfield and Ashland, monuments have been placed near the sites of his early nurseries. At Swinney Park in Fort Wayne, Indiana, is a huge boulder bearing a bas-relief of Johnny planting an apple tree.

The last year of his life was spent with some friends near Fort Wayne, Indiana. He died March 18, 1843, and was buried in a private cemetery two miles north of Fort Wayne. The cemetery has since been deeded to the township. His grave was neglected until 1912, when the Indiana Horticultural Society erected an iron fence around it. The Johnny Appleseed Memorial Commission of Fort Wayne has plans for a Johnny Appleseed Park which will contain every variety of apple.[5]

GREAT, WITHOUT SEEKING TO BE GREAT

POEM:

Father, I will not ask for wealth or fame,
Though once they would have joyed my carnal sense:
I shudder not to bear a hated name,
Wanting all wealth, myself my sole defense.
But give me, Lord, eyes to behold the truth;
A seeing sense that knows the eternal right;
A heart with pity filled, and gentlest ruth;
A manly faith that makes all darkness light:
Give me the power to labor for mankind;
Make me the mouth of such as cannot speak;
Eyes let me be to groping men and blind;
A conscience to the base; and to the weak
Let me be hands and feet; and to the foolish, mind,
And lead still further on such as thy kingdom seek.[6]

—THEODORE PARKER

PRAYER:

Thou, O God, hast provided for all of our needs with thy bountiful hand. Thou hast taught us that in quietness and in confidence shall we find strength. Endue us with thy spirit that in all of our dealings with others we may be kind, generous, patient, and forbearing. Enable us so to live together that there may be food for the hungry, comfort for the sorrowing, and serenity for the disturbed. We thank thee for thy servants who have mastered themselves, who have lifted drabness from the lives of others, and have found their greatest joy in serving thee. From their example we have learned that not only do we need thee, but that we need each other. From their lives may we gain inspiration to fight the good fight and obtain victory through Jesus Christ our Lord. AMEN.

HYMN: "Go, Labor On!" or
"Rise Up, O Men of God"

BENEDICTION:

Direct us in all that we do so that we may through our work praise thee. AMEN.

53

SERVICE 8

SHOWING KINDNESS

PRELUDE: "Largo Appassionato" by Beethoven

CALL TO WORSHIP:

> Lord, who shall abide in thy tabernacle?
> Who shall dwell in thy holy hill?
> He that walketh uprightly, and worketh
> righteousness, and speaketh the truth
> in his heart.[1]

HYMN: "Let All the World in Every Corner Sing" or
"Joyful, Joyful, We Adore Thee"

SCRIPTURE:

Brethren, if a man be overtaken in a fault, ye which are spiritual, restore such a one in the spirit of meekness; considering thyself, lest thou also be tempted. Bear ye one another's burdens, and so fulfil the law of Christ. For if a man think himself to be something, when he is nothing, he deceiveth himself. But let every man prove his own work, and then shall he have rejoicing in himself alone, and not in another. For every man shall bear his own burden. Let him that is taught in the word communicate unto him that teacheth in all good things. Be not deceived; God is not mocked: for whatsoever a man soweth, that shall he also reap. For he that soweth to his flesh shall of the flesh reap corruption; but he that soweth to the Spirit shall of the Spirit reap life everlasting. And let us not be weary in well doing: for in due season we shall reap, if we faint not. As we have therefore opportunity, let us do good unto all men, especially unto them who are of the household of faith.[2]

LEADER:

We will hear a story of Robert Louis Stevenson's kindness to the Samoans.

Story:

THE ROAD OF LOVING HEARTS

On the island of Upolu in Western Samoa a road leads from the shore town of Apia to the old home of Robert Louis Stevenson.

Many years have passed since the famous writer came to those islands and had all the white people wondering what he would do next to upset their established customs. First of all, he selected a spot three miles back in the woods to build his new home—a place that did not have even a road leading out of it. Then in his big house he ordered the building of an enormous fireplace costing more than a thousand dollars, something unheard of in that tropical climate.

But it was in his treatment of the natives that he sprang the biggest surprise. From the day of his arrival Stevenson set himself up as their champion. Any government official who tried to override them or take advantage of their trustfulness soon found himself "tangling" with this newcomer. The writer fought so hard for their interests and sympathized with them so in all their hardships that he won the friendship of the lowliest.

Of course a strong bond of understanding was bound to spring up between "Tusitala"—"the teller of tales"—and these simple island folk. They never came to him for advice without finding him ready to help. The Samoans never had known a white man so kind by nature and with a keener sense of justice. One and all were devoted to him, and the saying became common, "Once Tusitala's friend, always Tusitala's friend."

Stevenson's letters to English newspapers, presenting the grievances of the Samoans, often irritated the government officials in Apia. "What right has he, an outsider, to mix in island affairs?" they wanted to know. But Stevenson felt that since he had made Samoa his home, the Samoans had become his people; therefore he must see that no one took advantage of them.

Tusitala came to be held in such affection by the islanders that they wanted to show their love in some tangible form. After talking it over they came to a decision. No longer would their good friend be compelled to undergo a severe shaking-up as he rode the rough trail down to Apia, for they would build a road to his door.

They resolved that the highway should be as wide and as smoothly graded as any American road. "It shall never be muddy. It shall endure, forever, this road we dig," the natives vowed. It was an undertaking on which chieftains toiled side by side with their humblest tribesmen. When it was at last finished, the Samoans called it *Alo Lota Alofa*. Translated into English, this means "The Road of Loving Hearts." No Englishman had ever before been so highly honored by the native people, and Stevenson was deeply touched.

The writer's happy days in those islands came to an abrupt end all too soon. When he and his family settled at Upolu, he seemed to have found the place he long had been seeking. For years he had been a wanderer, traveling over Europe and the United States in a vain search for relief from lung weakness. Not until he reached the South Sea was he free at last from coughs and colds.

For four years life in the big home "Vailima" went by like a pleasant dream. Many a morning Stevenson and his wife found their porch heaped high with fruit, fish, turtles, even young pigs—all gifts from the islanders. In return Stevenson listened patiently while the chiefs, sitting cross-legged around his big stone fireplace, poured out their troubles and waited for Tusitala's words of counsel. Few white men have been so trusted and loved.

At sunset on the evening of December 3, 1894, Stevenson was talking gaily on the veranda. He had never seemed in better spirits and he went on in lively fashion about his plans for the future. Then suddenly he put his hands to his head, exclaiming, "What's that?" and had hardly added, "Do I look strange?" before he fell on his knees. Quickly he was borne into the great hall at Vailima. But he had already lapsed into unconsciousness and was breathing heavily. Two doctors from a naval ship were summoned, but both shook their heads. There was nothing they could do.

As soon as word got about that their beloved Tusitala was dying, the native servants stole silently in and seated themselves in a wide semicircle about him. All night long they kept their vigil beside the bed. When he breathed his last, they were still in their places. Reverently then someone hauled down the great Union Jack that flew over the house and laid it over the body.

When it became known that the master of Vailima was dead, a steady stream of his old friends came to the house. Chieftain after chieftain walked up the Road of Loving Hearts, bearing a fine mat to lay upon the bier. Masses of flowers carried into the hall turned it into a spectacle of color that the writer had so loved.

One of the callers, an old chieftain who had helped build the road, kneeling beside the body of his friend, poured out his lament:

"We were in prison and he cared for us. We were sick and he made us well. We were hungry and he fed us. The day was no longer than his kindness."

Next day a band of the strongest islanders bore the body up the steep face of Mount Vaca to the very top, where Stevenson had asked to be buried. In time a tomb of gray stone was set up, inscribed with his own poem "Requiem." But down in the valley, enduring to this day, winds "The Road of Loving Hearts," reminding travelers of how a great writer by his fairness and kindness won the love of the Samoans.[3]

LEADER:

Loving-kindness is greater than laws; and the charities of life are more than all ceremonies.—THE TALMUD.

A noble deed is a step toward God.—JOHN G. HOLLAND.

It is not enough to do good; one must do it in the right way.— JOHN MORLEY.

It is well for us to think that no grace or blessing is truly ours until God has blessed someone else with it through us.—PHILLIPS BROOKS.

HYMN: "O Perfect Love, All Human Thought Transcending" or "The King of Love My Shepherd Is"

STORY:

ROBERT E. LEE'S KINDNESS

One of the most interesting stories ever told of General Robert E. Lee has to do with the time when he was president of Washington College at Lexington, Virginia. One fall there came to the university a young student from Alabama. This boy's father had lost everything in the recent war, and the son was very poor. His clothes were so shabby that he shrank from association with other boys.

In order to support himself while studying, the boy made a bargain with a farmer living a few miles from Lexington. He was given a small hut to live in, and in return for his meals he did a certain amount of work about the farm. The young man walked to college, studied late each evening, kept to himself, and worshiped General Lee at a distance.

One day General Lee met the young fellow as he was leaving class. Drawing him aside, he asked what the boy did with himself between recitations. He knew the youngster lived in the country and had no room at the college. The student told him that he went from one classroom to another until he found one that was vacant, and then used that as a study until his next class.

"But that is going to too much trouble," said General Lee. "I'll tell you what you can do. I happen to have a little office and a good fire. You will not be disturbed there, so if you wish a regular place to study, you can start coming in tomorrow."

The student could hardly believe his good fortune. As it turned out, that was the beginning of a memorable experience. The next morning when the boy presented himself, he found General Lee had a chair and a desk all ready near the fire. There the president and the student sat together day after day throughout the session, General Lee occupied at his desk and the young chap absorbed in his studies.

One day the student had such a severe cold that he decided it would be unwise to risk the long walk through the cold to his classes. He stayed in his hut all day. Late in the afternoon he was surprised to hear the sound of a horse outside. A minute later the president of Washington College was knocking at his door.

Much taken back, the young fellow invited General Lee inside. The General complimented him on how nicely he had the place arranged, and pointed out what a fine place it must be to do his studying, with none of the distractions of the college to bother him.

This was not the last time this particular student was the object of General Lee's interest in his behalf. Not long afterward, during the harvesting season, the president took time to look him up again. As the boy could not afford to go home during vacation, he hired himself out to the farmer for the summer. One hot day he was busy helping his employer thresh wheat. He was standing under the threshing machine, and a grimier-looking farmhand hardly could have been found anywhere.

It was just at this time that General Lee rode up in the company of another man on horseback. The General beckoned to the boy and spoke of the usefulness of farm work, but informed him he had found a better opportunity. It was a job, he said, that he was sure would be more to his liking, since it was a teaching position in a neighborhood school for the rest of the summer. The salary alone would help greatly toward the boy's expenses in college the following year.

It goes without saying that the student was only too glad to avail himself of the offer. The money he earned was a lifesaver in his hard struggle for an education. As long as he lived he never forgot how General Lee went out of his way to do him a kindness.[4]

SHOWING KINDNESS

> I know that kindness can't be wrong,
>   That truth will not betray,
> That charity excels revenge
>   For this or any day.
>
> I know that verities endure,
>   That vanities will fade,
> That righteousness exalts a man
>   And makes him unafraid.
>
> I know that knowledge feeds the mind,
>   That beauty feeds the heart,
> That virtues are mosaic stones
>   In God's eternal art.
>
> I know good will bear good fruit,
>   That honesty is best,
> That faith and hope and love abide
>   Supreme in every test.[5]

—CHAUNCEY R. PIETY

PRAYER:

O Lord, grant us to love thee with all our heart, with all our mind, and all our strength; and to love our neighbors for thy sake, that the grace of charity and brotherly love may dwell in us, and that all envy, harshness, and ill will may die. Fill our hearts with kindness and compassion. May we constantly rejoice in the happiness and good success of others and sympathize with them in their sorrows. May we put away all harsh judgments and envious thoughts. So shall we follow thee, who art thyself the true and perfect Love; through Jesus Christ our Lord. AMEN.[6]

HYMN: "Rejoice, Ye Pure in Heart" or
    "Jesus, Thou Joy of Loving Hearts"

BENEDICTION:

The Lord bless you and keep you; the Lord make his face to shine upon you and be gracious unto to; the Lord lift up his countenance upon you and give you peace; both now and evermore. AMEN.

TO SET MEN FREE

PRELUDE: "Adagio" by Mendelssohn

CALL TO WORSHIP:

> Lord of all being, throned afar,
> Thy glory flames from sun and star;
> Center and soul of every sphere,
> Yet to each loving heart how near!

> . . . .

> Grant us thy truth to make us free,
> And kindling hearts that burn for thee;
> Till all thy living altars claim
> One holy light, one heavenly flame!
>
> —OLIVER WENDELL HOLMES

HYMN: "March On, O Soul, with Strength" or
"O Worship the King"

SCRIPTURE:

The Lord is my light and my salvation; whom shall I fear? the Lord is the strength of my life; of whom shall I be afraid? . . .

Though a host should encamp against me, my heart shall not fear: though war should rise against me, in this will I be confident.

One thing have I desired of the Lord, that will I seek after; that I may dwell in the house of the Lord all the days of my life, to behold the beauty of the Lord, and to inquire in his temple. . . .

Trust in the Lord with all thine heart; and lean not unto thine own understanding.

In all thy ways acknowledge him, and he shall direct thy paths. . . .

I can do all things through Christ which strengtheneth me.[1]

PRAYER:

Our Father, in the records of history we recognize thy spokesmen among the prophets, teachers, reformers, and other leaders, and we find in their example help for meeting our own problems. We thank thee for Wilberforce and his struggle to bring freedom to the Negroes. Grant us patience when success does not come at once to us. May our faith be a steadying influence which helps to make every experience of life a means of growth and development. Increase our faith, O Lord. May our religion give us courage, lift us over the rough places of life, and bring us peace, joy, and confidence. Give us such faith that we may never lack steadfastness as we strive to bring thy kingdom nearer; through Jesus Christ our Lord. AMEN.

HYMN: "When I Survey the Wondrous Cross" or
      "In the Cross of Christ I Glory"

POEM:

> I want to sing lyrics, lyrics
> Mad as a brook in spring
> I want to shout the music
> Of flushed adventuring.
>
> But how can I sing lyrics?
> I who have seen today
> The stoop of factory women,
> The children kept from play.
>
> . . . .
>
> I want to sing lyrics, lyrics
> But these have hushed my song.
> I am mute at the world's great sadness
> And stark at the world's great wrong.
>
> —AUTHOR UNKNOWN

LEADER:

William Wilberforce was small physically and in poor health most of his life, but what there was of him he threw in front of the British slave trade, one of the entrenched evils of his day. In spite of bitter opposition he did more than any other man to abolish slavery. He is remembered in England today as the "attorney general of the unprotected and the friendless." We will hear the story of the manner in which he invested his life.

STORY:

PIONEER IN THE FIGHT ON SLAVERY

On the night of July 31, 1834, thousands of Negroes of all ages crowded the churches of the British West Indies, their faces alight with expectation. Then at the first stroke of midnight they leaped to their feet with a shout of joy that seemed to lift the roofs. From that moment 800,000 slaves held under the British flag were free.

This great event was the climax of nearly fifty years of struggle by William Wilberforce, a frail little Englishman who seldom during his life was free from physical pain. To him more than to any other person goes the credit for abolishing slavery in the British Empire. His influence on the abolition cause in the United States was tremendous.

William Wilberforce was born in 1759, of a rich trading family in Hull. He was sickly from birth, but physical limitations did not hamper the development of his brilliant mind. By the time he was twenty-one he had graduated from Cambridge and been elected to Parliament.

The feebleness of Wilberforce's stunted body gave him a marked stoop. But his eyes sparkled with such kindliness and gaiety that people forgot his appearance. His eloquence and melodious voice made him known as "the nightingale of the House of Commons." There was every reason to believe that he was heading full tilt into a great political future.

Then when he was twenty-five years old, Wilberforce made a trip to the Continent with the Reverend Isaac Milner. Creeping by carriage over muddy, rutty roads, the two friends talked endlessly about religion and read the New Testament in Greek. Wilberforce was converted. He resolved to live to the glory of God and the good of his fellow creatures.

In view of its far-flung results, this conversion was one of the most important of Christianity. Soon under what he believed was divine guidance, the young MP began his lifelong crusade.

Wilberforce had seen the slave market when he was a child. Later he learned from the former captain of a slave ship how traders hired ruffians to invade West Africa villages, burn huts, kill the old and sick and take the able-bodied inhabitants in chains to the coast. He had heard of Negroes going mad and flinging themselves overboard.

Wilberforce knew that to consecrate his life to the abolition of the slave trade was to say farewell to his political ambitions, for no crusade was ever more unpopular. When he joined forces with ten Quakers, this little group made up the only antislavery society in England.

Against such a handful was arrayed much of the wealth and might of the empire. Many people, including the King, believed that if the trade was stopped, factories using slave-raised products would fall into ruin and England's prosperity would die.

In 1787 the twenty-eight-year-old MP gave notice in the House of Commons of his intentions. "Never, never will we give up," he said, "until we have extinguished every trace of this bloody traffic—a disgrace and dishonor to our country." This speech caused a sensation. The fight which Wilberforce began was to go on through nearly two decades of exhausting labor and heartbreaking disappointment.

The proslavery adherents, who spent months presenting their evidence before a parliamentary committee, said African Negroes were little more intelligent than orangutans and were better off as slaves; that most of them were convicts anyway; that the evils of the voyages had been grossly exaggerated.

To answer these statements Wilberforce began a monumental job of collecting evidence. It was dangerous work. Prospective witnesses were threatened with everything from loss of jobs to physical injury. A West Indian planter followed Wilberforce for months with threats to kill him.

Ignoring such attacks, Wilberforce proceeded to disprove the idea that African Negroes were hardly above the animal level. He collected examples of native handicrafts—skillfully dyed and woven cloth, pieces of jewelry, and artistically carved masks and pipe bowls. He brought out testimony from witnesses that the slaveship holds were so crowded and so closely hung with overhead shelves that the captives could neither sit up straight nor lie down. He produced proof too that at least a quarter of the captives were children.

The committee's investigation took nearly two years. Then in 1791 the slave trade abolition bill came to its first test in the House of Commons. It was voted down 163 to 88.

Having hoped that once Parliament had learned the facts victory would follow, the crusaders were bitterly disappointed. But Wilberforce was far from giving up. The thing to do, he decided, was to arouse public opinion. After sending out fifty thousand abridged copies of the evidence, he started on a nationwide speaking tour. He won thousands of adherents.

He went on introducing bills into Parliament. Through eleven discouraging years he drove his pain-racked body to miracles of exertion. Then in 1807, twenty years after he undertook his crusade, the bill finally passed. The vote was 283 to 16, and it culminated in one of the greatest ovations ever seen in the House of Commons.

Wilberforce looked forward to retirement but his hopes were soon dashed. Though the slave trade had officially been abolished, the slave ships began sneaking out again and Negroes were kidnapped in greater numbers than before. "I am sick of battle," the crusader said, "but I will not leave my poor slaves in the lurch." His decision committed him to twenty-six more years of struggle.

Wearily he decided to stand for Parliament. At first it looked as if he could not possibly win. But on the first day the polls were open strange processions began converging on York. When a large group of weary walkers were asked for whom they were voting, a shout went up: "For Wilberforce, to a man!" The little crusader won handily.

His new term in Parliament was marked by efforts to prevent slavery from spreading to new colonies and to keep British cruisers policing the seas. As late as 1810 smugglers carried eighty thousand slaves across the Atlantic. Spain and Portugal were then the only powers that legalized the trade. Wilberforce spent exasperating years working out agreements with these two nations for abolition of the traffic.

But Wilberforce began to realize that his days of great activity were over. In addition to his other handicaps he developed a chronic "inflamation of the lungs." In 1825 the aging crusader gave up his seat in the House of Commons. He still gave counsel, however, to those fighting for the cause.

It was not until 1833 that Parliament passed a bill which freed all slaves under the British flag. Wilberforce was on his deathbed when the news came that passage of the bill was assured. He was able to understand the message and to thank God for it. When he was buried in Westminster Abbey the streets were jammed, and at least every third person was in mourning.[2]

LEADER:

What constitutes the bulwark of our own liberty and independence? It is not our frowning battlements, our bristling seacoast, our army and our navy. Our reliance is in the love of liberty which God has planted in us. Our defense is in the spirit which prizes liberty as the heritage of all men in all lands everywhere. Destroy this spirit, and we have planted the seeds of despotism at our own doors.—ABRAHAM LINCOLN.

POEM:

> Is true Freedom but to break
> Fetters for our own dear sake,
> And, with leathern hearts, forget
> That we owe mankind a debt?
> No! True Freedom is to share
> All the chains our brothers wear,
> And, with heart and hand, to be
> Earnest to make others free! [3]
>
> —JAMES RUSSELL LOWELL

PRAYER:

O God and Father of mankind, who hast bound together all the generations of men; we rejoice in the communion of thy saints.

We praise and bless thee for all those thy faithful servants whose labor in thee has brought light and hope to the world. For those who were friend to the poor and weak, defending them against outrage and oppression; for those who went forth as sheep in the midst of wolves to declare thy truth and thy righteousness; for those who, being in thy service reviled and persecuted, did not turn back but continued steadfast to the end; for those who gave up their lives in love to thee and devotion to thy holy cause; for all who in ages past have helped to keep faith and hope and good will alive, we raise to thee our grateful praise.

Give to us thy grace, we beseech thee; that we also may enter into the company of thy saints, and have a part in thy great redemption; and that, with those who have been given the victory over sin and death, we may dwell with thee for ever and ever; through Jesus Christ our Lord. AMEN.[4]

HYMN: "Beneath the Cross of Jesus" or
"Lead on, O King Eternal"

BENEDICTION:

The Spirit of God remain with you evermore. AMEN.

SERVICE 10

MOUNTAIN MESSAGES

PRELUDE: Hymn tune "Creation"

CALL TO WORSHIP:
>   The Lord is in his holy temple:
>   Let all the earth keep silence before him. . . .
>   Oh come, let us worship and bow down:
>   Let us kneel before the Lord our Maker:
>   For he is our God.[1]

HYMN: "This Is My Father's World" or
"God, that Madest Earth and Heaven"

SCRIPTURE:
And the apostles gathered themselves together unto Jesus, and told him all things, both what they had done, and what they had taught. And he said unto them, Come ye yourselves apart into a desert place, and rest a while: for there were many coming and going, and they had no leisure so much as to eat. And they departed into a desert place by ship privately. . . .
And it come to pass about an eight days after these sayings, he took Peter and John and James, and went up into a mountain to pray.
I will lift up mine eyes unto the hills, from whence cometh my help.[2]

PRAYER:
God of the hills, grant us thy strength to go back into the cities without faltering, strength to do our daily task without tiring and with enthusiasm, strength to help our neighbors who have no hills to remember.
God of the wilderness, with thy pure winds from the northland blow away our pettiness; with the harsher winds of winter drive away our selfishness and hypocrisy; fill us with the breadth and

the depth and the height of thy wilderness. May we live out the truths which thou hast taught us, in every thought and word and deed. AMEN.

PRAYER:

Teach me the faith of the mountains, serene and sublime,
The deep rooted joy of just living one day at a time,
Leaving the petty possessions the valley-folk buy
For the glory of glad wind-swept spaces where earth meets
  the sky.

Teach me the faith of the mountains, their strength to
  endure
The breadth and the depth of their vision, unswerving and
  sure,
Counting the dawn and the starlight as parts of one whole,
Wrought by the Spirit Eternal, within His control. AMEN.

—AUTHOR UNKNOWN

HYMN: "When Morning Gilds the Skies" or
      "Be Still, My Soul"

LEADER:

We will hear the story of the man who loved mountains and would pass on their message to others.

STORY:

THE EVANGELIST OF THE MOUNTAINS

"I will lift up mine eyes unto the hills, from whence cometh my help," wrote the psalmist. In the calm majestic grandeur of the mountains there was peace—the tired soul harassed and spent by the cares and duties of life found in them a soothing and healing touch. They spoke of the great source of power, eternal and unchanging and inexhaustible; they were the handiwork of "the Lord, which made heaven and earth."

Down through the ages since the psalmist wrote the immortal words of Ps. 121, the message of the mountains has never failed those who have lifted up their eyes toward the heights. Always they found the assurance that "the Lord shall preserve thy going out and thy coming in from this time forth, and even for evermore."

That was the message John Muir, California's famous mountaineer-naturalist, received from the mountains, and passed on to us through his books and magazine articles. He loved and understood the mountains as few men have done—he had the "eye within the eye" which enabled him to see and interpret them to others.

Born on April 21, 1838, at Dunbar, Scotland, it was there he spent his boyhood. He seems always to have loved nature, the woods and meadows and wild creatures he met there. "Fortunately," he writes, "around my native town of Dunbar there was no lack of wildness. I loved to wander in the fields to hear the birds sing, and along the seashore to gaze and wonder at the shells and seaweeds; and best of all to watch the waves thundering on the black headlands."

When John was eleven years old the family emigrated to the United States, settling on a farm in Wisconsin. Here every bird, tree, and flower was novel and wonderful to him, and to his brothers and sisters, and they plunged into the study of nature with more eagerness than ever. They marveled at the woodpecker nests, the giant sandhill cranes, at the great variety of wild flowers. "How utterly happy it made us," he wrote. "Oh, that glorious Wisconsin wilderness!"

But there was much hard work too, for the land had to be cleared if it was to yield a living, and then there were always the chores. When they first came, they had four miles to the nearest neighbor and still farther to the school. John read every book he could get his hands on, borrowing them from other settlers. In this way parts of Shakespeare and Milton came into his hands, some of Scott's novels, and Mungo Park's travel books.

Every day, too, during his boyhood he had to memorize a certain number of verses from the Bible. His father, a very devout man, strictly enforced this rule. Muir wrote: "Father made me learn so many Bible verses every day that by the time I was eleven years of age I had about three fourths of the Old Testament and all of the New learned by heart."

Like many another boy he liked to whittle and make things, and though there was not much time to spare from the farm work, a most unusual lot of inventions resulted. Perhaps the strangest of all was the "early-rising bed"—when hooked up to one of his wooden clocks, it would stand on end at a certain hour in the morning, dumping its occupant out on the floor whether awake or asleep!

Since leaving Scotland, Muir's schooling had been limited to a winter term of two months, for he could not be spared from the farm. By working on the farm during summer vacations, selling some of his inventions, and one winter teaching a country school near Madison, he made his way, studying four years at the University of Wisconsin.

It was during his first year that he was introduced to the study that engrossed him the remainder of his life. Approaching the dormitory one day, he met another student who carried a flower in his hand. On being asked to identify it, he was forced to admit he could not. When his companion explained the flower to him, it was his first lesson in botany.

But even a botanist must eat, and so he worked for a while in a Canadian sawmill. An accident in which his right eye was so severely injured that he feared the sight was lost changed his plans, however. From that time on, he wrote, "I bade adieu to all my mechanical inventions, determined to devote the rest of my life to the study of the inventions of God."

A long walking trip took him to Florida and Cuba, and he had planned to go to the jungles of South America. Instead he went to California. Arriving there in March 1868, he set out to walk to Yosemite. His first views of the San Joaquin Valley, then one vast wildflower garden, and of the Yosemite Falls and mountain heights, made such a deep impression upon him that he at once decided to remain, taking any work he could find to earn his way between periods of mountain wandering.

One summer was spent in the high Sierras, in charge of a large flock of sheep, but with much time left for botanizing and mountain climbing. The notes he took were later used in his writing. When Emerson and Agassiz visited Yosemite, Muir met and talked with them. During the winter of 1871-72, he began turning his Yosemite experiences into articles, several of them being published in the *New York Tribune,* the *Atlantic, Scribner's,* the *Century,* and many other periodicals.

In the years which followed he explored the mountains and forests and glaciers of the Coast Ranges and of Alaska, altogether making five trips to Alaska. He also went to Europe, Africa, India, Australia, Japan, and South America.

Always in his articles and books he tried to draw people to the mountains, for their healthfulness, and purity, and beauty. He remarked to friends that he desired "to live only to entice people to look at nature's loveliness." He was America's great evangelist of the mountains.

Camping with Theodore Roosevelt among the big trees, he persuaded him to set aside the Grand Canyon as a national monument, Congress later making it a national park. It is largely because of John Muir that today we have Yosemite Park, and Sequoia National Park, and that California's groves of big trees have been preserved— these majestic forest giants which already were tall trees at the time of Christ.

In a letter to his mother he wrote: "Yosemite is one of many, one chapter of a grand mountain book written by the same pen of ice which the Lord long ago passed over every page of our great Sierra Nevadas. I know how Yosemite and all the other valleys of these magnificent mountains were made and the next year or so of my life will be occupied chiefly in writing their history in a human book —a glorious subject, which God helped me preach aright."

No one reading Muir long can remain unaware as to the main source of his literary pattern, for his sentences abound with biblical simile and metaphor. His familiarity with the Bible, gained during his youth, was the "well of springing water" from whence came his literary style. Even today his books carry the message of the mountains, and like the psalmist, invite us to look up to the hills of God wherein lies our source of strength.[3]

POEM:

> Nature never did betray
> The heart that loved her; 'tis her privilege
> Through all the years of this our life, to lead
> From joy to joy: for she can so inform
> The mind that is within us, so impress
> With quietness and beauty, and so feed
> With lofty thoughts, that neither evil tongues,
> Rash judgments, nor the sneers of selfish men,
> Nor greetings where no kindness is, nor all
> The dreary intercourse of daily life,
> Shall e'er prevail against us, or disturb
> Our cheerful faith that all which we behold
> Is full of blessings.[4]

—WILLIAM WORDSWORTH

PRAYER:

O God, who art the light of the minds that know thee, the life of the souls that love thee, take from our minds all anxiety and grant us thy peace. We fail to hear thy voice and to understand thy purpose because we have not been still; we fail to see thee for our eyes have been fixed upon material things; we have neglected spiritual values for our energy has been consumed on temporal things that pass away. Forgive us and lift us out of self-concern, purge us of all unworthy thoughts and low ideals, and lead us into a closer walk with thee. We thank thee for men like John Muir, who lived in thy presence and learned to think thy thoughts after thee. Through communion with thee may there come to us wisdom to face our problems, confidence to carry forward the building of thy kingdom, and inspiration for living by the truths which Jesus exemplified. Into thy hands we commit ourselves. In Jesus' name. AMEN.

HYMN: "My Soul, Be on Thy Guard" or
        "Go Forth to Life, O Child of Earth"

BENEDICTION:
            Father, give thy benediction,
               Give thy peace before we part;
            Still our minds with truth's conviction;
               Calm with trust each anxious heart. AMEN.
                              —SAMUEL LONGFELLOW

SINGING OF COURAGE

PRELUDE: Hymn tune "Finlandia" by Jean Sibelius

CALL TO WORSHIP:

Praise him with the sound of the trumpet:
Praise him with the psaltery and harp.
Praise him with the timbrel and dance:
Praise him with stringed instruments and organs. . . .
Let every thing that hath breath praise the Lord.
Praise ye the Lord.[1]

HYMN: "Fairest Lord Jesus" or
"God, that Madest Earth and Heaven"

SCRIPTURE:

Make a joyful noise unto God, all ye lands:
Sing forth the honor of his name: make his praise glorious.
All the earth shall worship thee, and shall sing unto thee; they shall
sing to thy name. . . .
O give thanks unto the Lord; call upon his name:
Make known his deeds among the people.
Sing unto him, sing psalms unto him: talk ye of all his wondrous
works.
Glory ye in his holy name: let the heart of them rejoice that seek
the Lord.
Seek the Lord, and his strength: seek his face evermore.[2]

PRAYER:

We bless Thee, O God, that Thou hast placed in the hearts of men
and women and little children the impulse to make music. By
manifold instruments devised by the art of men and by that greatest
of instruments, the human voice in song, our souls are stirred to
purer and more joyous living. We thank Thee, Lord.

By music men have praised Thee in all times and in all places. By music we proclaim our adoration beyond the power of our poor words to speak. By music hearts are knit together in common joyous praise to Thee. We thank Thee, Lord.

If perchance Thou hast imparted to us some power to make melody, help us to stir up the gift that is in us and to use it to Thy glory. Through Christ our Lord. AMEN.[3]

POEM:

> We are the music-makers,
>   And we are the dreamers of dreams,
> Wandering by lone sea-breakers,
>   And sitting by desolate streams;
> World-losers and world-forsakers,
>   On whom the pale moon gleams;
> Yet we are the movers and shakers
>   Of the world forever, it seems.
>
> With wonderful deathless ditties
> We build up the world's great cities,
>   And out of a fabulous story
>   We fashion an empire's glory:
> One man with a dream, at pleasure,
>   Shall go forth and conquer a crown;
> And three with a new song's measure
>   Can trample a Kingdom down.
>   —ARTHUR W. O'SHAUGHNESSY

HYMN: "Joyful, Joyful, We Adore Thee" or
      "Still, Still with Thee"

STORY:

HE SET FINLAND TO MUSIC

Finland is the home of Jean Sibelius, one of the greatest of contemporary musical composers. His music is typical of the land; it speaks of the Finn's intense love of freedom and hatred of oppression; it is full of the beauty of the lakes and hills and forests, of what the Finn loves in his homeland. The music of Sibelius is Finland set to music.

It is nationalistic, but not in a narrow and jingoistic sense. At the same time that it belongs to Finland and the Finns, it also belongs to every country in the world and to all people everywhere. For like all great music it speaks a universal language.

Jean Sibelius was born on December 8, 1865, of Finnish-Swedish parents, his mother's family having moved to Finland from Sweden. When Jean, or Johan, as he was christened, was less than three years old, his father died in a typhus epidemic. Even as a boy of five or six he liked to make music of his own on a piano. But when it came to taking regular music lessons, that was something else again! Like many another boy he disliked them. Still, at ten he turned out his first musical composition, a little piece called "Drops of Water."

As he grew older his love for music dominated his other likes and ambitions. He became interested in the violin, and began taking lessons from Gustaf Levander, who conducted the military band and was an excellent violinist. The young lad Jean soon mastered the violin. With his sister, who played the piano, and his younger brother, who played the cello, the Sibelius family had a trio of their own.

When he was about sixteen he began to study music seriously, and wrote several pieces of chamber music. In school two subjects held his interest—music and history. His home environment was a happy one. When his father died, his mother returned to her parental home to live. There the atmosphere was more Swedish than Finnish. He read Swedish books and became familiar with Swedish culture.

At the age of twenty he began studying law at the University of Helsinki. Not because he liked it, or desired to become a lawyer, but because his family wanted him to. They did not regard music as a really worth-while vocation for a man. As a pastime it was delightful and pleasant, but for making a living it would not do. And so young Jean Sibelius read law books for a year—when he was not working at his music!

Becoming a great composer was not in his thoughts when he was a student at Helsinki. But he did dream of becoming a violin virtuoso, and after plodding away for a year at his law course he gave that up, and with the consent of the family went back to music, particularly the violin.

At the university he came to know a man whose counsel and guidance were to mean much to him during the coming years—Martin Wegelius. He was the head of the university, a teacher who loved music, and above all, an idealist with dreams. The two did not always agree; Wegelius admired the German composer Wagner a great deal; Sibelius rather disliked his music, he thought it too loud and unrestrained. He preferred Grieg and Tchaikovsky. Wegelius was more than a teacher, however, he was also a wise man. He did not attempt to dictate what his young pupil should like or dislike, what he should think or do. The important thing was that he should, in his music and through his life, express himself clearly and honestly.

In 1889 Sibelius, aided by a $300 scholarship from a Finnish student association, went to Berlin to study under Albert Becker, the German musician and composer. Here he met Richard Strauss, and also Robert Kajanus, the Finnish composer and conductor. The latter had written a symphony based on the *Kalevala*, a great Finnish epic poem, and in Berlin young Sibelius heard Kajanus' symphony played for the first time. It awakened in him the desire to write music that would sing the beauty and courage of his native land.

The meter of the *Kalevala* is a familiar one to most Americans, for it is the same as that of *Hiawatha*. Longfellow read the *Kalevala* and was so impressed by the rhythm of its lines and the story contained in its runes, that he wrote his epic of Indian life on the same pattern.

A year in Vienna completed Sibelius' musical training. He returned to Finland to write a tone poem—*Kullervo*—based on the myths of the *Kalevala*. When it was played for the first time in April, 1892, Sibelius himself conducted the orchestra, it was accorded an ovation. Recognition was gratifying and the esteem of his friends and countrymen pleasant to have, but it does not always buy bread. A position as teacher in a musical academy in Helsinki provided enough for a comfortable living, however. A little later a government grant was awarded Sibelius, about $400 a year, which helped him financially so that he could spend more time on his music.

He wrote an opera which was never produced, but which contained some fine musical selections. One of these was the descriptive tone poem *The Swan of Tuonela,* now regarded as being among the loveliest of his works. It, too, is based on a legend of the *Kalevala*. In 1889 came the *First Symphony,* and it gained for him the plaudits of the world. After that Sibelius was a famous composer. As time went on he wrote six more symphonies and much other music. He set many of the poems of Johan Ludvig Runeberg to music, poems that sang of the valor and courage of the Finnish people.

In 1899, too, appeared the tone poem *Finlandia,* probably the most famous and best-loved of all the compositions of Sibelius. It was called forth by Russian oppression, Finland at that time being subject to and a part of Russia. The Russians at once forbade the playing of the song on any occasion. In spite of that it swept around the world in a very short time, a magnificent anthem which awakens the highest and noblest feelings in the hearts and minds of those who hear it.

In the spring of 1914 Sibelius visited the United States. He was the guest at the Litchfield (Connecticut) Music Festival, where his music was played. Later he received a degree from Yale University. The United States seemed a glorious country to him—"I have never, before or after, lived such a wonderful life," he once said, when talking about his experiences.

A great deal has been written, and much more might be said, about the music of Sibelius, its beauty and message. These lines from the *Kalevala,* however, sum it up as well as anything that might be said:

> "Good is won, and good brought homeward,
> Good decreed by the Creator,
> Good that's granted by his mercy." [4]

LEADER:

Finlandia has been arranged for the hymn "Be Still, My Soul," which we shall sing.

HYMN: "Be Still, My Soul"

PRAYER:

We thank thee, our Father, for thy interpreters, the great musicians, who serve humanity. We are grateful for Sibelius and his music, and for his determination to interpret beauty and to bring greater freedom to oppressed people. May his example inspire all who are struggling to gain freedom. We are thankful for the leaders who dedicated themselves to a great cause and who are an inspiration to us to hold fast to our faith in trying times. Support and sustain all who are tempted to lose courage when success does not come immediately. Give us a clearer vision of things we can do to aid those who are still oppressed. Guide us as we strive to bring thy kingdom nearer, and may we have the indwelling of thy spirit in our lives. AMEN.

HYMN: "God of Grace and God of Glory" or
       "Rise Up, O Men of God"

BENEDICTION:

May we go forth to be more faithful servants of thine. AMEN.

SERVICE 12

LET ANXIOUS HEARTS GROW QUIET

PRELUDE: "Guadeamus" by Rowley

CALL TO WORSHIP:

O Come, let us worship and bow down; let us kneel before the Lord our Maker.

For he is our God; and we are the people of his pasture, and the sheep of his hand.[1]

HYMN: "Breathe on Me, Breath of God" or
"'Mid All the Traffic of the Ways"

SCRIPTURE:

Trust in the Lord, and do good; so shalt thou dwell in the land, and verily thou shalt be fed.

Delight thyself also in the Lord; and he shall give thee the desires of thine heart.

Commit thy way unto the Lord; trust also in him; and he shall bring it to pass.

And he shall bring forth thy righteousness as the light, and thy judgment as the noonday. . . .

But the meek shall inherit the earth; and shall delight themselves in the abundance of peace. . . .

The steps of a good man are ordered by the Lord: and he delighteth in his way.

Though he fall, he shall not be utterly cast down: for the Lord upholdeth him with his hand. . . .

Mark the perfect man, and behold the upright: for the end of that man is peace.

Ask, and it shall be given you; seek, and ye shall find; knock, and it shall be opened unto you:

For every one that asketh receiveth; and he that seeketh findeth; and to him that knocketh it shall be opened. . . .

And all things, whatsoever ye shall ask in prayer, believing, ye shall receive.[2]

INVOCATION:

O God, who art the fountain of inner peace, may thy Spirit within our hearts become a source of strength and courage. Deepen within us a longing for fellowship with thee. May we through prayer and acts of Christian love keep open the channel between us and thee. Grant us wisdom to make wise choices and patience to follow thy guidance. Grant us renewal of spirit, and may we find joy and peace through a richer fellowship with thee; in Jesus' name, we pray. AMEN.

HYMN: "Dear Lord and Father of Mankind" or
      "Draw Thou My Soul, O Christ"

LEADER:

I have lived a long time, and the longer I live, the more convincing proofs I see of this truth: that God governs in the affairs of men. And if a sparrow cannot fall to the ground without his notice, is it probable that an empire can rise without his aid?—BENJAMIN FRANKLIN.

At all costs we must re-establish faith in spiritual values. We must worship something beyond ourselves, lest we destroy ourselves.—PHILLIP GIBBS.

An incident will be related from the life of one of the early missionaries to the Indians.

STORY:

MIRACLE ON THE SUSQUEHANNA

It was early summer in the year 1744. A young missionary walked along the lush green bank of the Susquehanna River. He was in Indian territory, and fearfully aware that there was no other white man for miles.

As David Brainerd walked he watched the flight of birds he never before had seen. Small animals ran off through the underbrush at his approach, and an occasional beaver slapped his tail and dived silently out of sight, leaving a circle of ripples to mark the spot.

When the missionary reached a small clearing at the riverbank, where there were footprints of many animals that had come to drink, he paused and dropped his pack to the moss-cushioned earth. A rattlesnake buzzed ominously at the edge of the clearing, then slithered off silently into the tall grass. It was nearing dusk, and from a rise a quarter hour ago Brainerd had sighted the smoke of the Indian village which was his destination.

But it was not safe to go on. The village did not know of his coming. The Indians in it were savage, hating the white man, and many who came this way had met death. Opening his pack, he determined to wait until morning to enter the village.

Brainerd spread his earthly goods on the ground. His knife, his blanket, and his Bible. A glow of red was showing through the trees at the western rim of the clearing, and he knew there would not be many minutes until dark. Suddenly there was a cracking of dry sticks in the underbrush. Brainerd looked up, startled. All the birds in the trees were instantly silent. The young missionary waited, watching, alert. Then a deer broke into the clearing and scampered away along the trail to the water hole, and gradually, as the birds once more took up their chatter, Brainerd began the task of preparing his dinner.

When he was about to eat, Brainerd paused, as was his custom, to offer prayer. Kneeling, he folded his hands in front of him, bowed his head, and closed his eyes. He could hear the sounds of beavers working at their dam in the crook of the river, the evening sound of insects, occasionally a distant cry of some larger animal falling on its prey. Once more came the sound of a creature stirring at the edge of the clearing, but this time Brainerd did not open his eyes, but continued his prayer.

When he had finished, he ate his supper and lay down for a night's rest just as darkness came, leaving a deep blue sky full of stars above him. His sleep was undisturbed.

Shortly after sunup the next morning the young man walked into the camp of the Indians. His heart beat furiously, and he could feel beads of perspiration breaking out on his face as he watched for the red man's reactions to his coming.

To his astonishment there was no rush of excitement. Squaws and children merely looked up from their work or their play, following him curiously with their eyes. The men did not move to intercept him. They merely watched, their faces expressionless, and Brainerd moved forward through the village toward the wigwam of the chief.

It was an eerie feeling. The suspense of it was nerve shattering.

But Brainerd continued his even stride, not showing any outward sign of fear, and when he faced the chief at the doorway to his wigwam, the young white man made a gesture of friendship, placing a bright, keen knife before the chief. Then he waited, not knowing whether the knife would be turned against him. If the chief raised his hand, braves would shout, bind him with leather thongs. . . .

At last the chief nodded and raised his hand in a gesture of good will, and Brainerd smiled, all his fears released, and he turned to look again at the large, well-kept Indian encampment.

For three years the young missionary stayed with the Indians of the village. He won their confidence, taught them the stories and the way of the Bible, worked with them, helped them, won their respect. But always in the back of his mind was the puzzling question: "Why did they accept me so easily? Why did they not kill me, as they had killed so many other white men?"

Only when he felt he had the complete confidence of the village did he dare ask the question. He was hunting with a young brave one afternoon. Their hunt had been successful and they were carrying game back to the village. He summoned all his courage.

"My friend," Brainerd said, "there is something I would ask you."

The brave nodded his willingness to answer.

"When I first came, how is it that you did not treat me as an enemy?"

The brave let the game on his shoulder fall to the grass beside the trail. He stood thoughtful a moment, then said: "When you come, we know you are friend. The forest brothers, they tell us. We come to capture you—to kill you. You are by the river on your knees. You pray. We watch, ready to spring. Then, big rattlesnake come. Snake coil, make ready to strike. We wait. Then, for no reason, he turn his head, go away. You still pray. We know you are friend, that Great Spirit is with paleface."

Brainerd blinked his eyes in astonishment. Then many things were clear to him—his acceptance by the Indians, his success in teaching and leading them—all because of a miracle beside the Susquehanna. Yes, it was a miracle. The Great Spirit was with him, guiding his every step, his every move.

Brainerd smiled, shouldered his share of the load. "That is an interesting story," he said. "I am thankful the Great Spirit watches over me." [3]

80

POEM:

O God, in restless living
We lose our spirits' peace.
Calm our unwise confusion,
Bid Thou our clamor cease.
Let anxious hearts grow quiet,
Like pools at evening still,
Till thy reflected heavens
All our spirits fill.

Teach us, beyond our striving,
The rich rewards of rest.
Who does not live serenely
Is never deeply blest.
O tranquil, radiant Sunlight,
Bring thou our lives to flower,
Less wearied with our effort,
More aware of power.

Receptive make our spirits,
Our need is to be still;
As dawn fades flickering candle
So dim our anxious will.
Reveal thy radiance through us,
Thine ample strength release.
Not ours but thine the triumph,
In the power of peace.[4]
—HARRY EMERSON FOSDICK

PRAYER:

O God, who hast taught us that in quietness and in confidence shall be our strength; make us to know that thou art with us, and that with thee is help adequate to our need.

We come to thee with our sins, asking thy forgiveness.

We come with our anxieties, needing courage and confidence such as are born of trust in thee.

We come with our manifold problems, knowing that wisdom dwells in thee, and that only in thy light shall we see light.

We come with our griefs, in the assurance that thou art able to revive the fainting soul and to comfort those who are crushed.

O thou who knowest us altogether and art acquainted with all our ways, show to us thy mercy and the wonders of thy grace. Grant us peace within our hearts. Grant us light upon our way. Grant us strength sufficient for the work we have to do and the burdens we have to bear. Enable us to fight the good fight, to endure to the end, and to obtain the victory; through Jesus Christ our Lord. AMEN.[5]

HYMN: "More Love to Thee, O Christ" or
      "Thou My Everlasting Portion"

BENEDICTION:
May the peace of God which passeth all understanding, keep your hearts and minds; through Jesus Christ our Lord. AMEN.

LOVE IS OF GOD

PRELUDE: "The Swan" by Saint-Saëns

CALL TO WORSHIP:

>   Beloved, let us love: love is of God;
>   In God alone hath love its true abode.
>
>   Beloved, let us love: for they who love,
>   They only, are his sons, born from above.
>
> .   .   .   .
>
>   Beloved, let us love: for love is light,
>   And he who loveth not dwelleth in night.
>
>   Beloved, let us love: for only thus
>   Shall we behold that God who loveth us.
>   —HORATIUS BONAR

HYMN: "Love Divine, All Loves Excelling" or
"Lord of All Being, Throned Afar"

SCRIPTURE:

>   The Lord is merciful and gracious,
>   slow to anger, and plenteous in mercy.
>   He will not always chide:
>   neither will he keep his anger for ever.
>   He hath not dealt with us after our sins;
>   nor rewarded us according to our iniquities.
>   For as the heaven is high above the earth,
>   so great is his mercy toward them that fear him.
>   As far as the east is from the west,
>   so far hath he removed our transgressions from us.

Like as a father pitieth his children,
   so the Lord pitieth them that fear him.
For he knoweth our frame;
   he remembereth that we are dust.[1]

POEM:

For all who watch tonight—by land or sea or air—
O Father, may they know that thou art with them there.

For all who weep tonight, the hearts that cannot rest,
Reveal thy love, that wondrous love which gave for us thy best.
. . . .
For all who fear tonight, whate'er the dread may be,
We ask for them the perfect peace of hearts that rest in thee.
. . . .
And all who pray tonight, thy wrestling hosts, O Lord,
Make weakness strong, let them prevail according to thy word.

                  —AUTHOR UNKNOWN

LEADER:
We will hear a story which illustrates God's love for us.

STORY:

THE WATCHER

"He sits there every day from the rising of the sun to the going down thereof. He is watching for his son."

The camel drivers of the caravan which had just arrived at the city's gate were busily engaged in the task of unpacking the huge bales of merchandise, and the master of the caravan was in merry but guarded conversation with Mordecai the merchant.

Gorgeous rugs from the East, exquisite tapestries from cities along the Tigris and Euphrates, finely tempered blades from the forges of Damascus, spices from far-off India, porcelains from Cathay, and sweet-scented wood from distant islands of the sea—these lay spread about in dazzling profusion.

As Mordecai made a furtive appraisal of the goods, he was attempting to conceal his interest in a flow of small talk. The bargaining which soon would begin would be a battle of wits in which he would need every advantage he could get.

The foundation of the great wall of the city formed a broad stone shelf, about four feet above the level of the street, and on that shelf in a shady corner beside the massive buttress on the east side of the gate sat an old man, cross-legged after the manner of the Orient. His thin white hair was a halo over stooped shoulders, and his misty eyes were fixed on the point where the caravan route disappeared beyond the limestone ridge on the other side of the valley. From his dress it might have been inferred that he was a man of substance, and the respectful way in which he was greeted by those who came out of the city indicated that he was well known and highly honored.

The master of the caravan was watching the old man through curious eyes, and, in answer to one of the master's questions, Mordecai was explaining his presence at the city's gate.

"Years ago he was one of the prosperous merchants of this city," Mordecai said, "and his caravans were on many highways. Jehovah had blessed him with much goods, so that he fared sumptuously every day. Moreover, he had two sons in whom his heart took great delight. But the burden of the day weighed heavily upon him, and he sighed for rest and ease. Therefore, when his youngest son besought him for the share of the inheritance that would fall to him, the old merchant divided his fortune between his sons, and retired unto his house. Not many days thereafter the younger one gathered his wealth together and journeyed into a far country, and every day the old man takes his seat beside the city's gate, scanning the caravans, in the hope that his son will return."

"Is this son a merchant, gone on some great enterprise?"

"No," Mordecai answered, "he was a youth of spirit and adventure, and his feet took him in the direction of much laughter, strong wine, and women with honeyed words upon their lips. Because of his long silence his father carries a deep sorrow within his heart, and because he loves him with an undying love he watches every day for his return."

"Whither did the boy go?"

"No one knows for a surety," Mordecai answered, with a little hesitancy, "though it is reported that he was last seen in Borsippa, on the lower reaches of the Euphrates."

At this the impassive face of the master brightened for a fraction of a second, as if the mention of Borsippa had stirred a flicker of interest in his heart. But before Mordecai's eyes could search his face, the crafty trader had assumed his mask again.

"Borsippa is a very great city," he said. "It has much that would be of interest to a comely youth with money to spend. I have seen young men from many lands rioting within its pleasure halls."

"He was a headstrong lad who would seek out the gayest crowd, but he was lovable and trusting withal, and for such there are many pitfalls," said Mordecai, pretending to examine a rug in which he had no interest in an effort to conceal his admiration for a piece of embroidered cloth which he hoped to buy at a bargain.

The master of the caravan, with the cunning of his craft, had noted the merchant's delight in the cloth with its design of scarlet and gold on purple; but he was as subtle as Mordecai, and went on with the conversation.

"My trade has carried me into many cities," he said, "and I have met many young men. Some of them have traveled with me in my caravans. Tell me the lad's name."

"He was known in this city as Shimron," Mordecai answered, "a lad of great might and stature, and skilled in the games of youth."

At the mention of the name Shimron the master's eyes opened wide and there was now no pretense in his voice or manner. "Did he have a scar over his left eye?" he asked.

"From being gored by a ram," Mordecai explained, the embroidered cloth forgotten for the moment.

"Then I have seen him!" the master exclaimed. "Only a fortnight ago I saw him in Racappa, a goodly city in the upper valley of the Euphrates. I believe he is returning to his father's house. But the lad has known much trouble.

"I saw him first three years ago, soon after he arrived in Babylon. His winsome ways and carefree spending made many friends for him among strange women and men without souls. And in time there was a famine in that land; and Shimron, his money and his jewels gone, was forgotten by all those who had consumed his treasure. In great loneliness he wandered from city to city in an effort to find food, and no man gave unto him. Finally he engaged himself to a rich farmer of Babylon as a swineherd. I saw him there when my caravan rested while I trafficked with his master.

"Long months of want have made many changes in him. The ways of sin have left their marks upon his countenance and the burdens of wickedness have laid grievous loads upon him. But who knows? The power of a father's love has worked much redemption, and Shimron may yet bring joy to his sire's heart."

"I pray you, tell this news to the aged one," Mordecai pleaded. "Lo, he has sat beside the gate for many days in heaviness of heart. His soul will rejoice in the word you bring."

The court outside the city's gate was filled with camels, drivers, merchants, idlers, and booths set up by tradesmen. On a little platform that lifted him up above the throng sat a judge hearing a case at law. Money-changers, jingling their coins, mingled with the crowd in search of clients. Buyers and sellers gesticulated besides piles of merchandise and shouted their last offers.

For more than an hour the master of the caravan and Mordecai had haggled over the price of the embroidered cloth. At last the purchase had been made, and Mordecai was left with the goldsmith who traveled with the caravan, while the master made his way over to the old man who sat beside the gate.

Saluting him respectfully, the master inquired, "Have you a caravan coming into the city, most noble sire?"

Upon the master of the caravan the old man turned faded eyes in which there was a light of a long-suffering hope. "It is no caravan that brings me to sit at the city's gate, my friend," he replied. "I have a son who has gone on a long journey. I await him."

"Is he to come this day?" the master asked, and in his voice there was an unaccustomed tenderness.

"That I know not. He has been gone in a far country for, lo, these many months, and has sent no word. But I come daily to the gate, so that when he comes, there shall be a father's welcome for him."

"But such waiting requires much patience. It may be the youth has met with misfortune, or it may be that he has grown enamored of the far country."

The old man's eyes were back upon the highway again, and the wistful look had spread over his features once more. Without looking at his questioner he replied: "These things may well be as you say, most honored sir, but I shall sit at the gate waiting to welcome my son, if it be even unto the day when I am gathered unto my fathers. If the Lord God will hear my prayer and send him unto me, I will not be found wanting in a father's love."

"But I have known young men in the far country, and they sometimes forget their father's love."

"I know the way of young men," the aged sire said, "and I know the evil ways of the far country. But none of these things will ever defeat the love I bear my son. If he be alive I will love him back."

The master of the caravan parted his lips to speak, and then, as if doubting his own words, he closed them again. All the time the old man stared past him, down the highway. At last the trader turned to go, and as he did so he said, "May the Lord God Jehovah grant thy prayer and add peace unto thy days."

"May the peace of God be upon thee likewise," the old man answered, turning his eyes toward him for a brief moment.

Nearly an hour later the master of the caravan found Mordecai beside a great pile of beautiful rugs. With a certain gentleness in his voice he told the merchant of his visit with the old man. "And who knows? He may be right. Love like his may bring the sinful son back to his father's house."

"I never knew there was such love in all the world," Mordecai declared, his voice trembling as he arose.

"There is a young prophet over in Galilee, whose name is Jesus," the master said, "who says that God's love is like that. I hope he is right!" [2]

POEM:

> I sought the Lord, and afterward I knew
>> He moved my soul to seek him, seeking me;
> It was not I that found, O Saviour true,
>> No, I was found of thee.
>
> Thou didst reach forth thy hand and mine enfold;
>> I walked and sank not on the storm-vexed sea;
> 'Twas not so much that I on thee took hold,
>> As thou, dear Lord, on me.
>
> I find, I walk, I love, but, O the whole
>> Of love is but my answer, Lord, to thee!
> For thou wert long beforehand with my soul;
>> Always thou lovedst me.
>
> —AUTHOR UNKNOWN

PRAYER:

Our Father, we are grateful for the revelation of thyself through thy Son, for the record of his life and teachings, and for the inspiration coming to us from a study of the Scriptures. We thank thee for thy watchful care over us. Forgive our willfulness, selfishness, and all the sins which keep us from having a close fellowship with thee. Make thyself known to us not only through our worship but in ordinary activities. Teach us to live in a manner that is pleasing to thee, and may we show our gratitude for all thy gifts by giving ourselves completely to thee and walking before thee in humility and righteousness. Lead us into a deeper loyalty to thee and a greater devotion to thy cause; through Jesus Christ our Lord. AMEN.

HYMN: "We May Not Climb the Heavenly Steeps" or
         "There's a Wideness in God's Mercy"

BENEDICTION:
    Help us to learn thy will and purpose for our lives as we continue to walk with thee. AMEN.

SERVICE 14

IN QUIETNESS AND IN CONFIDENCE

PRELUDE: Hymn tune "Morning Hymn" by Haydn

CALL TO WORSHIP:

> Jesus, thou Joy of loving hearts!
>> Thou Fount of life! Thou Light of men!
> From the best bliss that earth imparts,
>> We turn unfilled to thee again.
>
> . . . .
>
> O Jesus, ever with us stay;
>> Make all our moments calm and bright;
> Chase the dark night of sin away,
>> Shed o'er the world thy holy light!
>> —Ascribed to BERNARD OF CLAIRVAUX

HYMN: "Dear Lord and Father of Mankind" or
"Be Still, My Soul"

SCRIPTURE:

Happy art thou. . . . Who is like unto thee, O people saved by the Lord, the shield of thy help?

As thy days, so shall thy strength be. . . . The eternal God is thy refuge, and underneath are the everlasting arms.

Truly my soul waiteth upon God: from him cometh my salvation. . . . My soul, wait thou only upon God; for my expectation is from him.

He only is my rock and my salvation; he is my defense; I shall not be moved. . . .

Trust in him at all times; ye people, pour out your heart before him; God is a refuge for us. . . .

Thou wilt keep him in perfect peace, whose mind is stayed on thee: because he trusteth in thee.

Trust ye in the Lord for ever: for in the Lord our God is everlasting strength. . . .

Thus saith the Lord . . . , In returning and rest shall ye be saved; in quietness and in confidence shall be your strength. . . .

Be still, and know that I am God. . . .

And when he had sent the multitude away, he went up into a mountain apart to pray: and when the evening was come, he was there alone. . . .

And he said unto them, Come ye yourselves apart into a desert place, and rest a while.[1]

LEADER:

We will hear the story of one who discovered a new avenue of approach to God, and at the same time a solution to her problem.

STORY:

THE ANGELUS

To Hetty the world was a place of weary days and unrestful nights, and life was a thing of dishes that were never quite washed and of bread that was never quite baked—there was always something to be done.

First there was the breakfast for Theron and the hired man in the chill gray dawn of each day, for if one were to wrest a living from the stones and sand of the little hillside farm, one must be up and at work betimes. Then Harry, Tom, and Nellie must be roused, dressed, and fed . . . and made ready for the half-mile walk to the schoolhouse at the crossroads.

After that the day was a blur of steam, dust, heat and stifling fumes from the oven and the kettle, broken always at regular intervals by meal getting and chicken feeding. What mattered the blue of the heavens or the green of the earth outside? To Hetty the one was sky and the other grass. What mattered the sheen of silver in the emerald velvet of the valley far below? Hetty would have told you that it was the sun on Otter Creek down in Johnson's meadow.

And at night even sleep brought little relief to her, for her dreams were of hungry mouths that could not be filled and dirt-streaked floors that would not come clean.

Each day the sun rose, traveled its scheduled way across the sky and went to rest, and Hetty came to envy the sun. To her mind his work extended from the first rays that shot into her room in the morning to the last rose flush at night, while as for herself there were the supper dishes and the mending basket yet waiting.

Last summer Helen Raymond, Hetty's niece, had spent a week at the farm, and now a letter had come saying that she was to look out for an express package from New York.

When had she received a package by express before? Even Christmas brought to her no fascinating boxes or mysterious packages. It would be interesting to open it—and yet it probably held a book which she had no time to read, or a pretty blouse which she would have no time to wear.

Several days later her unaccustomed lips were spelling out the words on a small white card which had come with a handsomely framed picture: "The Angelus—Jean François Millet—1859."

Hetty looked from the card to the picture and then back again to the card. Gradually an angry light took the place of dazed wonder in her eyes. She turned fiercely to her husband. "Theron," she said, "why did Helen send me that picture?"

"Why, Hetty, I dunno, unless she wanted ter please yuh."

"Please me! Did she expect to please me with a thing like that? Look here. Theron, look here," she cried, snatching up the picture. "Look at that woman an' man! They're us, Theron; us, I tell you!"

"Oh, come, Hetty, they ain't jest the same yuh know. She didn't mean nothin'—Helen didn't."

"Mean nothin'! Then why didn't she send us something pretty, something that showed us pretty things, not jes fields an' farm folks? Why didn't she, Theron, why didn't she?" . . . "I know! 'Twas cause she thought that was all we could understand, dirt and old clothes an' folks that look like us! Don't we dig an' dig like them? Ain't our hands twisted an' old an' . . . ?"

"Hetty, yuh ain't yerself!"

"Yes, I am, I'm always myself. There's never anything else I can be, Theron, never!"

For some days the picture stayed on the kitchen shelf where it had been placed by Theron. Hetty did not seem to notice it after the first day and Theron was most willing to forget. It must have been a week after the picture's arrival that the minister from the village made his semi-yearly call.

"Oh, you have an 'Angelus'! That's fine!"

"Oh, that thing," said Hetty.

"That thing," repeated the man, quick to detect the scorn in her voice. "Why 'that thing,' as you call it, is a copy of the picture which in the original sold for one hundred and fifty thousand dollars!"

"Why, who could have bought it? That thing!"

But Hetty did not forget his words, for after the minister had gone she took the picture from the shelf and carried it to the light of the window.

"One hundred and fifty thousand dollars! And to think what I'd do with that money. . . . Well, they do look natural—but only think of payin' one hundred fifty thousand for a couple of farm folks out in a field. . . ." And yet, it was not to the kitchen shelf Hetty carried the picture that night but to the parlor, the somber sacred parlor where she propped it up among the plush photograph albums and crochet mats, her dearest treasures.

She scarcely could have explained to herself the reason for this change, but after the minister's call that day she went often to look at the picture. At first its famous price graced it with a halo of gold, but in time this was forgotten and the picture itself, with its silent bowed figures, appealed to her with a power she could not understand.

"There's a story to it," she said. "There's a story to it."

Then she hunted up an old pencil and a piece of yellow paper. Although she spent a long hour in labored thinking and careful guiding of cramped fingers along an unfamiliar way, the completed note, when it reached Helen Raymond, seemed very short.

The return letter was long. It answered not only her questions but attempted to respond to the longings and heart hunger Helen Raymond detected between the lines of Hetty's note. Twelve hours after it was written Hetty was on her knees before the picture.

"I know you now—I know you. I know why you're real and true. Your master, who painted you, was like us once—like us an' like you. He knew what it meant to dig an' dig. He knew what it meant to work and work till his back an' his head an' his feet an' his hands ached and ached—he knew, an' so he painted you.

"She says that you're prayin'—that you've stopped your work and turned to higher things. She says we should all have an Angelus in our lives . . . An Angelus. Good God! As if she knew! An Angelus. The dishpan? The washtub? The chicken yard? A fine Angelus that! And yet you look so peaceful, an' so quiet, an' so rested!"

It was not long after this that the picture disappeared from the parlor. Hetty had borne it very carefully to her room and hung it on the wall at the foot of her bed where her eyes would see it the first thing in the morning.

Every day she talked to it and every day it grew to be more and more a part of her very self. Not until the picture had been there a week did she suddenly realize that it represented the twilight hour. Then like a flash of light came her inspiration.

"It's the sunset! I'll go out at sunset an' my Angelus will come to me—I know it will."

Then indeed did the little hillside farmhouse see some strange sights. Each night as the sun dropped behind the faraway hills Hetty left her work and passed through the kitchen door, her face uplifted and her eyes on the distant skyline.

At first her eyes saw the grass, sky, and dull brown earth, and her thoughts turned in bitterness to her unfinished tasks, but gradually the witchery of the summer nights broke upon her. The grass assumed a deeper green and the trees stood out as sentinels along the hilltop. Even when she turned and went back to the kitchen and took up once more the accustomed tasks, her eyes still faintly glowed with the memory of what they had seen, and a peace and quiet entered her soul.

"It do beat all," said Theron a month later to Helen Raymond who was again at the farm, "it do beat all what's some over Hetty. She used ter be so sad like and fretted, and now she's calm and her eyes kind o' shine—'specially when she comes in from one o' them tramps out o' doors. She says it's because she has an 'Angelus!'" And Helen smiled in content.[2]

POEM:

> Draw thou my soul, O Christ,
>   Closer to thine;
> Breathe into every wish
>   Thy will divine!
> Raise my low self above,
> Won by thy deathless love;
>   Ever, O Christ, through mine
>   Let thy life shine.
>
> Lead forth my soul, O Christ,
>   One with thine own,
> Joyful to follow thee
>   Through paths unknown!

In thee my strength renew;
Give me my work to do!
  Through me thy truth be shown,
  Thy love made known.

—LUCY LARCOM

I need wide spaces in my heart
Where Faith and I can go apart
  And grow serene.
Life gets so choked by busy living,
Kindness so lost in fussy giving
  That Love slips by unseen.

—AUTHOR UNKNOWN

O Golden Silence, bid our souls be still,
  And on the foolish fretting of our care
  Lay thy soft touch of healing unaware.

—JULIA CAROLINE DORR

PRAYER:

O God, our Father, who art always ready to hear our supplication, grant unto each of us a sense of thy presence. May we put out of our minds all thoughts or attitudes which would keep us from a close fellowship with thee. Help each of us to have an Angelus in our lives—a time and place set apart for communion with thee. Teach us how to be still, to listen to thy voice, to follow thy leadership. Direct us as we strive to give thee first place in our lives, put thy will above our wills, and endeavor to live as sons and daughters of thine. Reveal to us ways by which we can help to bring thy kingdom on earth. In Jesus' name. AMEN.

HYMN: "Make Me a Captive, Lord" or
       "O Gracious Father of Mankind"

BENEDICTION:

May we show forth thy praise not only with our lips but in our lives, through Christ our Lord. AMEN.

SERVICE 15

VALUE OF THE INDIVIDUAL

PRELUDE: Hymn tune "Laudes Domini"

CALL TO WORSHIP:

> Stone walls do not a prison make,
> Nor iron bars a cage;
> Minds innocent and quiet take
> That for a hermitage:
> If I have freedom in my love,
> And in my soul am free,
> Angels alone, that soar above,
> Enjoy such liberty.[1]
>
> —RICHARD LOVELACE

HYMN: "Dear Master, in Whose Life I See" or
"O Thou Who Camest from Above"

SCRIPTURE:

Where the Spirit of the Lord is, there is liberty. . . .

Stand fast therefore in the liberty wherewith Christ hath made us free, and be not entangled again with the yoke of bondage. . . .

The fruit of the Spirit is love, joy, peace, longsuffering, gentleness, goodness, faith, meekness, temperance: against such there is no law. . . . If we live in the Spirit, let us also walk in the Spirit. . . .

Ye shall know the truth, and the truth shall make you free.[2]

LEADER:

The God who gave us life gave us liberty at the same time.—THOMAS JEFFERSON.

Personal liberty is the paramount essential to human dignity and human happiness.—BULWER-LYTTON.

The spirit of man grows in freedom; it withers in chains.—BERNARD M. BARUCH.

96

VALUE OF THE INDIVIDUAL

The only freedom worth possessing is that which gives enlargement to a people's energy, intellect, and virtue.—THEODORE PARKER.

Do you wish to be free? Then above all things love God, love your neighbor, love one another, love the common weal; then you will have true liberty.—SAVONAROLA.

We will hear the story of a Korean girl's attempt to understand democracy.

STORY:

I AM A CONVERT TO DEMOCRACY

I first heard about the United States many years ago when a small girl living with my family in North Korea. I heard about the wonderful American inventions, but what really impressed me was the idea of God's love as brought home to us by a group of simple, dedicated American missionaries.

My parents were ardent Buddhists, spiritualists, and Confucianists. No home had more idols than ours. When the dread cholera came and took my father and brother, it left my mother and me completely desolate. The idols were no comfort. In Korea a family with no men is no family at all.

It was at this time that a cousin who had recently become a Christian tried to comfort us.

"Is your God sympathetic?" my mother asked.

"Not only does this God love everyone, and grieves with those who have sorrow," our cousin said, "but this God has schools to which women can go as well as men."

This was a startling new thought for my mother. It turned her attention to me with new hope.

It was on Christmas Day that Mother and I walked three miles over snowy country roads to the nearest Christian church. Missionaries in the crude building greeted us warmly and presented me with a yellow pencil and a yellow writing pad. I was thrilled speechless. My mother was so touched that when we returned home that night, she burned all the idols in our home. Both of us accepted this new Christianity, and I set about learning to read and write the Korean alphabet.

"I wonder if she has enough brains to learn it," my mother thought to herself, wavering between her new hope and the common Korean conception that all females were stupid. I showed her. I learned the alphabet in two weeks.

What few Christian schools there were in our country at that time started at high school level. Meanwhile, I needed elementary grounding, so we moved to another area where there was a regular Korean school—for boys only. From that moment on I was a boy!

In those days both sexes wore the same long braided hair, with black ribbons tied at the end for boys, red ribbons for girls. Only slight changes were needed in my other garments—my jacket had to be lengthened and mother converted a skirt into a pair of trousers. My feminine-sounding name, Imduk, became, Induk.

Korean boys act like brats. The louder you read, the smarter you were. I shouted my head off. Boys were agile and athletic. I learned to climb trees, to play ball and to fish with the best of them. After two years I graduated without anyone knowing my real sex.

My mother, meanwhile, had saved enough money to buy me a railroad ticket to Seoul, home of Ewha Christian College for Korean women. Dressed now as a girl, I said good-by to her, clutching my few articles of clothing and ninety cents. When I arrived at the college, Miss Iula Frey, the principal, stared at me in dismay.

"But there's no money to feed you and no place for you to sleep," she said in answer to my request for admission. "I have fifty girls on the waiting list."

I looked around and saw an unused reception room. "I can sleep there," I pleaded. "I won't get in the way. I'll go to bed after the others and get up real early."

"But what will you eat?"

"I'll eat the scraps left by the others," I said desperately.

The kindly missionaries didn't have the heart to turn me away. An appeal was written to the United States, asking for additional funds to take care of just one more student. A man in Wilmington, Illinois, Mr. C. G. Steinhard, who himself had just gone blind, heard of my situation.

"My physical light is gone," he said to his sister, "but I would like to share my spiritual light with this Korean girl." Together they managed to send five dollars a month to Korea for seven years—the priceless sum needed to put a girl through school. (When I had a chance to thank this man in person many years later, he said: "You have caught the spiritual light, Induk. Share it with those who live in darkness.")

Upon my graduation from Ewha College, I became a schoolteacher and also took part in the Korean independence movement. Then a calamity happened. A number of us were rounded up and thrown into jail as agitators. Some were beaten to death. In my cold, bare cell, illuminated only by a tiny light from one slitlike window, I prayed: "If only I had a Bible to read and some rice to eat."

At the very same time Miss Frey at Ewha College was thinking: "I wonder what Induk needs most—probably some rice." So she began a systematic campaign to get some rice to me.

Meanwhile two of my missionary friends, Dr. and Mrs. Billings, remembered me. "What would be of most help to Induk?" they asked of each other.

A Bible was their decision.

They began to exert steady pressure on a judge they knew to have prison officials give me a Bible.

Several days later my prison door opened and guards handed me both a Bible and a container of rice.

How I pored over that book. Up to this time Christianity had meant an education and a new world of opportunities to me, but I had never really known God. In this grimy prison I was suddenly able to feel the presence of God through that Bible. New strength and faith came. I read the Bible through twice, then began memorizing passages. Death lost its terror because God was there to steady and comfort me. After six months officials set me free.

Strange how real and close God is to one in time of crisis, yet how easily we can let material interests and activities crowd him into the background again. My great plans to help improve the conditions of Korean women were forgotten after my release from prison. For I met a young man and fell in love.

My husband-to-be was an innkeeper. We had furnished a home with many lovely possessions, and one night while we were away, the home burned to the ground. As we stared at the ashes, stunned and heartsick, a neighbor dashed up with a silver vase.

"I'm so very sorry," she sympathized, proffering me the silver vase. "You lent me that last week—at least something has been saved."

Accepting the vase humbly, I suddenly felt the great truth of a phrase I had learned: *That which I kept I lost, that which I shared I have.*

That experience made me resolve all over again to share the benefits of my Christian education, and live the kind of life that I knew God meant for me. Soon after, an opportunity arose for me to go to the United States and do some speaking. With the money I earned, I was able to return and help my people. Other speaking invitations came, including one to the United Nations. Then I had an opportunity to bring a message to my people through the Voice of America.

During years of lecture trips I have traveled 434,020 miles with over 2,500 speeches made in 4 continents and 35 countries. My husband, mother, and first daughter are gone now, but I'll carry on my work as long as God gives me the strength. To American people who are disturbed over their responsibilities for world leadership, perhaps this message will help: *That which I kept I lost, that which I shared I have.*

And from my own experience I know that the greatest thing Americans have to sell is not their wealth and comforts, but that the United States is a country founded on belief in God, where man has freedom and opportunity to do, to think, to act, and to become just what he chooses.[3]

PRAYER:

As we look across the vast field of our work, O Master, we feel the challenge of thy call and turn to thee for strength. So much to do for thee, and so little wherewith to do it!

O Christ, thou who art touched with a feeling of our infirmities and hast been tempted even as we, look with thy great sympathy on thy servants. Thou knowest the drain of our daily work and the limitations of our bodies. Thou knowest that we carry but a little candle of knowledge to guide the feet of the erring amid the mazes of modern life. Thou knowest that our longing for holiness of heart is frustrated by the drag of our earthliness and the weight of ancient sins.

Fit us for our work, lest we fail thee. We lean on thee, thou great giver of life, and pray for physical vigor and quiet strength. We call to thee, thou fountain of life, to flood our minds with thy radiance and to make all things clear and simple. We submit our inmost desires to thy will, and beseech thee to make thy law sweet to our willing hearts.

Give, Lord, what thou askest, and then ask what thou wilt. We make our prayer, O God, by faith in Christ, our Lord. AMEN.[4]

HYMN: "My Soul, Be on Thy Guard" or
    "Dear Master, in Whose Life I See"

BENEDICTION:

Direct us, O Lord, in all we attempt to do, that we may in all our work glorify thy name, through Jesus Christ our Lord. AMEN.

SERVICE 16

HE WHO WOULD VALIANT BE

PRELUDE: "Melody in F" by Rubenstein

CALL TO WORSHIP:
Thou wilt keep him in perfect peace, whose mind is stayed on thee: because he trusteth in thee. Trust ye in the Lord for ever: for in the Lord Jehovah is everlasting strength.[1]

HYMN: "O Son of Man, Thou Madest Known" or
"Dare To Be Brave"

LEADER:
Be willing to have it so. Acceptance of what has happened is the first step to overcoming the consequences of any misfortune.—WILLIAM JAMES.

For those who will fight bravely and not yield, there is triumphant victory over all the dark things of life.—JAMES ALLEN.

> Cowards die many times before their deaths;
> The valiant never taste of death but once.[2]
>   —SHAKESPEARE

SCRIPTURE:
If thou faint in the day of adversity, thy strength is small. . . .

Be strong and of a good courage, fear not, nor be afraid of them: for the Lord thy God, he it is that doth go with thee; he will not fail thee, nor forsake thee. . . .

Wait on the Lord: be of good courage, and he shall strengthen thine heart: wait, I say, on the Lord.[3]

LEADER:
We will hear the story of one who conquered fear and stood steadfastly for what he believed to be right.

STORY:

INQUISITION . . . MY LORD MAYOR

His majesty Lord Mayor Franz Von Ross paced the floor of his study. Muttering angrily to himself he read a letter through for the fourth time. The study door opened letting in a young man.

"You called, my Lord?"

"Of course. Take a message to my son Wilhelm." The mayor read once more the last paragraph of the letter: ". . . and having heard Herr Martin Luther at Wittenberg, I have decided to leave the university and go study under this man. His viewpoints are mine. I agree with him and feel I shall be useful only after studying under him. The church will no doubt protest, but you will see what I have in mind and agree to my move."

The mayor turned to his waiting secretary. "Say this to my son . . . there has never been anything so confounding in all my life. You are a young student with just enough education to make you a fool. Leave Munich if you must, but as to your decision concerning this rebel Luther—hark these words! Go to him and you not only leave the church, but you leave your father's house. I will make no move whatsoever to aid you when trouble comes to you, as surely it will."

The secretary was dismissed. For a long time the mayor looked out the windows, seeing nothing in the street below.

Wilhelm let himself from the huge building that housed the students of Munich University. There was an ache in his heart but also a stern determination. He smiled and thought, "From now on I will be a poor scholar, for my father will turn against me." Somewhere along this road the young man would be given a ride and finally would arrive at Wittenberg.

The secretary announced, "This letter is from the archbishop."

The longer the mayor read, the redder his face became. "That young scoundrel of mine has disobeyed me and gone to Wittenberg. The Munich authorities reported his move to the archbishop, and I am to appear before him to explain the movement of Wilhelm. Send a message to the archbishop with word that I shall appear before him this afternoon."

Sometimes the mayor felt an urge to rage against the practices of the church, but habit of a lifetime forced his lips to remain silent. Martin Luther in posting his ninety-five theses on the church door at Wittenberg had fired him with a strange ecstasy of reform. But he had made no move or even given a hint to his feeling. He could truthfully say that no comment he might have made had caused his son's decision.

The mayor was ushered in, and without any preliminaries the archbishop remarked: "Von Ross, word came to me that your son Wilhelm has denied the teachings of the church and is listening to Herr Martin Luther. Is this true?"

"I have not talked with my son. I do not know with surety just what has occurred."

"Let there be no evading. What a son thinks is implanted within him by his parents. Von Ross, you are secretly leading or teaching against the doctrines of the Catholic Church? That is heresy, and you know the consequences."

Hatred against this domineering attitude flared up in the breast of the mayor. Maybe Luther was correct. Reform was needed. He looked the old man in the eyes and spoke calmly. "What are the consequences?"

The archbishop pointed a shaking finger at the mayor as he snarled: "Consequences? Inquisition, my Lord Mayor. Inquisition for you and your whelp."

A door opened and two soldiers led a young man in. Von Ross gasped. Before he could speak the archbishop was addressing the young man.

"Wilhelm Von Ross, answer truthfully before God these questions. Were you a student at Munich University? And did you leave that university to sit under the teachings of Martin Luther?"

"I did!"

"In doing so you violated the rules of your church. Were you aware?"

The young man replied: "I was aware of the consequences when I went to Wittenberg. But I would do likewise were I released this minute. The church needs reform. Who indeed but the foolish in his heart believes in good works to bring him to his Creator? Or that indulgences assure a place in paradise? Morality is good, but it does not assure immortality. Luther teaches salvation by faith and the priesthood of all believers."

"Enough of this heresy! You young fool! It will take much penance and many indulgences to atone for your sins now. Do not add to them." The young man was taken out of the room without an opportunity to speak to his father.

Von Ross was pale. But he was a wise man. No rash, foolhardy statements were forthcoming. Instead, a plan was already forming in his mind.

"Von Ross, you heard the words of your son. No doubt some of them can be laid to the rashness of youth. However, he has listened to Luther and you know his influence is strong."

"What would you have me do, sir?"

"There will be the matter of penance. Much penance to atone for your negligence in the upbringing of your son. Then there will be some indulgences, of course; perhaps furnish funds for a new church."

"Very well, sir. May I beg your pleasure to let me abide a day to decide what I shall do to atone for my sins and those of my son?" The archbishop nodded and the mayor bowed out of the room.

No time was lost by the mayor. First he dispatched a message to Martin Luther, telling him what had occurred. Then with boldness he moved about the city and countryside talking to anyone who would listen. When midnight came he had his plan in motion.

Early next morning the jailers received orders from the archbishop to bring Wilhelm to the monastery before dawn. Needless to say, before the guards and their prisoner had traveled many streets, they were surprised by a group of citizens, but the prisoner was whisked away before the guards could gather strength enough to resist. Bewildered, they went on to the monastery and reported the incident.

An excited monk broke in upon the archbishop's morning meal. "Majesty, there is something happening that you should know. In the courtyard are two hundred peasants with spikes and clubs and led by the lord mayor himself. And there must be a thousand without the court, waiting to enter."

"Why? What is their purpose?"

"Come and see. They are calling for you."

The archbishop appeared on the balcony. Seeing the mayor, he addressed him, "What is the meaning of this?"

"We are a simple people coming to you for a simple cause. My son Wilhelm will tell you the reason."

The young man stepped forward and faced the old man: "Sir, as time passes, the idea of good works as a means of salvation has appeared unsatisfactory. We believe, through the works of Luther, that all men should be able to read the Word of God and pray for themselves, and that salvation comes through faith in our Lord and Master Jesus of Nazareth. We come to allow you grace to leave Frankfurt unharmed. We will escort you to the city limits safely, with your monks. Never will you return to this monastery unless you have reformed according to the lights of Martin Luther."

The old man was a wilted figure on the balcony. He nodded silently and disappeared into the rooms behind him.

The mayor faced his son, "When will you return to Wittenberg to continue your studies?"

"Today the man will arrive who will take over as Luther's representative in Frankfurt. He is to turn the monastery into a school to help educate all who seek knowledge of the truths so long kept from men. He is a man, once a cardinal in the old church, who heard Luther, and believed him and reformed himself. Now he conducts services in German instead of Latin, and the Scriptures are read to all who will listen."

"And you—?" asked the father softly.

"I shall return to Wittenberg tomorrow, with the carriage that returns from bringing him here."

Franz Von Ross arose and stepped around the desk. The hands of father and son met in a handclasp of understanding far surpassing any words that might have been spoken.[4]

Poem:

> O God, whose smile is in the sky,
> Whose path is in the sea,
> Once more from earth's tumultuous strife,
> We gladly turn to Thee.
>
> Now all the myriad sounds of earth
> In solemn stillness die;
> While wind and wave unite to chant
> Their anthems to the sky.
>
> We come as those who toil far spent
> Who crave Thy rest and peace,
> And from the care and fret of life,
> Would find in Thee release.
>
> O Father, soothe all troubled thought,
> Dispel all idle fear,
> Purge Thou each heart of secret sin,
> And banish every care;

Until, as shine upon the sea
The silent stars above,
There shines upon our trusting souls
The light of Thine own love.[5]

—JOHN HAYNES HOLMES

PRAYER:

Our Father, help us to realize that there are many injustices and inequalities in life, that poverty, hardships, and suffering are often the lot of good people, and that evildoers are not always punished immediately for their wickedness. Help us to understand that we can take any experience of life and use it as a means of growth and development of Christian character if it is accepted in the right attitude. Clarify our thinking and enable us to know what is right. Grant that we may accept our full share of responsibility in every situation. When times of testing come and we are tempted to lower our standards, give us the power to make each decision as thou wouldst have us do, and to meet each experience courageously and victoriously. In Jesus' name. AMEN.

HYMN: "Be Strong!" or
"Courage, Brother! Do Not Stumble"

BENEDICTION:

Now may the Lord of peace give you peace always. The Lord be with you all. AMEN.

SERIES THREE
MESSENGERS OF HOPE

SERVICE 17

MESSENGERS OF GOOD NEWS

PRELUDE: Hymn tune "Mornington"

CALL TO WORSHIP:

I look to thee in every need,
   And never look in vain;
I feel thy strong and tender love,
   And all is well again;
The thought of thee is mightier far
Than sin and pain and sorrow are.

. . . .

Thy calmness bends serene above,
   My restlessness to still;
Around me flows thy quickening life,
   To nerve my faltering will:
Thy presence fills my solitude;
Thy providence turns all to good.

—SAMUEL LONGFELLOW

HYMN: "O For a Heart to Praise My God" or
"Lift Up Our Hearts, O King of Kings"

SCRIPTURE:

And the same day, when the even was come, he saith unto them, Let us pass over unto the other side. And when they had sent away the multitude, they took him even as he was in the ship. And there were also with him other little ships. And there arose a great storm of wind, and the waves beat into the ship, so that it was now full. And he was in the hinder part of the ship, asleep on a pillow: and they awake him, and say unto him, Master, carest thou not that we perish?

107

And he arose, and rebuked the wind, and said unto the sea, Peace, be still. And the wind ceased, and there was a great calm. And he said unto them, Why are ye so fearful? how is it that ye have no faith? And they feared exceedingly, and said one to another, What manner of man is this, that even the wind and the sea obey him? . . .

And the apostles said unto the Lord, Increase our faith.[1]

LEADER:

We will hear the story of the dauntless faith and courage of two pioneer missionaries who served in the northwestern part of our country.

STORY:

NARCISSA AND MARCUS WHITMAN

Over a hundred years ago in the little Presbyterian church in Angelica, New York, a blue-eyed, blond-haired girl stood beside a stalwart, bronzed man and repeated her marriage vows. Their names were Narcissa and Marcus Whitman. Immediately afterward the minister announced that the choir would sing a missionary hymn. The words of the beloved old song drifted softly over the little church like a benediction. And then came the last stanza. Members of the choir faltered, their voices clouded, and one by one they stopped, overcome with emotion. It was then the bride took up the thread of the music, her voice clear and full of conviction.

"Yes, my native land . . . I love thee,
All thy scenes I love them well—
Friends, connections, happy country.
Now, I bid you all farewell."

She didn't know it, but the words of that hymn were prophetic.

Narcissa's story really begins on a day when all the women of the Ladies' Aid of Angelica, New York, were in a great flutter. Young Dr. Marcus Whitman, just back from the West, was to tell about his work among the Indians, and he proposed to go back to found a mission. When Marcus strode into the room a gasp could be heard. Dr. Marcus didn't appear in black broadcloth and white shirt. He entered softly on moccasined feet, buckskin shirt open at the neck, breeches of leather, arms and face as bronze as copper. All the ladies were shocked . . . all except one. She was touched by a very strange emotion. Maybe it was the call of adventure, or just old-fashioned "love at first sight." At any rate the next day lovely Narcissa Prentiss asked to be sent as a missionary to the West!

Narcissa's father rebelled; her mother protested; friends told her no white woman had ever gone overland to the West, but Narcissa was adamant. Dr. Marcus came back often those next few months, and he wooed and won lovely Narcissa. Perhaps she planned it that way. You know the ways of a maid with a man. One year later they were married. Narcissa, just past twenty, blond and delicate, didn't look like pioneer stock.

The next day they started on their honeymoon, a honeymoon across the United States to a place vaguely called "The Oregon." Months later they stepped from the flatboat at Liberty, Missouri. It hadn't been bad this far. Every day had been fun, on the stages, on the river, three days in a Conestoga wagon, and every minute a honeymoon. Now they faced the real West, two thousand miles of travel, mostly afoot. There were no roads, no blazed trails, only a rough map made from the reports of Lewis and Clark. Still they looked westward eagerly. Why? Let Narcissa's diary tell.

"We are now halfway to the Rocky Mountains. The country grows rough and travel is slow. My hands are calloused, my feet blistered, and I now wear moccasins. Marcus has been ill, so I made camp, cook, pack, help portage. But we are both so anxious to found a mission in this new country; our sacrifices are petty. This is the most thrilling honeymoon any woman could dream of. At night on the prairie I often wake and see stars so close I can almost touch them. The howl of a coyote and the hoot of an owl are real music. I pray our honeymoon will never end."

From the Missouri to the Columbia there were five posts where white men were stationed, five small dots on a vast country. They must find them or die. They found them one by one, and months later faced the Great Divide. Now came a new problem. They must discard all but essentials to lighten weight. Food, medicine, bedding are vital; a bride's trunk of personal treasures is surplus weight. Narcissa wrote:

"Discarding my small trunk cut the last tie to the world I knew. I was ashamed to show emotion in front of the men. I took the trunk into the forest, opened it, touched each precious thing, my bridal veil, the wedding gown, pieces from my trousseau I had hoped to pass on to my children. I put them back, closed the lid, covered it with fragrant pine needles, wept a moment, and left it."

The weeks stretched to months and the months almost to a year, and then, one clear morning as the fall sun tipped the fir trees . . .

the boy and girl from Angelica looked down on the broad waters of the Columbia River. They went downstream on a raft and then bought horses near Vancouver. Narcissa rode into the fort, her long skirt tattered, her tight-fitting bodice buttoned up to her dimpled chin. Rough woodsmen cheered her as the first white woman to make the overland journey, east to west.

Marcus and Narcissa built a rough log cabin at Waiilatpu in the Cayuse land. Narcissa's chores were without end that first winter, for on her own birthday, March 14, Alice Narcissa arrived, the first white baby born in the territory. Dr. Marcus built a small chapel that served as church and doctor's office, and that fall Narcissa opened the first schoolroom in the Oregon. She loved this new life, enjoyed every day; that is, almost every day—for tragedy was to knock twice at Narcissa's door. The first time was that quiet warm day when Baby Alice slipped away to play by the wide brook. A baby's cry cut through the silence. Narcissa ran screaming to the brook but it was too late.

Narcissa was childless, but not for long. First the Whitmans adopted a half-breed girl, then Mary Ann Bridger, and next, an orphan. Then, one October dawn, a wagon rolled slowly up the trail, an emaciated boy of fourteen half collapsed at the reins. Narcissa ran out. In the wagon were six more half-starved children, one a tiny baby. History knows this family: the "Sager children"; their parents died on the trail to their new Oregon home.

Narcissa adopted all of them, on the spot. Now she had ten! The farm grew, the mission grew, school and church grew, and every day now wagon trains passed on their way to the Yakima or the Willamette, beating the trail of Narcissa Whitman into a road.

Eleven years passed and though Narcissa's hair had streaks of gray, and she was only thirty, and Marcus was gaunt from endless hard work, they were lovers still . . . still on their honeymoon. They would walk of an evening to the top of the knoll when the prairie rose was in bloom and the bobwhite calling. They would sit and talk of the little intimate things that only a man and woman in love can understand. Eleven years is such a short time with the man you love. Eleven years that held great hardship and complete happiness. Of course, there were worries, like this past month, with the epidemic of measles spreading throughout the mission. Marcus tended the sick day and night, making the Cayuses well, while their medicine men blamed the measles on the doctor's black bag, tore down the faith he had spent eleven years building.

110

Fate has uncouth manners, and on a quiet autumn day tragedy knocked once more on the door of the Whitman cabin. Tomahas, chief of the Cayuse, stood there. Anger darkened his face. He demanded medicine. Marcus stepped outside and told Narcissa to lock the door behind him. But Narcissa Whitman had faced every crisis of the eleven years at Marcus' side. She would face this one the same way. She stepped outside, softly closed the door so the baby would not waken. News of the Whitman massacre spread like wildfire throughout the nation. Only four had survived, three Sager children and Narcissa's adopted baby, Henriette.

From the college that bears her name, carefree boys and girls often walk out to visit the green knoll at Waiilatpu, the knoll Narcissa loved; and the afternoon sun slants across the simple stone shaft and lights the name "Narcissa Whitman." This was the end of the trail from Angelica to Oregon . . . the honeymoon trip that never ended for Marcus and Narcissa Whitman.

POEM:

Give me Thy strength for my day, Lord,
　That wheresoe'er I go,
There shall no danger daunt me
　And I shall fear no foe;
So shall no task o'ercome me,
　So shall no trial fret,
So shall I walk unwearied
　The path where my feet are set;
So shall I find no burden
　Greater than I can bear,
So shall I have a courage
　Equal to all my care;
So shall no grief o'erwhelm me,
　So shall no wave o'erflow:
Give me Thy strength for my day, Lord,
　Cover my weakness so.[2]

—ANNIE JOHNSON FLINT

PRAYER:

O Thou who art the Light of the world, have compassion upon those who are still sitting in darkness. We thank thee for thy servants who have gone into other lands to proclaim thy gospel. Increase our faith that we may attempt greater things for thee. Give us courage to pray and to give more liberally of our means that other workers may be sent into the field. Grant us a greater vision of things we can do for thee as we strive to carry thy gospel throughout the world. Forgive our selfishness, dullness, and complacency. Guide and direct us, and make us more worthy of the great trust thou hast given us. Pardon all our sins and mistakes, and give us grace to do our part in bringing the lost unto thee; all of which we ask for Jesus' sake. AMEN.

HYMN: "O Zion, Haste, Thy Mission High Fulfilling" or
     "Heralds of Christ"

BENEDICTION:
   The Lord bless thee and keep thee; the Lord make his face to shine upon thee and be gracious unto thee; the Lord lift up his countenance upon thee and give thee peace. AMEN.

SERVICE 18

DISPLACED PERSONS FIND A FRIEND

PRELUDE: Hymn tune "Sicilian Mariners' Hymn"

CALL TO WORSHIP:
Enter into his gates with thanksgiving, and into his courts with praise:
Be thankful unto him, and bless his name. For the Lord is good.[1]

HYMN: "Where Cross the Crowded Ways of Life" or
"Father in Heaven, Who Lovest All"

SCRIPTURE:
Blessed is the man that walketh not in the counsel of the ungodly, nor standeth in the way of sinners, nor sitteth in the seat of the scornful.

But his delight is the law of the Lord; and in his law doth he meditate day and night.

And he shall be like a tree planted by the rivers of water, that bringeth forth his fruit in his season; his leaf also shall not wither; and whatsoever he doeth shall prosper.

The ungodly are not so: but are like the chaff which the wind driveth away.

Therefore the ungodly shall not stand in the judgment, nor sinners in the congregation of the righteous.

For the Lord knoweth the way of the righteous: but the way of the ungodly shall perish.[2]

PRAYER:
We humbly pray, O Father, that we may be honest and true in all our dealings, and gentle and merciful to the faults of others, remembering of how much gentleness and mercy we stand in need ourselves; that we may earnestly try to live in thy true faith, honor, and love, and in charity and good will with all our fellow creatures; that

we may worship thee in every beautiful and wonderful thing thou hast made, and sympathize with the whole world of thy glorious creation. AMEN. —CHARLES DICKENS

HYMN: "There's a Wideness in God's Mercy" or
"We May Not Climb the Heavenly Steeps"

LEADER:

Worship is the noblest response of man to the worth-ship of God:
The realization of his Presence,
The greeting of his Majesty,
The welcoming of his cleansing Holiness,
The unifying of the finite with the infinite will and purpose,
The sharing of human life with the Divine,
Communing, singing, witnessing, giving, and serving.

Worship is the glorious response of God to the worth-ship of man:
The pouring of love into hearts of brotherhood,
The bestowing of pardon with peace that passeth understanding,
The giving of truth to light humanity's gloom,
The imparting of power and courage to edify and stabilize,
The sharing with his children of his wisdom,
Beauty, comfort, abundant life, and everlasting joy.[3]
—CHAUNCEY R. PIETY

LEADER:

Robert Montgomery said, "All men of good will readily admit they are against grafters, gangsters, Communists. If I have learned anything in my attempts to expose these godless scuttlers of our way of life, it is this: to be *against* evil is never enough. We must be *for* the answer to evil.

"And the answer is not one big blazing action, but many little ones, fought on many different fronts—usually by unsung people who believe like giants.

"Such a giant is Ethar Milliken, a Maine farmer." You will now hear his story.

STORY:

FLAMES THAT LICK THE IRON CURTAIN

With his huge bare hands Milliken beat at the flames of a raging forest fire that threatened farm property around Kennebunkport,

Maine, in 1947. For several days and nights Ethar battled the flames and smoke until exhausted.

Milliken's condition made complete rest necessary the following winter. Doctors said he would never again be able to work on his land the way he did before—from sunup to sundown. It was his heart.

As he lay there in his farmhouse bed he did not curse the darkness of his day. He looked back into the valley at yesterday and over the mountain to tomorrow.

Oh, there had been hard times. Once almost all his cattle had been wiped out by disease. Several times he had been forced to borrow money to start all over again. But there had been good years too. He now had two farms. Surely God had been good to him.

"What can I do to repay my debt to him?" Ethar asked himself.

And in asking he little realized that he was starting a chain of events that would one day affect people he did not know in far-off Estonia, behind the Iron Curtain.

"Two farms are too many for one man," he thought to himself. "One could easily be used to help those in need. But who? And how?"

Milliken's first thoughts were of those who had suffered terrible tribulations during the war in Europe. What better way to show his gratitude to God and country than to give his farm for the use of those who wanted to build a new life in America? Why, whole families could live there—to learn about farming and American freedoms.

It would be called Freedom Farm.

After exploring the idea further he decided it would be best if an agency administered the project. The farm was turned over to the United Baptist Convention of Maine, and through this organization Freedom Farm became a state-wide project with co-operation from the Federal Displaced Persons Bureau.

The farm itself contains 156 acres, 50 of which were cultivated land. There was work to be done, especially on the muchly built onto, eleven-room farmhouse.

The community caught Ethar's enthusiasm. With true New England thoroughness housewives scrubbed the farmhouse floors; husbands painted and papered walls. A crew of ministers shingled the roof. The Baptist Youth Fellowship raised funds for a team of horses; a church in nearby Farmington Falls gave the first cow. Other contributions included twenty-five hens, a cat and dog, gifts of canned goods and clothing.

In June, 1949, the first foreign family moved into Freedom Farm. Ants Parna, his wife Agnes, and ten-year-old daughter Lembi. The Parnas had fled from Estonia just in time to miss being drafted into a Russian work camp. For days they traveled by foot, begging food wherever possible. For a week they traveled by hiding in a freight car. At nights Parna would sneak out and forage for potatoes, which they ate raw. Little Lembi nearly went blind from malnutrition. Finally they reached an American camp in the United States zone of Germany. Soon came the invitation to Freedom Farm.

Parna, however, had been a supervisor in an Estonian shoe factory. He knew nothing about farming. Strangely enough, this factor proved a disguised blessing. The Parnas arrived too late for the planting season. A drought which followed raised the price of hay. On the unplanted acres of Freedom Farm hay grew plentifully, nourished by water below the surface.

Three ministers from nearby towns, Archibald Craig, Chauncey Stuart, and Harold Bonell, gathered in a bumper hay crop, worth $2,500, and the plan to make the farm self-supporting was off to a good start.

Soft-spoken Ethar Milliken was not at all surprised. "God is taking care of these people," he said.

In July, 1949, a dedication service was held at Freedom Farm to honor the "American-to-be" (a name Baptists prefer to D.P.'s).

Mrs. Parna was asked what she thought of her adopted country. She replied, "Happy Land!" Then grinned broadly.

The Parnas remained at Freedom Farm for over a year, the shoe-maker becoming a competent farmer. Soon it was apparent that they not only could earn their bread by themselves, but also be an asset to any community. Parna then obtained employment in Illinois, making room for another family. Since then, twenty-five other Americans-to-be have "graduated" from the farm, including Alexander Wowk, a Ukranian farmer, whose mother, father, six brothers and sisters were killed by the Communists. Wowk himself lost an eye through torture. With him are his wife and two charming children, Alex and Luda.

After a week at Freedom Farm Mrs. Wowk, watching her young-sters play in the sun without fear, said almost reverently: "America is what I thought heaven would be like."

The Parnas, Wowks, Gontschars, Milenkas, Wolotschajs, Zahaladas —these are some of the Ukranian and Estonian people who found the answer to Communism on a farm in Maine, thanks to a real twentieth-century minuteman, Ethar Milliken.[4]

POEM:

> Lord God, we lift to thee a world hurt sore.
>> Heal it and let it be wounded no more!
> Lord, when this year is done, or e'en this day,
>> Many shall pray to thee who do not pray.
> Let all lips comfort them, all hearts be kind,
>> They who this year shall leave their joys behind.
> They have thy comforting, help them to know
>> That though their hopes are gone, thou dost not go.
> They who shall give for thee lover and son,
>> Show them thy world set free, thy battles done.

—AUTHOR UNKNOWN

PRAYER:

Almighty Father, who art full of compassion and tender mercy, hear our prayer for those who suffer from any cause; for displaced persons, the insecure, who would work but lack the opportunity; for those who try bravely to face illness and suffering; for those who have lost loved ones; for those who are depressed and fearful; for those who try to bear their burdens alone; for those who are handicapped through no fault of their own; and for all who face a dark future. Grant to all these unfortunate ones a knowledge of thy love as revealed through Jesus, an awareness of thy presence, and a peace and contentment which the world cannot give.

Touch our hearts and give us a sense of comradeship with those who are afflicted; touch our sympathy to the extent that we will be willing to share with them to our utmost and thus relieve their suffering. Thou, O God, hast provided with thy bountiful hand enough for all thy children. May we so live that there will be sufficient food for the hungry, shelter and security for the homeless, and comfort for the sorrowful. This we pray in the spirit of Christ. AMEN.

HYMN: "O Brother Man, Fold to Thy Heart Thy Brother" or
"The Voice of God Is Calling"

BENEDICTION:

May the Father give you fullness of life in his service. AMEN.

BROTHER TO THE POOR

Prelude: "Pastorale" by Rowley

Call to Worship:
Wherewith shall I come before the Lord, and bow myself before the high God? . . .
He hath showed thee, O man, what is good; and what doth the Lord require of thee, but to do justly, and to love mercy, and to walk humbly with thy God? [1]

Hymn: "The Voice of God Is Calling" or
      "Where Cross the Crowded Ways of Life"

Scripture:
Now when Jesus was in Bethany, in the house of Simon the leper, there came unto him a woman having an alabaster box of very precious ointment, and poured it on his head, as he sat at meat. But when his disciples saw it, they had indignation, saying, To what purpose is this waste? For this ointment might have been sold for much, and given to the poor. When Jesus understood it, he said unto them, Why trouble ye the woman? for she hath wrought a good work upon me. For ye have the poor always with you; but me ye have not always. . . .
And he lifted up his eyes on his disciples, and said, Blessed be ye poor: for yours is the kingdom of God. . . .
Verily I say unto you, Inasmuch as ye have done it unto one of the least of these my brethren, ye have done it unto me. . . .
And when he had called the people unto him with his disciples also, he said unto them, Whosoever will come after me, let him deny himself, and take up his cross, and follow me. For whosoever will save his life shall lose it; but whosoever shall lose his life for my sake and the gospel's, the same shall save it.[2]

PRAYER:

O God, we humbly beseech thee to purify our hearts from all vain and worldly and sinful thoughts, and thus prepare our souls to worship thee this day acceptably, with reverence and godly fear. O Lord, set our affection on things above, all the day long, and give us grace to receive thy word which we shall hear this day, into honest and good hearts, and bring forth fruit with patience. Hear us, O God, for the sake of Jesus Christ, our Saviour. AMEN.

POEM:

> O Lord, who knowest every need of mine,
> Help me to bear each cross and not repine;
> Grant me fresh courage every day,
> Help me to do my work alway
>   Without complaint!
>
> O Lord, thou knowest well how dark the way,
> Guide thou my footsteps, lest they stray;
> Give me fresh faith for every hour,
> Lest I should ever doubt thy power
>   And make complaint!
>
> Give me a heart, O Lord, strong to endure,
> Help me to keep it simple, pure,
> Make me unselfish, helpful, true
> In every act, whate'er I do,
>   And keep content!

—AUTHOR UNKNOWN

HYMN: "At Length There Dawns the Glorious Day" or
      "O Brother Man, Fold to Thy Heart Thy Brother"

LEADER:

It has been said that about one half of the people of the world go to bed hungry every night. People who are haunted by the fear of hunger do desperate things to avoid starvation. Should we not be concerned about the suffering of the poor? If Christians worked together, could they not solve this problem?

We will hear the story of a man who gave himself in service to the poor.

STORY:

THE LITTLE POOR MAN OF GOD

Among all those who have followed Christ very few can stand beside Francis of Assisi. To have founded a religious order which has lasted for seven centuries, to have been the inspiration for poets and painters and sculptors, to have captured the admiration of churchmen and skeptics, to have influenced the heart, if not the mind, of the church: this was the accomplishment not of a great scholar or of a statesman, but of a simplehearted man who began seven hundred years ago to follow Christ as literally as he could.

Francis, who lived in the thirteenth century, was the son of an Italian merchant. In his youth he was gay, thoughtless, and extravagant. After a severe illness and an unsuccessful experience in the army, Francis turned to religion. He began to give all that he had to the poor and to the church, until his father, alarmed for fear that his hard-earned wealth would be given away by his seemingly overgenerous son, went to court to have the young man declared incompetent to handle his father's goods. Francis renounced his inheritance and declared himself a servant of the church. With a few companions he became a religious beggar, doing the most menial services such as waiting upon lepers in hospitals, and giving all that he could beg or earn to the poor and for the purpose of building chapels in the city of his birth, Assisi, in central Italy.

A few years later Francis offered his own services and those of his followers to the Pope, who was wise enough to allow Francis to found an "order," an organization within the church which could have its own rules and could devote itself to what we would call evangelistic and missionary work. Francis called himself "the little poor man of God" and his followers the Little Brethren, Friars Minor. He bound his brethren under obligations to remain poor, to obey unquestioningly the orders of their superiors, and to keep themselves pure.

Francis believed that the ideal life was one of perfect poverty. In a day when business was organizing itself along the lines which we know as capitalistic, Francis sought to re-establish what he believed to be Christ's ideal, servants of God who were unhampered by the possessions of things. He did not allow his followers to own even a prayerbook. If one owned anything, he believed, it became a temptation to pride and led eventually to strife and wars.

Pity for all poor and all suffering was a passion with Francis. Beggars and lepers received the kindest and most deferential treatment from him. Even birds and animals came within the circle of his ministry. He seems to have been one of those people to whom the wild things come fearlessly, and whenever he stopped in the fields, birds came about him unafraid. Once he is said to have preached to them: "Always praise your Creator wherever you are, for he gives you the air of heaven for your kingdom, the rivers and springs to quench your thirst, the mountains and valleys for a place of refuge, and also gives you warm clothing for yourselves and your children."

When at last Francis came to die, he asked to be laid on the floor of the infirmary in his church at Assisi. He had read to him his poem, the "Canticle of the Creatures," in which he had praised God for "brother sun," "brother wind," "sister water," "brother fire," and "our mother the earth"; and to this he added a verse in praise of "our sister, the bodily death, from which no living man can flee." It was on an evening in early October, 1226, that Francis, surrounded by his brethren of the order, bade farewell to his children, as he called them, and committed his soul to God. His followers said that when he breathed his last, a flock of larks, who never sing except in the daytime, lighted on the roof of the Church of St. Mary of the Angels and lamented in song the passing of their friend.

Aside from founding an order whose members have been missionaries in China, in Africa, in North America, and wherever the gospel has been preached in a new land, Francis did something to the Christian world. After his time even the rich sculpture on the walls of churches began to show the effects of his preaching. Artists no longer portrayed Christ as a stern judge but as a pitying friend of man. Pity and humility have always been characteristics of Christianity, but in the stern days following the fall of the Roman Empire, when the remnants of law and order fell into the hands of scattered nobles and cities, there seemed little room for the gentler aspects of the gospel.

But Francis did more. The monks in their cells and great houses had held together the remnants of culture and order during the dark days following the breakup of the great empire. Francis sent his Little Brethren out into the world. They were not to retire into monasteries to promote their own devotion but to go out to serve their unfortunate fellows. In the truest sense Francis instituted a great missionary movement at home and abroad.

For the problem of wealth and poverty Francis had a simple solution.

Own nothing, then there can be no pride of possession, no strife for goods. He sincerely believed that this was Christ's way and that it is the best way. As a student of Francis has said: "We are accustomed to think of a poor man as one who lacks riches; St. Francis thought of a rich man as one who lacked the inestimable boon of poverty." Francis would have had a revolution; but in his revolution the poor would not have seized the riches of the rich but would have given up what little they themselves had.

We do not believe today that the solution of our social problems is for everyone to be poor; but Francis made two contributions which ought not to be lost. In the first place, he realized with Paul that the love of money is the root of all kinds of evil. And he knew that no solution of the vexing problem of riches and poverty will succeed unless attention is paid to man's greed and his resulting inhumanity to man. In the second place, Francis taught Christians that the Christ of the Gospels is a friend of the poor, and that no services in rich churches and no power in church organizations can be substitutes for humble service to the poor and suffering. Among all the church's great men, one of the very greatest was "the little poor man of God." [3]

POEM:

Christ was life, creative, growing,
    Life unfolding power and beauty,
Life of holy thinking, knowing,
    Life of service, love, and duty.

Christ was life, abundant, glorious,
    Life adventuring for right,
Life that dared and life victorious,
    Revolution, peace, and might.

Christ was life of joy and sorrow,
    Life that conquered death and grave,
Life that lights each tomb and morrow,
    Life eternal, strong to save.

Christ is life, dynamic, surging
    Through the hearts of faith today,
Guiding, succoring, and urging
    Up to God the glory way. [4]

—CHAUNCEY R. PIETY

BROTHER TO THE POOR

LEADER:

It is not the possession of extraordinary gifts that makes extraordinary usefulness, but the dedication of what we have to the service of God. —FREDERICK W. ROBERTSON.

No one is useless in this world who lightens the burden of it for anyone else.—CHARLES DICKENS.

> That best portion of a good man's life,
> His little, nameless, unremembered acts
> Of kindness and of love.[5]
>
> —WILLIAM WORDSWORTH

POEM:

> If there be some weaker one,
> Give me strength to help him on;
> If a blinder soul there be,
> Let me guide him nearer thee.
> Make my mortal dreams come true
> With the work I fain would do;
> Clothe with life the weak intent,
> Let me be the thing I meant;
> Let me find in thy employ
> Peace that dearer is than joy;
> Out of self to love be led
> And to heaven acclimated,
> Until all things sweet and good
> Seem my natural habitude.[6]
>
> —JOHN GREENLEAF WHITTIER

PRAYER:

O God, who art the Father of all mankind, we are grateful for thy faithful servants who have gone into the far corners of the world to bring light and hope to the needy. We thank thee for Francis of Assisi, for his unselfish service to the poor and needy. Reveal to us ways by which we can help thy faithful servants who are ministering to the poor and destitute in every country. Grant us a victory over every temptation, and may we be numbered with those who have a part in spreading thy truth throughout the world. Enable us to put our selfish interests into the background and to show more concern about others, and be willing to sacrifice in order to bring the lost to a saving knowledge of thee; through Jesus Christ our Lord. AMEN.

HYMN: "Saviour, Thy Dying Love" or
"The Light of God Is Falling"

BENEDICTION:
May the spirit of our Master lead us as we strive to serve the poor and destitute. AMEN.

SERVICE 20

BUILDING A FRIENDLY WORLD

PRELUDE: "Pilgrim's Chorus" from Tannhauser

CALL TO WORSHIP:
>Who shall ascend into the hill of the Lord?
>or who shall stand in his holy place?
>He that hath clean hands, and a pure heart;
>who hath not lifted up his soul unto vanity,
>nor sworn deceitfully.
>He shall receive the blessing from the Lord, and
>righteousness from the God of his salvation.[1]

HYMN: "When Morning Gilds the Skies" or
"O Worship the King"

SCRIPTURE:
And when he had called unto him his twelve disciples, he gave them power against unclean spirits, to cast them out, and to heal all manner of sickness and all manner of disease. . . .

These twelve Jesus sent forth, and commanded them, saying, Go not into the way of the Gentiles, and into any city of the Samaritans enter ye not: but go rather to the lost sheep of the house of Israel. And as ye go, preach, saying, The kingdom of heaven is at hand. Heal the sick, cleanse the lepers, raise the dead, cast out devils: freely ye have received, freely give. . . .

Behold, I send you forth as sheep in the midst of wolves: be ye therefore wise as serpents, and harmless as doves. But beware of men: for they will deliver you up to the councils, and they will scourge you in their synagogues. . . .

The disciple is not above his master, nor the servant above his Lord. . . .

He that loveth father or mother more than me is not worthy of me:

125

and he that loveth son or daughter more than me is not worthy of me. And he that taketh not his cross, and followeth after me, is not worthy of me. He that findeth his life shall lose it: and he that loseth his life for my sake shall find it. . . .

In him was life; and the life was the light of men. . . .

I am come that they might have life, and that they might have it more abundantly.[2]

POEM:

> We live in deeds, not years; in thoughts, not breaths;
> In feelings, not in figures on a dial.
> We should count time by heart-throbs.
> He most lives
> Who thinks most, feels the noblest, acts the best.
> Life's but a means unto an end; that end
> Beginning, mean, and end to all things—God.[3]
> —PHILIP JAMES BAILEY

The great use of life is to spend it for something that will outlast it.—WILLIAM JAMES.

We find in life exactly what we put into it. Live truly and thy life shall be a great and noble creed.—RALPH WALDO EMERSON.

HYMN: "In Christ There Is No East or West" or
"The Morning Light Is Breaking"

LEADER:

We will hear the story of one of the greatest missionaries of our time, who went to what he considered the neediest part of the world.

STORY:

ALBERT SCHWEITZER

Albert Schweitzer's life reads like a fairy story, except that in fairy tales the unbelievable things happen by magic. Albert Schweitzer has made them happen without any magic, and he seems to take it all quite as a matter of course.

Albert was born in a parsonage in a village of Upper Alsace in 1875. His people were German, and both his father and mother came of families of education and culture. His mother's father was a musician who was greatly interested in beautiful and fine old organs. One of Schweitzer's earliest memories is that of sitting by the hour to listen to his grandfather play. Of course the boy wanted to play

126

too, and it was not long until his teachers discovered that he had an unusual talent for music. Before many years he was playing on the great church organ.

Albert did not particularly like school. Arithmetic and languages were especially hard for him, and he liked to think things out for himself instead of learning what the books said. Once when he had done very poorly in school, he discovered that one of his teachers prepared very carefully the lessons he was to teach each day. It suddenly dawned upon Albert that it was important to do hard things well. From that time on whenever he had a task that was especially hard or disagreeable he took pains to do it as well as he possibly could. He then found that the sense of mastery over the hard task was rather fun. Many of the most interesting experiences of his later life never would have been possible without this habit of doing well the hard or unpleasant things that came his way.

When Albert was eighteen he entered the university to study theology and philosophy, and of course he was still studying music. By the time he was thirty he might be said to have "arrived." He had a doctor's degree in theology and another doctor's degree in philosophy. He had traveled over Europe. In spite of his early difficulties with languages he could speak English, French, and German, and could read Latin, Greek, and Hebrew. He had written several important books. He was in demand for organ concerts in various parts of Europe, and he had the reputation of knowing more about Bach than did any other person. He held the position of principal of the Theological College of St. Thomas. It looked as if he had all that any man of thirty could possibly ask for.

Then Albert Schweitzer wrote two letters that caused a perfect storm of protest, ridicule, and suspicion to break upon his head. He wrote one letter resigning his position as principal of the college. He wrote the other to his family. In each letter he announced that he planned to take up the study of medicine, after which he expected to go to Central Africa as a missionary doctor. Nobody could believe it. Here was a man who had two of the highest degrees that a university can bestow, and was a successful preacher, teacher, author, and musician. And he was preparing to start to school again in a medical course that would take from five to seven years of the hardest possible work! Worst of all, he then expected to bury himself in Africa. It was too much.

During the year that followed, Albert Schweitzer passed through one of the hardest periods of his life. He had thought his plans out very carefully. He felt that he had had many advantages that most people do not have. He was a preacher and had talked a lot about a religion of love. He thought that he should put his teaching into practice. He says: "I wanted to be a doctor so that I might be able to work without having to talk. I wanted to show people love, not just tell them about it." He chose Africa because he felt the need there to be so great, and because he knew that the white nations of the world had carried to Africa so many of the curses of their civilization. He knew that some of the worst diseases of Africa had been carried there by white men. And he had heard how whole villages had been wiped out by alcohol traded by white men to the natives in the form of rum. Then there was the dark story of the slave trade and of forced labor. Schweitzer felt he had to go as a sort of atonement for all the wrongs white men had done to the African people. He wanted to go as a doctor because he could then relieve pain and cure disease, and thus show them the love of God.

Schweitzer could not tell people all these thoughts and reasons. He was too sensitive and reserved, and he knew that many people would not understand. So he merely said that he was going. Some people tortured him with their questions. Others accused him of being disappointed in love. Some of the doctors at the medical school thought he was the victim of a morbid idea and wanted to have him examined at a mental hospital.

To make his troubles worse, Schweitzer found his medical course very hard. His studies had all been along another line. Now he had to begin again with chemistry, physiology, and anatomy. In order to pay his expenses he had to continue writing and giving concerts. Some nights he did not go to bed at all. Fortunately he was very strong physically or he never could have stood it. Yet he never complained and was never discouraged. In writing of his experiences he says: "Anyone who proposes to do good must not expect people to roll stones out of his way, but must accept his lot calmly if they even roll a few more upon it."

It was seven years before Schweitzer was ready to go to Africa. He had studied tropical medicine and had served his internship, and then had raised the money to run his hospital for two years. He had married and his wife had studied nursing so to be able to help him with his work. He planned to build his hospital on the Ogowe River near a mission station in a region where there was no doctor. The missionaries there had pleaded for a long time for someone to come out to do the medical work that was so desperately needed. It was a French mission in French territory and Schweitzer was a German, but he did not feel that it mattered.

Schweitzer found that being a doctor in primitive Africa was very hard. The other missionaries helped all they could, but even so, his first clinics were held outdoors and his first operations were performed in an old chicken house. White ants got into this packing cases, his boxes and bottles gave out, the ignorant patients would not obey orders, he could not get reliable helpers. Through it all he worked patiently, finding time at night to write and to play on the little organ which his musical friends in Europe had given him.

The Schweitzers had planned to stay two years in Africa and then go back to Europe to give organ recitals and raise money to carry on the Hospital for another period. Before they were ready to leave news came of World War I. One of the most awful tragedies of war is that otherwise sensible people seem then to lose their reason completely. It is only on such a basis that one can explain the things the Schweitzers had to endure for the next few years. Schweitzer was a German musician, scholar, and surgeon, who at his own expense was serving as a missionary doctor in a French territory in Africa. He was not remotely suspected of any war activity. Yet immediately after the declaration of war, word was sent to the French officials in Africa that Schweitzer and his wife must be arrested and put under guard as prisoners of war. And so with sick persons all about him needing his help, the doctor who went out to show people love, was locked up in his own house and guarded by native soldiers.

Schweitzer accepted this astounding situation with his usual calm and spent his time practicing on his organ and writing a book which he hoped would, after the terrible war was over, help people see that civilization must be built on a foundation of love and respect for life.

Both the missionaries and the natives complained so bitterly about the doctor being kept away from his hospital that he was finally released. As the war went on, however, word came that the Schweitzers must be taken to France as war prisoners. So the doctor and his wife were put on a French ship under guard and taken to a prison camp in France. The Schweitzers had been too long in the tropics and both were suffering from ill health. However, they adjusted themselves to the camp and soon were favorites of both their fellow prisoners and their guards. One of the grateful fellow prisoners made Schweitzer a table of packing boxes and on this the doctor practiced as though it were an organ.

After a long period the German prisoners were exchanged for an equal number of French ones, and the Schweitzers found themselves once more in Alsace, but this time without funds and in broken health. But the war ended at last and Schweitzer found that in Sweden and Switzerland people still had money and wanted to hear him play. So after numerous concerts to raise funds, and after two operations which somewhat restored his health, Schweitzer, still believing in love, went back to his little hospital in the African forest. He found the whole ground overgrown with the jungle, the roof falling in, and all his labor to be done over again. When workers were not to be had, or when native men would not work alone, he with his own hands plaited palm fibers for the roof, rolled logs, and cleared brush.

If one should land on the west coast of Africa just a little below the equator, he would find the Ogowe River. A little boat would take him up the channel to Lambaréné. There he would find Albert Schweitzer, philosopher, theologian, author, musician, and surgeon, removing tumors, treating sleeping sickness and leprosy, and bringing freedom from pain and fear to countless black people in order to show them love and respect for life.[4]

. . . .

When Dr. Schweitzer visited the United States in 1949 a committee of prominent Chicago citizens waited in one of the city's railroad stations. They were to welcome one of the greatest men in the world. He arrived and greeted them in three languages. He was a giant of a man, six feet four inches tall, with bushy hair and a walrus mustache. The reception committee stood talking about how honored they were to meet him and how the important people of the city were waiting to entertain him. Reporters took down his every word. Flash cameras were busy taking his picture. Suddenly he asked to be excused. He walked rapidly through the crowd on the station platform. Coming to an old woman who was struggling with heavy suitcases, he scooped up her bags with his great hands. Then he told her to follow him. He worked his way through the throng and took the woman to her coach. After wishing her a good journey he returned to the committee. "Sorry to keep you waiting, gentlemen," he said to the astonished group. "I was just having my daily fun."

A member of the reception committee remarked, "A lot of us

stuffed shirts were unstuffed that moment." Well might they be. A man with a world mission, engaged in writing a profound history of civilization, was demonstrating in a simple, unaffected way the love of God for the least individual.[5]

It is very fitting that the 1952 Nobel Peace Prize was awarded to Dr. Albert Schweitzer, world-famous philosopher, musician, and missionary.

POEM:
> This is no time for fear, for doubts of good,
> For broodings on the tragedies of fate.
> It is a time for songs of brotherhood,
> For hymns of joy, of man's divine estate.
> Though echoes of old wars depress the heart,
> Though greed and hate still curse men's nobler ways,
> Though strife and tumult blast our life apart,
> It is a time for confidence and praise.
> Let prophets prophesy, let poets sing,
> Our dreams are not in vain. The night is past.
> Together, as new hopes are wakening,
> Let us proclaim, The Kingdom comes at last!
> Our Babels crash. Let selfish flags be furled.
> As brothers all, we build a Friendly World.[6]
> —THOMAS CURTIS CLARK

PRAYER:
O Thou, who art the Light of the world, have compassion upon those who are still sitting in darkness. Touch our hearts that we may be more zealous in sending the gospel to them. Bless the workers like Albert Schweitzer who have gone to the difficult fields to carry thy message. May we learn from their example the right attitude toward peoples of other races. Forgive us for our false ideas of greatness. Help us to find ways of living peaceably with all people and sharing with them the good things which we enjoy. AMEN.

HYMN: "O Master of the Waking World" or
"Jesus Shall Reign"

BENEDICTION:
Now may the blessing of God be with you as you go forth to support the weak, help the afflicted, and love all men as brothers. AMEN.

SERVING THE OUTPOSTS

PRELUDE: Hymn tune "The Kingdom Coming"

CALL TO WORSHIP:
> The earth is the Lord's, and the fulness thereof;
> The world, and they that dwell therein. . . .
> Let the people praise thee, O God;
> Let all the people praise thee.[1]

HYMN: "O Master of the Waking World" or
"Eternal God, Whose Power Upholds"

SCRIPTURE:
The Gentiles shall come to thy light, and kings to the brightness of thy rising. . . .

For God, who commanded the light to shine out of darkness, hath shined in our hearts, to give the light of the knowledge of the glory of God in the face of Jesus Christ. . . .

Other sheep I have, which are not of this fold: them also I must bring, and they shall hear my voice; and there shall be one fold, and one shepherd. . . .

They shall come from the east, and from the west, and from the north, and from the south, and shall sit down in the kingdom of God. . . .

Then saith he unto his disciples, The harvest truly is plenteous, but the laborers are few; pray ye therefore the Lord of the harvest, that he will send forth laborers into his harvest. . . .

All power is given unto me in heaven and in earth. Go ye therefore, and teach all nations, baptizing them in the name of the Father, and of the Son, and of the Holy Ghost: teaching them to observe all things whatsoever I have commanded you: and, lo, I am with you alway, even unto the end of the world.[2]

132

POEM:

O God, our supreme Father,
Supreme in wisdom, power, and love,
We magnify and glorify thy name.
Thanks for thy supreme Gift, Jesus Christ,
And for the Church of his love,
Thanks for thy supreme book, the Bible,
And thanks for thy supreme Kingdom
in Heaven and on earth. AMEN.[3]

—CHAUNCEY R. PIETY

LEADER:

What is our attitude toward non-Christians? Many people are still bound by superstition, fears, and frustration. Only the gospel of Christ can raise them from their low estate. Are we responsible for sharing the gospel with them?

As the following poems are read, let us look within, examine our attitudes, and try to decide whether we have done everything possible to send the gospel to those who sit in darkness.

O Spirit, that dost prefer
Before all temples the upright heart and pure,
Instruct me, for thou knowest. . . .
What in me is dark
Illumine; what is low, raise and support;
That to the height of this great argument
I may assert eternal Providence,
And justify the ways of God to men.[4]

—JOHN MILTON

I—who have the healing creed,
The faith benign of Mary's Son,
Shall I behold my brother's need,
And, selfishly, to aid him shun?
I—who upon my mother's knee,
In childhood, read Christ's written word,
Received his legacy of peace,
His holy rule of action heard;
I—in whose heart the sacred sense
Of Jesus' love was early felt;
Of his pure, full benevolence,
His pitying tenderness for guilt;

133

His shepherd-care for wandering sheep,
For all weak, sorrowing, trembling things,
His mercy vast, his passion deep,
Of anguish for man's sufferings;
I—schooled from childhood in such lore—
Dared I draw back or hesitate
When called to heal the sickness sore
Of those far off and desolate? [5]

—CHARLOTTE BRONTE

LEADER:

We will hear the story of the first medical missionary who went to Labrador to serve.

STORY:

THE MAN WHO WENT TO LABRADOR

"The religion of Christ never permitted me to accept the idea that there is 'nothing to do, only believe,'" wrote Dr. Wilfred T. Grenfell in his autobiography. And because it did not, it sent him to Labrador and Newfoundland, where he spent his life ministering to people who desperately needed just the assistance he could give them.

When he first came, there were no hospitals and but little in the way of medical help for the thousands of people, most of them fisherfolk of small means, scattered along hundreds of miles of bleak and barren coast. Starting from "scratch" he first operated from a hospital ship, then built a hospital at Battle Harbour, and later others at various points. Years afterward it was mainly through his efforts that a large Seaman's Institute was erected at St. Johns. And although he was primarily a medical missionary, he ministered not alone to physical needs, but to mental and spiritual needs as well.

The second of four boys, Wilfred T. Grenfell was born on February 28, 1865, in Parkgate, near Chester, England. His father was a clergyman-schoolmaster who conducted a school for small boys in the seaside town. The Grenfell boys attended their father's school until they grew out of it, after which they were sent to schools elsewhere; Wilfred to Marlborough in Wiltshire. At home they spent their leisure time much as other young boys; they had a pony and guns, and a boat they used on small streams in the vicinity. And of course they collected butterflies, birds' eggs, and rocks. When Wilfred was away at school, his mother sent him each week a little box of flowers, one of which he wore in his buttonhole at morning chapel on Sunday.

134

When his father was offered the chaplaincy of a large hospital, he gave up teaching and the family moved to London. There Wilfred, having completed his courses at the preparatory school and Oxford, began studying medicine at London University and to take up work at the hospital. He took an active part in athletics at the university— rowing, cricket, and football, especially the latter.

Then an event occurred which made a great change in his life. This was in 1885, during his second year at the university. Returning home from a visit to a patient in the Shadwell district of the city, he passed by a huge tent. Wondering what was going on, he stepped inside and found himself at a Moody and Sankey meeting. A man on the platform was praying as he entered, and it soon became apparent the prayer would become a long dissertation. Suddenly another man stepped forward and called out to the audience: "Let us sing a hymn while our brother finishes his prayer." That interested young Grenfell and he stayed for the preaching and the rest of the service. The second man, he later learned, was Dwight L. Moody. When he walked home that night, he was filled with determination to make his life count for something, and the best way clear to him was to follow in the footsteps of the Master.

Having spent his boyhood in a seaside town he loved the sea, and so during vacations he and his older brother hired a fishing smack and with it explored the coastal regions of England, Ireland, and Scotland. On some of these trips they would take groups of boys from the London slums, teaching them how to cook and camp and manage the boat, and taking them on hikes through the countryside where they saw and learned about nature. On the agenda too was Sunday school, when they sang hymns and heard Bible stories.

His course at the university completed, Grenfell joined the Mission to Deep Sea Fishermen, visiting the fishing fleet in the North Sea as a medical missionary. There he found the great curse of the men was drink. But he liked the work because it gave him the opportunity to help his fellow men build not alone new bodies but new lives. In all this the example he set by a life devoted to working for others counted for more than the mere words he spoke, or the medical assistance he gave in the carrying out of his daily duties.

In 1892 the Deep Sea Mission outfitted a vessel as a hospital ship and sent him to Newfoundland and Labrador, to work among the fishermen who fished the Grand Banks, and to visit the little coastal villages in which they lived. He found that a large part of the population was living far beyond the reach of medical aid, that many of the fisherfolk and natives were desperately poor and could not afford to pay a doctor. After spending the summer in Labrador waters the ship returned to England in the fall. The next spring they were back again, this time with a larger force, two doctors and two nurses in addition to Grenfell. Two "cottage hospitals" were established on land, at Battle Harbour, and at Indian Harbour.

By the turn of the century the work had expanded to such an extent that the Deep Sea Mission no longer could raise the funds necessary to carry it on. So Dr. Grenfell took to the lecture platform to raise money, lecturing in Canada, the United States, and Great Britain. From that time on, as the need arose, he went on lecture tours. It helped to make his work known too, and interested people of means on both sides of the Atlantic contributed large amounts. The Labrador Mission was never supported by any denomination or church, that is, none assumed responsibility for its financial needs. The cost of maintaining it had to be met by voluntary donations.

After the mission was established on a permanent basis, Grenfell spent winters as well as summers on the field. He often visited his patients in outlying districts, traveling there by sledge and dog team. This led to his great adventure of the ice-pan, a story of the North that has come to be a classic. It happened on April 21, 1908, in northern Newfoundland. Spring comes late so far north and the ground was still covered with snow. He received a message that a young man was acutely ill some sixty miles away and set out at once to answer the call. On his way there he decided to take a short cut across an inlet of the sea, the ice appearing to be safe. When he was almost across, the wind suddenly shifted and blew offshore, breaking up the ice and blowing it out to sea. It happened so quickly that he barely had time to cut the traces of his dog team and release them from the sledge before it sank and they were all plunged into the icy water.

A small pan of fairly solid ice drifted by and he was able to crawl up on this, his dogs with him. During the following night he killed and skinned three of his dogs, wrapping the skins about him for warmth, the temperature being below freezing and a cold wind blowing him out to sea. In the morning he made a flag out of his shirt, using the frozen legs of the dogs he had killed for a staff. Hour after hour he stood on his little ice raft waving his crude flag, hoping someone would see him. Four men seal hunting on a headland did see him, and at once organized a rescue party which came out in a boat and picked him off his perilous perch, so small it might at any moment break up in the rough sea. His hands and feet were frozen, otherwise he suffered no ill effects from his icy and dangerous ordeal. The young man he had started out to see was brought in by boat to the hospital and his life was saved too.

A graphic chapter of his autobiography describes the adventure. He tells of his thoughts during the time it seemed most unlikely he would be rescued. "My own faith in the mystery of immortality is so untroubled that it now seemed almost natural to be passing to the portal of death from an ice-pan. Quite unbidden, the words of the old hymn kept running through my head:

> 'My God, my Father, while I stray
> Far from my home on life's rough way,
> Oh, help me from my heart to say,
> Thy will be done.' "

Grenfell tried to better the life of the people of Labrador and northern Newfoundland in other ways beside bringing them medical care and the gospel. He built co-operative stores where they could sell their furs and produce, and buy food, clothing, and other necessities.

Before that everything had been handled through the large trading concerns who often took an unfair advantage of the poor people they dealt with. In another experiment he purchased and introduced a herd of reindeer. These, he hoped, would provide food as well as draft animals for the natives.

In 1909 Grenfell married an American girl, Anna MacClanahan, of Chicago. Mrs. Grenfell joined him in his mission work and they lived in the North where their children, two boys and a girl, were born. Grenfell died in 1940.

In the last chapter of his book is a summation of his religious beliefs: "What . . . D. L. Moody did for me was just to show that under all the shams and externals of religion was a vital call in the world for things that I could do. . . . He started me working for all I was worth, and made religion real fun—a new field brimming with opportunities." And then he concludes: "If there is one thing about which I never have any question, it is that the decision and endeavour to follow the Christ does for men what nothing else on earth can." [6]

POEM:

> Set us afire, Lord,
> Stir us, we pray!

While the world perishes
  We go our way,
Purposeless, passionless,
  Day after day.
Set us afire, Lord,
  Stir us, we pray!

Set us afire, Lord,
  That we may be
Thy word to the millions
  Who hunger for Thee;
Stir us, empower us
  By Calvary;
Give us the passion
  To set the world free! [7]
      —RALPH S. CUSHMAN

PRAYER:

Our Father, we thank thee for the missionaries who have gone into all parts of the world to teach, heal, and preach. Bless those who have gone into distant lands to carry the gospel. Be near to them, fill them with thy spirit, strengthen them for their tasks, comfort them in times of loneliness, and give them a sense of thy presence at all times. May we support the work of missions by praying for the success of the work, by giving liberally of our means, and by living in such a manner as others will be drawn unto thee. Hasten the coming of thy kingdom when all people will be brought to thee, and prepare our hearts that we may be able to take our place in that kingdom. In Jesus' name we pray. AMEN.

HYMN: "Take My Life, and Let It Be" or
       "Lord, Speak to Me"

BENEDICTION:

The grace of the Lord Jesus Christ, and the love of God, and the communion of the Holy Spirit, be with you all. AMEN.

SERVICE 22

MINISTERING TO THE SICK

PRELUDE: Hymn tune "Tidings"

CALL TO WORSHIP:

> O Master of the waking world,
>   Who hast the nations in thy heart—
> The heart that bled and broke to send
>   God's love to earth's remotest part:
> Show us anew in Calvary
> The wondrous power that makes men free.
>   —FRANK MASON NORTH

HYMN: "Christ for the World We Sing" or
      "Jesus Shall Reign"

SCRIPTURE:

And a woman having an issue of blood twelve years, which had spent all her living upon physicians, neither could be healed of any, came behind him, and touched the border of his garment: and immediately her issue of blood stanched. And Jesus said, Who touched me? When all denied, Peter and they that were with him said, Master, the multitude throng thee and press thee, and sayest thou, Who touched me? And Jesus said, Somebody hath touched me: for I perceive that virtue is gone out of me. And when the woman saw that she was not hid, she came trembling, and falling down before him, she declared unto him before all the people for what cause she had touched him, and how she was healed immediately. And he said unto her, Daughter, be of good comfort: thy faith hath made thee whole; go in peace.

Come unto me, all ye that labor and are heavy laden, and I will give you rest.[1]

Hymn: "We Thank Thee, Lord, Thy Paths of Service Lead" or "We Bear the Strain of Earthly Care"

Poem:

> The sweetest lives are those to duty wed,
>   Whose deeds, both great and small,
> Are close-knit strands of unbroken thread
>   Where love ennobles all.
> The world may sound no trumpet, ring no bells;
> The book of life the shining record tells.
>
> The love shall chant its own beatitudes
> After its own life working. A child's kiss
> Set on thy sighing lips shall make thee glad;
> A sick man helped by thee shall make thee strong;
> Thou shalt be served thyself by every sense
> Of service which thou renderest.[2]

Leader:

Various members of the Scudder family gave more than a thousand years of service to missions in India. We will hear a story of one outstanding member of this family.

Story:

ONE THOUSAND YEARS OF SERVICE IN INDIA

One of the outstanding union institutions is the Christian Medical College at Vellore in South India. Its founder, Dr. Ida Scudder, has long been one of the most beloved missionaries in India.

The story of the medical school and of Dr. Scudder should properly begin with the death of a young missionary more than 130 years ago. In spite of the opposition not only of friends and family, but also of the church, this young man sailed for India. He had been told no white man could live in that climate. The warning proved all too tragically true in his case. Within six weeks of his arrival he died on the steps of a Hindu temple, the victim of one of India's diseases. Who can assess the value of a life? Certainly in that brief space of time on the field he could not have been thought to have given a valuable contribution to the cause of missions. His death, however, was not a useless sacrifice.

His story was published in a little pamphlet, and a copy found its way into the hands of a leading New York physician, Dr. John

Scudder. The story found its way into his heart also. So deeply was he moved by it that he determined to answer the missionary call. Ten years earlier he had been challenged by the same call, but he had decided against it. Now he surrendered to it and became the first American medical missionary to India, being sent in 1819 to North Ceylon, later serving in Madura and the neighborhood of Madras. He was an indefatigable traveler and preacher. In the morning he devoted himself to medical work, but the afternoons were reserved for evangelistic work. His itinerating was not without its dangers. As he preached and distributed tracts, the crowds were sometimes hostile. On one occasion his interpreter was stoned. This outstanding pioneer missionary founded a family whose members have given more than a thousand years of service to missions in India. He gave seven sons, two daughters, and ten grandchildren to this work.

One of the most renowned members of this family is a granddaughter, Dr. Ida Scudder. She was the daughter of Dr. John Scudder's second son, who was also named John and also a physician. Like other members of her family, Ida had no intention of spending her life in India as a missionary. She preferred life in the United States. She did, however, sign up as a short-term missionary in order to be with her mother who was ill.

It was during this three-year term that she received and answered the call to missions. Her call came three times on the same night as three callers came on a similar errand. Each begged her to help their child-wives who were near death in childbirth. Having no medical training, she was forced to tell them she could do nothing. All three refused to accept the help of her father, saying they would prefer to see their wives die than permit a man to attend them. Early the next morning she learned that the three women had died. Since men were not allowed to treat women, Ida Scudder decided the only solution was women doctors. She dedicated herself to this work.

On returning to the United States Ida Scudder studied at the Women's Medical College in Philadelphia and Cornell Medical School. Without waiting to intern she returned to India, arriving on January 1, 1900. Just before she sailed word came from Dr. Louisa Hart, who had gone to India while Ida was in medical school, that there was a desperate need for $10,000 to start a women's hospital at Vellore. She called on Miss Harriet Faber, the president of the Missionary Society of Marble Collegiate Church in New York, intending to ask that society for funds. In the next room Robert Schell overheard her tell of this need. He gave her $10,000 with which he had intended to endow a library in memory of his wife.

The Mary Tabor Schell Hospital, completed in 1902, was the first unit of the medical center at Vellore, which has become one of the finest in all India. One of the most valuable services of this center is the roadside clinic; work started in 1906 and continues today. Villagers often cannot reach or do not even know how to find medical help. The station wagon brings the hospital to them.

One of the big medical problems in India is leprosy. Dr. Scudder and her staff have treated as many as a thousand lepers a day. Another major problem is eye disease. India has a million blind, perhaps half of them with cataracts. One Vellore doctor has set up eye camps, operating from dawn to dusk. The patients remain in these makeshift camps for a week. When the doctor returns, many have the joy of knowing their sight has been restored. In addition to performing minor operations, dispensing medicines, and taking to the hospital those who need hospitalization, the station wagon workers teach health and sanitation. Also a Bible woman is one of the team for these hospitals on wheels.

Since medical missionaries could not begin to meet India's needs, Dr. Scudder dreamed of a school to train Indian women in medicine. This school was opened in 1918, and 17 students were selected from 151 applicants. The school was organized under the Reformed Church Board, but soon aroused the interest of other denominations and has long been a union institution. The medical school includes dormitory, laboratories, lecture and assembly rooms, administration building, and a beautiful chapel. This campus was Vellore's share in a $3,000,000 building fund, for seven Christian colleges in Asia, raised during the depression years. John D. Rockefeller had offered $1,000,000 if the other $2,000,000 was raised. Dr. Scudder returned to the United States to help in this project.

The hospital is also very complete with surgical, maternity, gynecological pavilions, a dispensary, private wards, a children's hospital, and a chapel. Despite all this, in 1942 Vellore faced a crisis and was in danger of being closed. The government raised its requirements. In order to meet these, the hospital had to be almost doubled, the staff increased, and new equipment added. The medical school had to be raised to university standing. At the age of seventy-one Dr. Scudder traveled all over the United States and Canada to raise $1,000,000 to enlarge the hospital and school.

It would have been a tragedy if this institution had been closed. It is the only Christian school in south or central India training women doctors. Moreover, its students absorb and reflect the radiant Christianity of its founder. In the staff house Indians and missionaries live together. On Sunday mornings students and faculty gather together in the chapel and pour out their hearts in spontaneous prayer.

Today Christian Medical College at Vellore trains men as well as women doctors and nurses. It supplies some nine hundred medical units in India. It is now supported by more than thirty Protestant denominations. On January 7, 1950, it celebrated the golden jubilee of medical work of the beloved Dr. Ida Scudder. A new psychology and biochemistry building was officially opened by the governor of Madras, and additions to the nurses' buildings were dedicated by the Maharani of Bhavanagar.[3]

POEM:

> O thou best gift from heaven,
> Thou who thyself hast given,
> For thou hast died—
>
> This hast thou done for me—
> What have I done for thee,
> Thou crucified?
>
> I long to serve thee more,
> Reveal an open door
> Saviour, to me.
>
> Then counting all but loss,
> I'll glory in thy cross,
> And follow thee.
>   —AUTHOR UNKNOWN

PRAYER:

O God, who art the light of the world, hear our prayer for thy servants who have gone into distant lands to carry thy message of salvation. Prosper them in their labors and give them a bountiful harvest. Frequently we pray for the coming of thy kingdom, but fail to do our part in sharing the gospel with those who are still in darkness. Show us definite ways by which we can help to bring thy kingdom nearer. Touch our hearts and make us willing to share our means in the spread of the good news of the gospel. Hasten the time when we shall make the welfare of those who have not heard the message of Christ our chief concern. In Jesus' name we pray. AMEN.

HYMN: "From All the Dark Places" or
"We've a Story to Tell to the Nations"

BENEDICTION:
Now may the peace of God abide with you now and evermore. AMEN.

SERVICE 23

THANKS BE TO GOD
(*Thanksgiving*)

PRELUDE: Hymn tune "St. George's, Windsor"

CALL TO WORSHIP:

> For all the blessings of the year,
> For all the friends we hold so dear,
> For peace on earth, both far and near,
> > We thank thee, Lord.
>
> For life and health, those common things,
> Which every day and hour brings,
> For home, where our affection clings,
> > We thank thee, Lord.
>
> For love of thine, which never tires,
> Which all our better thought inspires,
> And warms our lives with heavenly fires,
> > We thank thee, Lord.
> > > —ALBERT H. HUTCHINSON

SCRIPTURE:

All the commandments which I command thee this day shall ye observe to do, that ye may live, and multiply, and go in and possess the land which the Lord sware unto your fathers. . . . For the Lord thy God bringeth thee into a good land, a land of brooks of water, of fountains and depths that spring out of valleys and hills; a land of wheat, and barley, and vines, and fig trees, and pomegranates; a land of oil olive, and honey; a land wherein thou shalt eat bread without scarceness, thou shalt not lack any thing in it; a land whose stones are iron, and out of whose hills thou mayest dig brass. When thou hast eaten and art full, then thou shalt bless the Lord thy God for the good land which he hath given thee. Beware that thou forget not the Lord thy God, in not keeping his commandments, and his judgments, and his statutes, which I command thee this day; . . . and thou say in thine heart, my power and the might of mine hand hath gotten me this wealth. But thou shalt remember the Lord thy God: for it is he that giveth thee power to get wealth, that he may establish his covenant which he sware unto thy fathers, as it is this day.[1]

HYMN: "Now Thank We All Our God" or
"My God, I Thank Thee"

POEM:

> Thank the Lord for earth and Heaven,
>   Sun and moon and stars and sky,
> Mountains, plains, and valleys given
>   Flowers and fruits, and birds that fly;
> Thank him for the farms and fact'ries,
>   Mines and shops and towers of trade,
> Churches, homes, and schools, and vict'ries,
>   Numberless good things he made.
>
> Thank the Lord for works of wonder,
>   Power and order over all,
> Frost and snow and rain and thunder,
>   Summer, winter, spring, and fall;
> Thank him for the things of spirit,
>   Faith and love and brotherhood,
> Life eternal we inherit,
>   Through his grace and mercy good.[2]
>   —CHAUNCEY R. PIETY

LEADER:

As we approach another Thanksgiving Day let us think of some reasons that we have for being thankful. We have peace within our borders, general prosperity, and plentiful harvests. As we thank God, the Giver of every good and perfect gift, let us remember those whose lives are shattered by war, the displaced persons without a home or country of their own, and the poor of every country. Are we really concerned about these needy persons? Are we willing to share with them that they may have the necessities of life? Are we ready to help put into operation plans by which they can have a higher standard of living?

As the Thanksgiving story is brought to us, let us ask God to deepen our sympathies for others and save us from self complacency.

General Douglas MacArthur said: "This is the story of a Thanksgiving dinner given in a small home in Midwest America over forty years ago. It might easily never have happened at all, yet it may affect the future of the Orient."

STORY:

MY FAVORITE THANKSGIVING STORY

In 1908 Hachiro Yuasa, a seventeen-year-old Japanese boy, said good-by to his parents and sailed for the United States. Raised in an earnest Japanese Christian family, Hachiro had long dreamed of coming to America to live the simple Christian life of an American farmer and later to get his university education.

On ship, thin, young Hachiro composed an imaginary letter telling of his long-awaited arrival in California. He pictured his father at dinner, holding the letter, as be bowed his head for grace:

"Our Heavenly Father, we come together again, as a family. Yet one of us is away. May Hachiro's presence be with us through the warm letter he has written. In Christ's name. . . ."

But Hachiro did not write that letter—not for eleven years. His words about the United States always seemed to come out bitter. He did not find the Christianity he expected. In the restaurants no one said grace. Once at a YMCA he laid his pocket change on a dresser in the men's dormitory before going out to look for a job. When he returned, the "Y" secretary gave him a stern lecture about the care of money.

"But why?" Hachiro wanted to know. "Isn't this the Young Men's *Christian* Association?"

And where was this respect for individuals? California in 1908 was not an easy place for an Oriental to live. Prejudice ran high. In time Hachiro did find work picking cherries in the fruit fields near San Jose; but his hours were from sunup to sundown, and at irrigation time, far into the night. Evenings, when he was not working in the fruit fields, he would wash dishes in the farm kitchen. There he attacked the pots and greasy water that were to become such a part of his life.

Standing over the sink full of dirty dishes and some of his own tears, he again composed in his mind a letter about the United States. But again he did not write it, because it would be bitter:

"I am not a brother to Americans. Our working crew is Japanese. Only the foreman is American. He spoke to me once. He said: 'See? Them too green. No pick 'em.'

"But I feel better now. I have formed a layer of ice around my heart which protects me."

After two years of farm labor during the day and dirty dishes at night, Hachiro realized he was not making the headway in English he would need to enroll in an American university. So in 1910, still thin and frail, Hachiro Yuasa moved to Oakland and went for a few months each to grade school, then high school.

He supported himself by housecleaning, window washing, and lawn mowing, at twenty-five cents an hour . . .

At the end of four years in this country, Hachiro, thinner than ever, had put aside seven $10 gold pieces and learned enough English to be accepted as a freshman at Kansas State. He had reached his goal, but he was not ready, even yet, to let the ice melt from his heart.

For one thing, the only work he could find was washing dishes again and cleaning floors.

Each morning Hachiro swept out laboratories in the school's department of entomology. Through sheer loneliness he went over each bit of floor three times to wipe up every speck of dust.

In time he was given work grinding up bones for laboratory examination. But he grasped at the opportunity, instantly buried himself in his science, still making no friends and now wanting none. Cut off from the human life around him, memories of the old dream about an individual's dignity were stuffed into a forgotten corner of his mind.

What letters Hachiro's family had from their son were brief and contained little about the United States.

Eleven years passed.

While Yuasa was doing graduate work in Urbana, Illinois, the Reverend Roger Augustine and his wife of that town decided to share their Thanksgiving with a foreign student. Hachiro was invited.

Hiding behind a shell of scholarly and scientific reserve, Hachiro arrived at the modest home. But at the door he was greeted by a real smile, and Mr. Augustine took Hachiro's hand in both of his. Hachiro smiled back reluctantly, on his guard.

Dinner was ready. He sat down at the table with the family of four: mother, father, and two children. Behind a set smile Hachiro was watching closely for the first sign that they might be fooling. Perhaps they really wanted him to do the dishes.

Then, carving knife in hand, the father bowed his head. "Our Father: We have come together strangers. Let us part forever friends."

They meant him! Struggle as he might against it, memories came flooding back of Hachiro's own family. Grace before meals. The warm, close-knit family circle. He looked at the faces around him. There could be no doubt about it: these people liked him, wanted to know him, thought of him not as an Oriental, but as a person, an individual.

That night Hachiro wrote to his mother the letter about the United States which he had put off for so many years.

"I was wrong when I looked for a whole government or a job or a school to respect me as an individual," he wrote. "This is not where to find Christianity. Love and kindliness are things that happen inside each separate man. The individual, the person-to-person relationship —that is the important thing."

Hachiro soon began to find friends. He told one of his instructors about a research problem that had been bothering him. The professor said: "Drop up to my house tonight, and we'll go over it. I'm glad you asked me. I've been interested in your work."

He told a fellow graduate student he had not made many friends. "We'd like to have you in our science fraternity," said the young man. "But you always seemed so busy."

When Hachiro completed his work at the university, he had a new goal firmly rooted in his mind: show Japan the importance of the individual human being.

Hachiro returned to the Orient in 1924 and took a post as professor of entomology at Kyoto Imperial University, the center of Japan's scholastic life. But while his reputation as scientist and teacher quickly soared, his own dissatisfaction with the kind of education offered at Kyoto grew too.

The formal, stereotyped schools in Japan offered no chance for the personal relationships that Yuasa had found all important. There was no discussion, no questioning of what was spoken from the lectern. Student and teacher were separated by an impassable gulf of formality.

Finally Yuasa could stand it no longer. He spoke out against god-shelves in schoolrooms, the bowing to imperial portraits. He took a stand for Christian principles. Young students, feverish over Japan's successes in China, reported him to their military instructors. Hachiro began to see his name chalked on the walls: "Down with the traitor Yuasa!"

Forced to resign, Yuasa left Japan for the United States. Many of his friends think it was just in time. During the years of World War II that followed, it seemed to Dr. Yuasa that his life was a failure.

Five months after the bomb was dropped on Hiroshima, Dr. John MacLean, minister of a large church in Virginia, made a suggestion that the United States, by some act of love, should show the world a Christianity more powerful than war. His idea spread, and the "act of love" soon focused on a new kind of university for Japan, the International Christian University. Plans were drawn up.

The school would be for students of all faiths, an experiment in stressing the importance of the individual in contrast to the dictatorship teachings of prewar Japan. Living rooms in faculty apartments, for instance, would be oversized to encourage informal discussion groups right in the professors' homes. On school property was planned a co-operative farm. Allowing professors to pitch in and work with their hands beside the students would develop a new kind of relation to authority. On-campus dormitories would encourage students to make friends more easily in democratic situations.

Before long the proposed university had the backing of more American churches than had ever before co-operated on a single project. Help came too from labor and from management; from pacifist Quakers and from military men; from liberals and from conservatives.

In Japan, meanwhile, the response to the idea of this new school has been amazing. Out of a crippled economy, Japanese people in 1949 raised over $450,000 for the building fund, 95 per cent of the money coming from non-Christians. This interest by Japanese of all religious faiths is very significant.

Ironically enough, the site chosen for the school was where an aircraft factory turned out fighters during the war, a few miles from Toyko. There in 1952 the entire Orient watched as International Christian University was formally opened amid much fanfare by its president Hachiro Yuasa.[3]

POEM:

Father all bountiful,
  Thee we adore,
Filling our treasure house
  Out of Thy store.
By Thee our years are blest;
  By Thee we live.
Grateful, we take from Thee
  All Thou dost give.

. . . .

Father who givest all,
  To Thee we bring
Tribute of grateful hearts;
  Thy praises sing.
Help us to use Thy gifts
  To spread Thy peace;
Give us Thy Spirit, Lord,
  Our love increase.[4]

—GEORGIA HARKNESS

PRAYER:

O God, from whom all blessings come, we are grateful for health, strength, and every good and perfect gift which we receive from thee. Touch our hearts that we may show our gratitude for these gifts by sharing with others less fortunate than ourselves. Be thou at this time very near to bless all who suffer from any cause. Forbid that we should be indifferent to the suffering of the sick, the poor, and the needy. Forgive our complacency and lack of sympathy to the needs of others. Reveal to us the means by which we can help to lighten the burdens of the unfortunate and bring joy and abundant living to the oppressed and downtrodden people of every country. Fill us with thy spirit that we may serve thee in newness of life; through Jesus Christ our Lord. AMEN.

HYMN: "Come, Ye Thankful People Come" or
      "O Lord of Heaven and Earth and Sea"

BENEDICTION:

May the God of peace be with you now and evermore. AMEN.

SERVICE 24

THE SHEPHERD SPEAKS
(*Christmas*)

PRELUDE: "The Pastoral Symphony" from *The Messiah* by Handel

CALL TO WORSHIP:
>As with joyful steps they sped
>To that lowly manger-bed,
>There to bend the knee before
>Him whom heaven and earth adore;
>So may we with willing feet
>Ever seek thy mercy seat.[1]
>
>—WILLIAM C. DIX

HYMN: "Joy to the World" or
"Hark! the Herald Angels Sing"

SCRIPTURE:

And there were in the same country shepherds abiding in the field, keeping watch over their flock by night. And, lo, the angel of the Lord came upon them, and the glory of the Lord shone round about them; and they were sore afraid. And the angel said unto them, Fear not: for, behold, I bring you good tidings of great joy, which shall be to all people. For unto you is born this day in the city of David a Saviour, which is Christ the Lord. And this shall be a sign unto you: Ye shall find the babe wrapped in swaddling clothes, lying in a manger. And suddenly there was with the angel a multitude of the heavenly host praising God, and saying, Glory to God in the highest, and on earth peace, good will toward men.

And it came to pass, as the angels were gone away from them into heaven, the shepherds said one to another, Let us now go even unto Bethlehem, and see this thing which is come to pass, which the Lord hath made known unto us. And they came with haste, and found

Mary and Joseph, and the babe lying in a manger. And when they had seen it, they made known abroad the saying which was told them concerning this child. And all they that heard it wondered at those things which were told them by the shepherds. But Mary kept all these things, and pondered them in her heart. And the shepherds returned, glorifying and praising God for all the things that they had heard and seen, as it was told unto them.[2]

HYMN: "O Little Town of Bethlehem" or
    "Angels from the Realms of Glory"

LEADER:
We will hear the story of the shepherd who missed the song of the heavenly host.

STORY:
THE SHEPHERD WHO WAS NOT IN THE FIELD

Benjamin climbed slowly toward the little town of Bethlehem. City of David, it was called, after the king who had been a shepherd boy on the same hills.

Benjamin was thinking of this as he trudged along beside his plodding oxen, and his reflections were bitter because he too had been a shepherd until that night, just a short while ago, when he had failed to hear the wolf which had slipped into the fold while he was sleeping. One lamb had been killed and another carried off by the wolf. After that night Benjamin's father would no longer trust him with the sheep. He was given less responsible work to do. Benjamin's father was the host of a small inn at Bethlehem, but he had also a flock of sheep pastured on the slope of one of the hills outside the town.

Benjamin looked resentfully at the patient-eyed beasts he was leading. He felt it was humiliating for a fifteen-year-old boy to perform such a stupid task. He must take the oxen to the stable of the inn and put their supper of beaten straw and barley in the manger. Then he would be free to go out in the fields with the other shepherds but he could not bear to see Caleb taking his place. His father had hired Caleb to care for his flock, instead of his own son who could call each sheep by name. Benjamin's cheeks felt hot as he remembered how the boy, whom he had asked to watch for him while he slept, had run away in fear of the dark shape that crept so silently out of the shadows. When he, Benjamin, was awakened by the bleating of the lambs, it was too late to save the poor victims.

Of course Benjamin knew the blame was his own, for he was in charge of the flock and had no right to pass his responsibility on to someone else, so he said nothing to his father about the other boy, and accepted his punishment with a heavy heart. He missed the companionship of the shepherds who roamed the hills and valleys with their sheep.

Bethlehem, thought Benjamin, would be crowded tonight. He doubted if his father's inn would hold all the people. Many were coming to their home city to be enrolled, in obedience to a decree of the Roman emperor requiring that a census should be taken of all the Jews of his empire.

A hand on his shoulder startled Benjamin. Turning quickly, he found himself facing a man who looked as though he had traveled a long distance. The dust of the road clung to his cloak and was caked on his sandaled feet. His face was tired, and a deep line between his eyes showed strain and anxiety. He was leading a small donkey on which the figure of a woman, wrapped in a heavy woolen shawl, drooped with weariness.

"My son," said the man, "can you direct me to an inn, or some place where we may find lodging? We have had a long journey, and my wife is very tired."

"An inn," said Benjamin, "is on this road. You will come to it if you keep straight ahead into the city, but you must hurry because it is a small inn and many will be looking for lodgings tonight."

"Yes, I know," answered the man, "but surely there must be a room somewhere for us to rest."

It was past sunset when Benjamin reached the outskirts of Bethlehem. He paused a moment to watch Obed ben Levi, who spent most of his time studying the stars. It was not yet dark, but Obed was evidently excited about what he saw. His fingers were curved around his eyes to sharpen his vision as he gazed fixedly at the eastern sky.

Benjamin, following his gaze, thought he could detect an unusual brightness on the horizon. "What are you looking at, Obed?"

"A new star is rising," answered the old man. "It is the brightest I have ever seen. When darkness comes you will see how great it is— as though several stars were joined together."

The main street which led to the inn was crowded, so Benjamin led his oxen around through a narrow lane and approached a cave which

154

served as the stable of the inn. At this moment Benjamin heard voices at the entrance to the cave. "It is a poor place," Benjamin's father was saying, "but it will shelter you for the night, and you are welcome to use it if you wish."

"Thank you," said a second voice, and a moment later the travelers, who had inquired their way of him on the road, came through the low doorway. The man had his arm around the woman, and was leading the donkey by a bridle.

Could they be going to spend the night here with the animals? "Wait," cried Benjamin, "I will brush the floor clean and give you fresh straw to put under your mats."

"You are kind," said the woman, smiling at Benjamin, but her voice was tired and faint.

Benjamin piled up some clean straw, and the woman lay down with a grateful sigh. Then he ran to get a wooly lambskin rug and a saucer lamp with oil and a floating wick in it. "Here," said Benjamin, handing the lamp and rug to the man, "it may be cold tonight."

"You are a good lad," said the husband. "We shall be comfortable now, and we are grateful."

Benjamin went out into the darkening streets where people jostled each other looking for their lodgings. Turning, he saw the boy who had run away from the wolf that night on the hills. "What do you want, Arni?" Benjamin asked.

"Benjamin," he said, "why didn't you tell your father it was my fault the wolf got in the fold?"

"What good would that have done?" asked Benjamin. "He would have told me that a good shepherd does not trust someone else to see that his sheep are safe. He guards them with his own life. It was my fault that I put my task upon your shoulders, Arni."

"But you haven't told anyone what a coward I was," said Arni.

Benjamin's father called: "I have been looking for you. I have important guests tonight and you must help me to serve them. Arni, I shall need you, too."

It was past midnight when the innkeeper released them and the boys could steal out into the night. The courtyard seemed as bright as day, and Benjamin turned his face up to the sky in surprise. This was different from the usual starlight; there was a glow, as from some heavenly fire. "Let's go to Obed," Benjamin said to Arni, "he will tell us what this means."

Suddenly Benjamin heard a sound near the entrance to the cave, and he remembered the guests who were in this humble lodging. He remembered the weariness of the young woman and the anxious face of her husband as he bent over her, for Benjamin was realizing that the sound he had heard was a baby's cry. "Let us find Obed," he whispered.

They found the old man still on his rooftop. The panorama of the sky from Obed's rooftop was enough to hold them all speechless. The star seemed to hang low in the sky and to shed its radiance over all the surrounding country. "It is a sign," said Obed, "that a great and holy One has been born tonight. Could it be the long expected One? And where shall we look for him?"

A baby? Benjamin's thoughts raced back to that cry he had heard outside the stable. But, no, those were simple folk whose child had been born in a stable. Theirs could not be the child, foretold by the prophets, who should be the king of the Jews.

The boys thanked Obed and started toward the city gate. Suddenly Benjamin discovered a group of men and boys hurrying up the hillside. "Look, aren't those the shepherds from the valley yonder? Why are they leaving the sheep?" The shepherds came nearer and Benjamin saw that Caleb was with them.

Caleb's face was pale and he breathed hard as he spoke. "Benjamin," he said, "we have had heavenly visitors in the fields tonight. As we sat around the fire, an angel appeared to us in a great light, and when we hid our faces for fear he said to us: 'Be not afraid; for behold, I bring you good news of a great joy which will come to all the people; for to you is born this day in the city af David, a Saviour, who is Christ the Lord. And this will be a sign for you: you will find a babe wrapped in swaddling clothes and lying in a manger.' And suddenly there was with the angel a multitude of the heavenly host praising God and saying, 'Glory to God in the highest, and on earth peace, good will among men.' And when the angels went away, we came with haste to find this child. Have you heard any news of him?"

"Come," said Benjamin, and he felt his heart swell as he spoke, for even though he had missed those heavenly messengers in the field, had he not heard the first faint cry of the babe, and would he not be the one to lead the shepherds to the humble place of his birth? "Come," he said again.

And so they came to the doorway of the little stable, and one by one crept into the quiet place where a young mother lay resting on a bed of straw, her dark eyes turned toward the babe cradled in a manger, while her husband kept vigil beside them both. Then the man lifted his head and saw them all kneeling there, and Caleb told the story of the heavenly visitation. The mother listened with wonder in her eyes, but Benjamin had the feeling that it was not so much the wonder of the story Caleb was telling as the marvel of her newborn son. Then the shepherds rose to their feet and followed Caleb out of the stable.

"Benjamin," said Arni, "I told your father how I ran away the night the wolf got into the fold."

"You were brave to tell my father the truth. Anyhow none of that seems to mean so much tonight. I feel, Arni, as though we were making a fresh start—as though this day meant a new beginning for everyone, because of what happened in there."

"What was it the angel said to the shepherds?" Arni asked.

" 'I bring you good news of a great joy which will come to all people; for to you is born this day in the city of David a Saviour, who is Christ the Lord.' "

They stood looking into each other's eyes, trying to comprehend the full meaning of the angel's announcement, but all Benjamin could think of was the face of the sleeping baby and the love in the mother's eyes; and this, Benjamin felt suddenly, was the whole story.

POEM:

> Behold the people of the earth
>   In all the nations striving!
>   Seeking, longing, not arriving;
> They know not of the Savior's birth.
>
> Behold the people of the earth
>   In armaments confiding!
>   Fearing, shrinking, crouched in hiding;
> They know not of the Savior's birth.
>
> Behold the peoples of the earth
>   In love and peace residing!
>   Trusting God, in Grace abiding;
> They know full well the Savior's birth.[3]

—MACK B. STOKES

LEADER:

At this season when there will be much giving, let us think of making a gift to him whose birthday we celebrate. What more appropriate gift could we offer than that of ourselves to Christ? And for those of us who have committed ourselves previously, let us renew our vows along with others who take the step for the first time. Let us make a new beginning by offering ourselves wholeheartedly to Christ and his cause.

PRAYER:

Our Father, as we commemorate the birth of thy Son, grant that his spirit may be born anew in our hearts and that we may give him first place in our lives. As we renew our vows to thee today, help us to understand clearly what it means to live as Jesus lived. During this season of joy and gladness may we not forget those who are lonely and discouraged. Touch our hearts that we may share with them the good things that we enjoy. Lead us into larger fields of usefulness as we dedicate ourselves anew to thee. In Jesus' name. AMEN.

HYMN: "While Shepherds Watched Their Flocks" or
       "It Came upon the Midnight Clear"

BENEDICTION:

Now unto him who is able to lead you into the way of love and service, be glory and honor, now and evermore. AMEN.

MINISTERING TO LEPERS
(*Missions Sunday*)

PRELUDE: Hymn tune "Russian Hymn"

CALL TO WORSHIP:
> Great art thou, O Lord, and greatly to be praised;
> Great is thy power, and of thy wisdom there is no end.
> And man, being a part of thy creation, desires to
> praise thee—
> Man, who bears about with him his mortality,
> The witness of his sin, even the witness that thou
> "resistest the proud"—
> Yet man, this part of thy creation, desires to
> praise thee.
> Thou movest us to delight in praising thee;
> For thou hast formed us for thyself,
> And our hearts are restless till they find rest in thee.
> —ST. AUGUSTINE

HYMN: "We May Not Climb the Heavenly Steeps" or
"Dear Lord and Father of Mankind"

SCRIPTURE:

Then shall the King say unto them on his right hand, Come, ye blessed of my Father, inherit the kingdom prepared for you from the foundation of the world: for I was ahungered, and ye gave me meat: I was thirsty, and ye gave me drink: I was a stranger, and ye took me in: naked, and ye clothed me: I was sick, and ye visited me: I was in prison, and ye came unto me. Then shall the righteous answer him, saying, Lord, when saw we thee ahungered, and fed thee? or thirsty, and gave thee drink? when saw we thee a stranger, and took thee in? or naked, and clothed thee? or when saw we thee sick, or in prison, and came unto thee? And the King shall answer and say unto them, Verily I say unto you, Inasmuch as ye have done it unto one of the least of these my brethren, ye have done it unto me.[1]

LEADER:

We will hear the story of the man who dedicated himself to the task of alleviating the suffering of the lepers of the island of Molokai.

STORY:

BENEATH THE LEPER TREE

There were hundreds of them on the island. All were hungry, ragged, forsaken, their only friendship that which misery invents for itself. As you may have guessed, I am writing of the men, women, and children of Molokai—they who exist on living death.

Molokai is an island in the Hawaiian group. Its population is listed as five thousand. Its area is two hundred sixty-one square miles. It boasts a pleasant climate, shady palms, and glorious resortlike beaches. But there are few sight-seers or travelers to its shores. For Molokai is a leper island.

It was a number of years ago that Father Damien determined to go to these outcasts with the message of Christianity and any joy that he could bring to their forsaken lives. But, like Francis of Assisi, when he saw the wretchedness of their condition, the utter ugliness of their disease, he turned away from them. Living apart in a little hut of his own, he cooked his own meals, washed his own clothes, and would not allow a leprous person to come inside. He had come to minister to them, but he lived apart.

Then something strange happened. I can liken it only to what must have taken place in the mind of Francis of Assisi as he rode on horseback along a narrow mountain trail in Italy. Suddenly as he rounded a curve a wretched, maimed leprous man stood right in the path. Francis was repelled. Rather than brush past this man, he turned his horse and started back to the place from which he had come.

But something happened within Francis. He paused, got down from his horse, and went back to the leprous man. He put his arms about him as a token of brotherliness, much to the astonishment of the man who had known nothing but ill-treatment all his life. Then taking his moneybag from his tunic, Francis gave what was in it to the man, and went away strangely refreshed for the deed he had performed.

It must have been such an experience that impelled Father Damien at Molokai to abandon his isolation. "For how," he thought, "can I help them if I try to avoid them?" Completely denying his own desires, he helped the lepers build better homes. He organized the colony in such a way that one would help another. He dressed their infectious wounds, secured pure water, sent out a request for clothing and food. Because of his complete self-sacrifice, Father Damien won the confidence of the people who never before had witnessed such a demonstration of friendship.

Father Damien died a leper. But before his death he had won the entire colony to Christ.

On August 19, 1947, a fifty-three-year-old Chicago telephone operator, Miss Margaret Haven, retired from her job and sailed for Molokai. "God has always given me a marvelous health," she says, "and now I just want to share it with others."

This was no sudden decision on the part of Miss Haven, who was deeply impressed with the work of Father Damien. She and her sister had thought often of the possibility. But when her sister died a year and a half before their sailing date, Miss Haven almost gave up her plan. But now she looks forward to the career from which there is no turning. The possibility of getting leprosy and being unable to see friends or family again does not bother her.

"It makes no difference," she said.

She is helping to ease the suffering of the between five and ten million people of our world who are afflicted with leprosy. Perhaps nowhere is religious fellowship so greatly needed, so deeply appreciated, as among those who have the dreadful disease, leprosy.

Ruth Winant Wheeler has expressed well in the following lines the need which is in part being met by our churches:

> Beneath the leper tree the leper waits.
> Before him are the white, white wooden gates
> Closed to him still. The evening air is chill.
> He waits for you and me, beneath the leper tree.
> Under the leper tree the lepers call:
> "Christians, in Jesus' name, I pray you all
> Bring healing help; we stretch our hands to thee,
> Bleeding and crippled hands, under the leper tree." [2]

SOLO: "Come unto Me, When Shadows Darkly Gather" or
"O Jesus, Master, When Today"

POEM:

> Father, whose will is life and good
>   For all of mortal breath,
> Bind strong the bond of brotherhood
>   Of those who fight with death.
>
> Empower the hands and hearts and wills,
>   Of friends in lands afar,
> Who battle with the body's ills,
>   And wage thy holy war.
>
> Where'er they heal the maimed and blind,
>   Let love of Christ attend:
> Proclaim the good Physician's mind,
>   And prove the Saviour friend.
>
>   .   .   .   .
>
> O Father, look from heaven and bless,
>   Where'er thy servants be,
> Their works of pure unselfishness,
>   Made consecrate to thee!
>
> —HARDWICKE D. RAWNSLEY

LEADER:

A visitor to a leper colony relates the following incident:

One day I walked through the stone gateway to a leprosy colony in India. Great trees shaded the road, but the red dirt burned redder than ever in a footworn square before the superintendent's cottage.

There I saw a man squatting. He did not move. He only squatted abjectly. The red dust streaked his white shirt and dhoti. The sun beat cruelly on his bare head and sweating body. As I passed him he lifted his face very slowly. Under a tangled mop of hair his forehead was plowed deep by wrinkles of anxiety. He looked at me with eyes of pathos and despair, and raising a fingerless hand, saluted me in the ancient gesture of salaam.

A week before, he had asked for admission to the colony but had been refused because there was no room. Not the space of one bed, not the little extra food to keep one extra man alive. But he would not leave. He squatted, and waited, and somewhere behind his hopeless eyes, hoped. Against all evidence and all denial, hoped.

The American Mission to Lepers exists to justify such hope. I works through 40 Protestant mission boards and their missionaries, in 125 places in 29 countries, to give care, and often healing, to men, women, and children. Through our offering we will have opportunity to help in this worthy cause.[3]

OFFERTORY:

Let us remember the words of Jesus: Inasmuch as ye have done it unto one of the least of these my brethren, ye have done it unto me.

POEM:

The cry of man's anguish went up to God,
"Lord, take away pain!
The shadow that darkens the world thou hast made;
The close coiling chain
That strangles the heart: the burden that weighs
On the wings that would soar—
Lord, take away pain from the world thou hast made
That it love thee the more!"

Then answered the Lord to the cry of the world,
"Shall I take away pain,
And with it the power of the soul to endure,
Made strong by the strain?
Shall I take away pity that knits heart to heart,
And sacrifice high?
Will ye lose all your heroes that lift from the fire
White brows to the sky?
Shall I take away love that redeems with a price,
And smiles with its loss?
Can ye spare from your lives that would cling
    unto mine
The Christ on his cross?"

—AUTHOR UNKNOWN

PRAYER:

O God, from whom cometh every good and perfect gift, and who hast bidden us to seek heavenly treasure, grant unto us a proper sense of values. May we show our gratitude for all that comes from thee by giving a portion of it to thy service. May we give cheerfully and wholeheartedly.

Bless those who have gone into the far corners of the world to serve the sick and to carry thy message. Endue them with thy spirit, enrich them with thy fellowship, and may they have an abiding sense of thy presence at all times. Give them grace to bear the loneliness and separation from their families and friends. We thank thee that we may have a part in this worthy work by sharing our means. Touch our hearts and make us generous in our giving. In Jesus' name. AMEN.

HYMN: "O Jesus, I Have Promised" or
    "We Thank Thee, Lord, Thy Paths of Service Lead"

BENEDICTION:
  May the blessing of God our Father be with you both now and evermore. AMEN.

SERVICE 26

YE ARE MY WITNESSES
(*Dedication Day*)

PRELUDE: "Intermezzo" by Mascagni

CALL TO WORSHIP:

> LEADER: Lift up your heads, ye mighty gates,
> Behold, the King of glory waits;
> The King of kings is drawing near;
> The Saviour of the world is here!

> GROUP: Fling wide the portals of your heart;
> Make it a temple, set apart
> From earthly use for heaven's employ,
> Adorned with prayer, and love, and joy.

> UNISON: Redeemer, come, we open wide
> Our hearts to thee; here, Lord abide.
> Thine inner presence let us feel;
> Thy grace and love in us reveal.
> —GEORG WEISSEL

HYMN: "Breathe on Me, Breath of God" or
"Holy Spirit, Truth Divine"

INVOCATION:

O God of peace, we turn aside from an unquiet world, seeking rest for our spirits and light for our thoughts. We bring our work to be sanctified, our wounds to be healed, our hopes to be renewed and our better selves to be quickened, so that we may not sin but serve and walk humbly with thee. O thou in whom there is harmony, thou alone canst silence the discords of our lives. Thou whose greatness is beyond our utmost thought dost alone lift us above our common littleness and sendest visions of the beauty that is in thy world, of the love that is in thee, and of the good that may be in us. AMEN.[1]

—AUTHOR UNKNOWN

SCRIPTURE:

And Jesus returned in the power of the Spirit unto Galilee: and there went out a fame of him through all the region round about. And he taught in their synagogues, being glorified of all.

And he came to Nazareth, where he had been brought up: and, as his custom was, he went into the synagogue on the sabbath day, and stood up for to read. And there was delivered unto him the book of the prophet Esaias. And when he had opened the book, he found the place where it was written, The Spirit of the Lord is upon me, because he hath anointed me to preach the gospel to the poor; he hath sent me to heal the brokenhearted, to preach deliverance to the captives, and recovering of sight to the blind, to set at liberty them that are bruised, to preach the acceptable year of the Lord. . . . But ye shall receive power, after that the Holy Ghost is come upon you: and ye shall be witnesses unto me both in Jerusalem, and in all Judea, and in Samaria, and unto the uttermost part of the earth. . . . Every good gift and every perfect gift is from above, and cometh down from the Father of lights, with whom is no variableness, neither shadow of turning.[2]

LEADER:

Let us consider the joy of helping others.

One act of charity will teach us more of the love of God than a thousand sermons.—AUTHOR UNKNOWN.

He that turneth from the road to rescue another, turneth toward his goal; he shall arrive by the footpath of mercy; God will be his guide.—HENRY VAN DYKE.

Do not wait for extraordinary circumstances to do good actions; try to use ordinary situations.—JEAN PAUL T. RICHTER.

God has so constituted our nature that we cannot be happy unless we are, or think we are, the means of good to others. We can scarcely conceive of greater wretchedness than must be felt by him who knows he is wholly useless in the world.—ERSKINE MASON.

HYMN: "Lord, Speak to Me" or
        "Master, No Offering Costly and Sweet"

166

POEM:

> Oh, what is Christianity?
>   No holy creed or theory,
> No mystic law or cult or band,
>   No formal rite, but life's best brand,
> Such life as Jesus lived for me,
>   Oh, that is Christianity.
>
> Oh, what is Christianity?
>   Not anything we hear or see,
> Not value by mint-measure told,
>   Not born of force, but love controlled,
> Such life as Jesus lived for me,
>   Oh, that is Christianity.
>
> Oh, what is Christianity?
>   Not something past eternally,
> Not what the future may allow,
>   But life of my life even now,
> Such life as Jesus lived for me,
>   Oh, that is Christianity.[3]

—CHAUNCEY R. PIETY

LEADER:

We shall hear a story of one who found pleasure through serving others.

STORY:

THE YOUNG MONK'S DREAM

A monk once sat by the window of his rude hut on the mountainside looking down upon the little village below. The years seemed long since as a busy, happy lad he had played in its streets and climbed its hills to care for the goats—then left for the city to complete his education. The burdens of sin and sorrow, suffering and ignorance that pressed upon him in the crowded city streets made him long for release. Then came a day when he returned to the little village. Here he might find refuge. But he was to meet disappointment. Poverty and sin were there in the valley, and evil lurked where his boyish eyes had never seen it. As the days passed the village seemed accursed, and so he left it, climbed the mountainside, built his hut, planted his garden, listened to the singing of the birds and the winds, cared for his sheep and goats, read, played, grew strong in body and content in mind—until the day of his dream.

He had been reading in the glory of the sunset the story of Calvary, and fell to wondering whether Jesus Christ ever felt for a moment that his task was hopeless. It must have been a shock to him when he uncovered the sin, hypocrisy, greed, and littleness of man. If ever there was a reason for loss of faith in one's mission Jesus had it, thought the monk. The snobbery of the Pharisees, the ambition of the disciples, the cowardice of Pilate, the jealous envy of the priests—these might easily have made him lose all hope that the thing he had come to do ever could be done.

"But there is no hint of any such spirit in any of the words he spoke," the monk said to himself. "Looking unto the hard, shrewd faces of those about him, Jesus said, 'Do unto others as you would that they should do unto you.' In the presence of evil he said, 'Blessed are the pure in heart, for they shall see God.' Looking over a group of self-seekers, he declared, 'He that saveth his life shall lose it.'"

The monk's meditation on Jesus' life and teachings thrilled his soul and sent him to his knees in prayer. As night came over the valley he fell asleep and dreamed that he walked upon a road from earth to heaven. It was dark at first and hard to travel. There were many weeds, the rocks were jagged, and the brambles sharp. Then it grew lighter and beautiful with flowers. Suddenly at a turn in the road he met the Master whose words he had been reading.

"O Master," he cried, kneeling at his feet, "art thou on thy way back to earth?" The Master shook his head.

"But men need thee so badly. Thou shouldst have stayed," said the monk.

The Master answered softly, "I finished the work I had to do."

"O Master," said the monk, made bold by his eagerness, "but the burden, the burden of sin and poverty. It is still with us. There is no escape. Who can bear the burden of man's stupid blundering, his hate and greed, his love of goods and gold?"

The Master smiled. "I share with those who understand my mission the burden of man's need," he said.

"But, Master," cried the monk in sorrow and in fear, "what if no man understands thy mission? What if men fail thee? What then?"

"I am counting on them," said the Master, and his voice thrilled the monk to the depth of his being. "I am counting on those who love me and who understand."

When the monk awoke, so real had been the dream and so clear the vision that he gazed for some moments about the tiny room, then out into the moonlight, half expecting to see the road from earth to heaven. Then in the silence of his retreat he considered the meaning of the dream. The hut had been so quiet, so comfortable; there was time for worship, for study, for prayer and meditation. He had been well content. But the dream disturbed him. He could not close his eyes to its message or his mind to its demand.

It was sunrise when for a moment he knelt once more, a new light upon his face. When he arose, he took off his robe and folding it neatly with the cross and beads laid it away. With mingled feelings of fear and hope he dressed in the clothes he had worn when he had awaited ordination. "Now," he said softly, "again I am one of them." Carefully he set his room in order and closed and barred the door of his hut.

A moment he paused to look at the world below him, just waking to life in the morning mist. Then he grasped his mountain stick firmly and started down the trail. As he walked fear and dread were changed to joy.

"I am going back," he said aloud, "back into the midst of it all where a Christian belongs, with his fellow men, to be a part of their lives, to share their burdens, to struggle with them and on their behalf for a better day. I am going back into the midst of problems that must be met and solved, where life is hard, where men must toil, into the thick of the battle with selfishness and greed, into the homes where men and women struggle to be true and fail. The Christ, with his faith that the kingdom of God could be built upon the earth, has given the challenge from which for me henceforth there is no turning back. The battle is mine, the struggle mine, the burden mine. I take it upon myself." [4]

POEM:

> Stay, Master, stay upon this heavenly hill;
> A little longer, let us linger still;
> With all the mighty ones of old beside,
> Near to God's holy presence still abide;
> Before the throne of light we trembling stand,
> And catch a glimpse into the spirit-land.

Stay, Master, stay! we breathe a purer air;
This life is not the life that waits us there:
Thoughts, feelings, flashes, glimpses come and go;
We cannot speak them—nay, we do not know;
Wrapt in this cloud of light we seem to be
The thing we fain would grow—eternally.

"No!" saith the Lord, "the hour is past," we go;
Our home, our life, our duties lie below.
While here we kneel upon the mount of prayer,
The plough lies waiting in the furrow there!
Here we sought God that we might know his will;
There we must do it, serve him, seek him still.

If man aspires to reach the throne of God,
O'er the dull plains of earth must lie the road:
He who best does his lowly duty here,
Shall mount the highest in a nobler sphere:
At God's own feet our spirits seek their rest,
And he is nearest to him who serves him best.

—SAMUEL GREG

PRAYER:

Our Father, may thy Holy Spirit bring to our remembrance that we are to seek first thy kingdom and righteousness; that we are to desire not to be ministered unto but to minister; and that we are to love not only our friends but our enemies also. May we realize that one of the greatest privileges we enjoy is that of communion with thee, that thy Spirit is ever present with us to give us strength when we are weak, to give us courage when we are fearful, and to grant us wisdom with which to meet the many problems of life. We are reminded that the building of thy kingdom on earth is left to thy followers. May we be instruments in thy hands to carry out thy purpose in the world, through Jesus Christ our Lord. AMEN.

HYMN: "Lord, Speak to Me" or
       "O Master, Let Me Walk with Thee"

BENEDICTION:

Thou who art able to keep us from falling, and to present us faultless before thy presence, unto thee be glory forever and ever. AMEN.

SERVICE 27

THE LIVING WORD
(*Universal Bible Sunday*)

PRELUDE: "Consolation" by Mendelssohn

CALL TO WORSHIP:
>Draw nigh to God, and he will draw nigh to you.
>Humble yourself in the sight of God, and he shall
>lift you up.

HYMN: "A Glory Gilds the Sacred Page" or
"Book of Books, Our People's Strength"

SCRIPTURE:
>Wherewithal shall a young man cleanse his way?
>by taking heed thereto according to thy word.
>With my whole heart have I sought thee: O let me
>not wander from thy commandments.
>Thy word have I hid in mine heart, that I might
>not sin against thee.
>Blessed art thou, O Lord: teach me thy statutes.
>With my lips have I declared all the judgments of
>thy mouth.
>I have rejoiced in the way of thy testimonies, as
>much as in all riches.
>I will meditate in thy precepts, and have respect
>unto thy ways.
>I will delight myself in thy statutes: I will not
>forget thy word. . . .
>Teach me, O Lord, the way of thy statutes; and I
>shall keep it unto the end.
>Give me understanding, and I shall keep thy law;
>yea, I shall observe it with my whole heart.

Thy word is a lamp unto my feet, and a light unto
my path. . . .

All Scripture is given by inspiration of God, and is profitable for
doctrine, for reproof, for correction, for instruction in righteousness:
that the man of God may be perfect, thoroughly furnished unto all
good works.[1]

PRAYER:

Direct us, O Lord, in all our doing, with thy most gracious favor, and
further us with thy continual help, that in all our works, begun,
continued, and ended in thee, we may glorify thy holy Name, and
finally, by thy mercy, obtain everlasting life, through Jesus Christ our
Lord. AMEN.

HYMN: "Break Thou the Bread of Life" or
"Behold a Sower!"

POEM:

Beautiful Bible,
Glory of the ages,
God's victor over every foe,
Truth-brightened pages,
Lamp of the sages,
God's wisdom that all men should know.

Wonderful Bible,
Message of salvation,
Telling God's love for every man,
Word of conversion,
And consecration,
The revelation of God's plan.

Glorious Bible,
God's mighty man-changer,
And guide to vanquish daily strife,
Light for the stranger,
World's rearranger,
God's word of everlasting life.[2]

—CHAUNCEY R. PIETY

LEADER:

We will hear a story of a Bible, one of William Carey's translations
into Bengali, which was lost for many years, yet its influence lived on.

THE LIVING WORD

TALES OF LOST BIBLES

When William Carey made shoes in a Northampton village, he had a Latin and Greek grammar propped up in front of him, for it seemed as if languages were food and drink to him. The heat of the sun in England was such a menace to him that he had to take a job indoors. Little did he think that in a few years' time he would be studying Indian languages under the relentless heat of an Indian sun.

Stranger than the strangest fairy tale does it seem that this cobbler from Northampton should arrive in India and should there translate the Bible, or parts of it, into thirty-five different languages.

His first translation was of the New Testament into Bengali. Who knows what thoughts filled his mind as he fingered the little pile of that first edition of the book as it lay on his study table? Here was something never done before. The Word of God in an Indian language, a language spoken by nearly fifty million people. Carey wondered where those books would go, and what fruit they would bear.

One was indeed lost for many years, but it lived in spite of it. It passed from hand to hand in the crowded city of Calcutta, and then, as a much-treasured possession, it was taken by a village schoolmaster when he went back to his far-off village. He traveled for days by the Bengali waterways, lying under a thatched roof in a country boat, listening to the monotonous singing of the coolie with the pole who punted the boat along. The boat moved quietly from one reach to another, past mangrove swamps, and great wide jheels covered with wild duck, and through narrow reed passages, until he reached his secluded village. Here none could read but he, and books were not to be reckoned with. This one was, though. In the evening, just before dusk, he used to read it to his friends under the great banyan tree in the middle of the village. The green parrots darted and shrieked above their heads, and the air was thick with dust as the cows and goats came by, their musical bells chiming slowly and gently.

The villagers pieced together by themselves a picture of what Jesus was like and what he expected of them. Gradually they left off worshiping at the shrines of their gods, the marigold wreaths were absent, and the little offerings of rice and millet were no longer left before the grinning wooden figures. When the conch blew in the evenings, the worshipers became fewer and fewer. They were all under the banyan tree, listening to the words of life.

Slowly these words changed their lives. They became truthful instead of lying, gentle instead of rough, merciful instead of grasping, and always they were asking for and searching for a Teacher sent from God.

Other peasants from other villages came to listen to the reading of the Book, and they too carried away the idea of a gentle and more honest way of life and worshiped the Teacher they could not find.

The schoolmaster died and his son read in his stead, keeping the sacred Book in a painted wooden box by day and taking it out in the evening as a kind of evening service.

No one from the outside world came to that remote village, but the Book lived on, its words treasured and learned by heart and pondered over by the villagers. They came to be called the disciples of truth, and gradually news of their way of life penetrated down the waterways and quiet canals to the great capital of Calcutta.

Filled with curiosity, one of the younger missionaries made the long journey into the heart of Bengal to see for himself these seekers after truth and to hear where they got their new faith.

They offered to show him their holy book, and there, wrapped in a gaudy cloth, and reposing in a painted box, lay a copy of Carey's first Bengali Testament, lost for so many years, yet still alive.[3]

LEADER:

Let us notice what some great men have said about the Bible.

FIRST SPEAKER:

John Quincy Adams said: "Search the Scriptures. The Bible is the Book of all others to read at all ages and in all conditions of human life." Daniel Webster said: "If religious books are not widely circulated among the masses in this country, and the people do not become religious, I do not know what is to become of us as a nation."

SECOND SPEAKER:

William Lyon Phelps said: "I am not sorry that when I was a child, I read every word of the Authorized Version of the Bible, from the first chapter of Genesis to the end of the last chapter of Revelation. The Bible contains within its covers the greatest literature in the world. . . . It is the foundation of modern civilization; our ideas, our art, our way of thinking, our ideals come more from the Bible than from all other books put together."

THIRD SPEAKER:

Ulysses S. Grant said: "Hold fast to the Bible as the sheet anchor to your liberties. Write its precepts in your hearts and practice them in your lives. To the influence of this Book we are indebted for all the progress made in true civilization, and to this we look as our guide in the future."

FOURTH SPEAKER:

Lincoln said: "The Bible is the best gift which God has ever given to man—but for that book we could not know right from wrong."

Sir Walter Scott wrote:

> Within that awful volume lies
> The mystery of mysteries!
> Happiest they of human race
> To whom God has granted grace
> To read, to fear, to hope, to pray,
> To lift the latch and force the way;
> And better had they ne'er been born
> Who read to doubt, or read to scorn.[4]

POEM:

> Thy Word, O God, the Book of Life,
> That tells Thy will and way,
> Let this now be a beacon light
> Upon our stricken day.
> When nations quake and systems shake,
> Here find our souls release;
> Within this Book the longer look
> Brings vistas of Thy peace.
>
> For here is told the best we know
> Of wisdom, faith and good;
> The story of Thy Father-love
> Is seed of brotherhood.
> In Thy command our duty lies,
> In Christ our goal we see;
> Our freedom and our strength are won
> Through Him who makes us free.
>
> Be Thou, O Lord, from sacred page
> A lamp unto our feet.

As Thou hast led our fathers forth,
  So may we scorn retreat.
To Thee, O God, we pledge our all,
  Heart, soul, and strength and mind;
In Christ our Lord known through Thy Word
  Thy saving health to find.[5]

—GEORGIA HARKNESS

PRAYER:

Our Father, help us to appreciate the fact that we may find thy word for us in the Bible. Forbid that we should ever read casually the record of the experiences that people of the past have had with thee. Grant that we may treasure the truths found in the Scriptures, make an effort to understand their meaning for us, and strive to live by them. We are grateful for the freedom which we enjoy. Help us to realize that freedom has come to us because many people of the past and present have tried to live by the principles taught in the Bible. Help us to turn to the Bible with open minds and with teachable hearts and find therein a guide for daily living; through Christ our Lord. AMEN.

HYMN: "O Word of God Incarnate" or
  "Thy Word Is Like a Garden, Lord"

BENEDICTION:

O God, may the meditations of our hearts be acceptable in thy sight as we strive for a better understanding of thy Word and a more complete obedience to thy commands. AMEN.

Part II. For Intermediates

SERVICE 28

FINDING GOD THROUGH BEAUTY

PRELUDE: "The Lark's Song" by Tchaikovsky

CALL TO WORSHIP:

> Serve the Lord with gladness;
> Come before his presence with singing,
> For the Lord is good, his mercy is everlasting,
>   and his truth endureth to all generations.[1]

INVOCATION:

O God, thou art the creator of beauty and hath implanted within our hearts the love of the beautiful. We thank thee for all thy gifts, but especially for the beauty of nature, its varied colors and delightful forms. Broaden our minds, open our eyes, and enlarge our capacity to appreciate beauty. Forgive our narrowness, dullness, and lack of gratitude for all of thy gifts. Guide and direct us as we strive to use our talents and our means to make the world more beautiful; through Jesus our Master and Lord. AMEN.

SCRIPTURE:

O sing unto the Lord a new song: sing unto the Lord, all the earth. . . .

For the Lord is great, and greatly to be praised. . . .

He hath made every thing beautiful in his time: also he hath set the world in their heart. . . .

Honor and majesty are before him: strength and beauty are in his sanctuary. . . .

O worship the Lord in the beauty of holiness: fear before him, all the earth. . . .

Let the heavens rejoice, and let the earth be glad; let the sea roar, and the fulness thereof.

Let the field be joyful, and all that is therein: then shall all the trees of the wood rejoice before the Lord: for he cometh, for he cometh to judge the earth: he shall judge the world with righteousness, and the people with his truth.[2]

POEM:

> O Lord of heaven, and earth, and sea,
> To thee all praise and glory be!
> How shall we show our love to thee,
>   Who givest all?
>
> . . . .
>
> We lose what on ourselves we spend,
> We have, as treasures without end,
> Whatever, Lord, to thee we lend,
>   Who givest all.
>
> Whatever, Lord, we lend to thee,
> Repaid a thousandfold will be;
> Then gladly will we give to thee,
>   Who givest all!
>   —CHRISTOPHER WORDSWORTH

OFFERTORY:

Offering Response:

> All things are thine, no gift have we,
> Lord of all gifts, to offer thee;
> And hence with grateful hearts today,
> Thine own before thy feet we lay. AMEN.

HYMN: "For the Beauty of the Earth" or
"My God, I Thank Thee, Who Hast Made"

LEADER:

We will hear the story of a man who gave to the American people a beautiful tower and sanctuary in appreciation for the opportunities the United States had given him.

STORY:

THE SINGING TOWER

There was once a little boy named Edward Bok who liked to listen to stories. One he liked particularly. It was about a dreary island which had been made beautiful. He liked it particularly because it was his own grandfather who had brought the trees to the island and had made it beautiful. He liked to remember the words his grandmother had said to her boys and girls before they left their own home: "Make your world a bit more beautiful and better because you have been in it."

"I'd like to do that, mother," said Edward. "Do you suppose I could?"

"Time only will tell, little son," she would reply, "but it is something to remember and to dream about."

And Edward did remember. He remembered his grandmother's words and his own plan.

"Sometime I will make the world more beautiful and happy because of me," he often thought. He thought it when he was a little boy, he thought it when he was a big boy, and he thought it when he grew to be a man.

It was not easy, for there was not much money, and Edward had to leave school early to help make a living for the family, but he did not forget. From a little boy he grew into a big boy, a big boy who helped his mother and then went out to work to bring more and more money home. Years passed by and the little Edward grew to be the editor of a big magazine, and a very rich man.

"Now is my time to make my dream come true," he thought. "Like my grandfather, I will build a place of safety for the birds. It shall be called a sanctuary, for the word sanctuary means a place of rest and safety, but it shall not be only for birds. Men, women, and little children need places of beauty where they can rest and think. I will make a sanctuary for them, too."

For a long time he thought about his plan.

"I will take some ugly place and make it beautiful," he said. He chose a barren sand hill in Florida, so dry and hot that many things would not grow there.

"I must have water brought," he said.

Trenches were dug and water pipes laid. There were enough to bring a great deal of water to his new park—enough to fill a lovely pool.

Often when Edward Bok was thinking of his dream, he had heard the church bells ring. Sometimes when they rang they seemed to say, "Come! Come!" Sometimes they played beautiful tunes. Some had only a few bells; others had many. When he heard the music of the bells, it filled his mind with beautiful thoughts. Once he went to Malines to hear the lovely carillon, which is another name for many bells singing together. Malines is in Belgium. The bells hang in a very beautiful tower. It was the most beautiful bell tower that Edward had ever seen.

"I will have a beautiful tower in my sanctuary," thought Edward. "It shall be the most beautiful in all the world. The bells will sing to the people and will give them rest. They will bring beautiful thoughts to the people."

He went to see a man who drew plans and pictures of churches, homes, and other buildings. This man was called an architect.

"What do you want?" asked the architect.

"The most beautiful tower in the world," said Edward Bok.

"Do you know the tower at Malines?" asked the architect. "Do you expect me to beat that."

"Yes," said Edward Bok.

"I will try," said the architect.

It was a lovely tower that he planned, a tower built of pink marble and Florida coquina stone. On part of it flowers and animals were carved. At its top hung seventy-one bells. At its foot was a lovely pool which formed a giant lookingglass for the tower and the trees about it.

Hundreds of people came to see the beautiful tower and to hear the marvelous bells. Hundreds of birds flew to the sanctuary, for they knew that no harm could come to them there. There were many fruit and berry trees which had been planted for them. There were fifty birdbaths for them to bathe in and drink from.

Carved on a tablet near the tower are Miss Gurney's beautiful lines:

> The kiss of the sun for pardon,
>   The songs of the birds for mirth—
> One is nearer God's heart in a garden
>   Than anywhere else on earth.

Truly the world is a lovelier place because Edward Bok's dream came true, and well has he followed in the footsteps of his grandfather who made a barren island the Island of Nightingales.[3]

Poem:

> We thank thee, Lord, for eyes to see
>   The beauty of the earth;
> For ears to hear warm words of love,
>   Or happy sounds of mirth;
> For minds that find new thoughts to think,
>   New wonders to explore;

For health and freedom to enjoy
   The good thou hast in store.

May we remember that to some
   The eye and ear and mind
Bring sights and sounds of ugliness,
   And only sadness find;
May we remember that to them
   The world has seemed unfair;
That we must strive to bring to them
   The beauty all may share!

Oh, may our eyes be open, Lord,
   To see our neighbors' need,
And may our ears be kept alert
   Their cries for help to heed;
Keen be our minds to plan the best
   For one another's good,
That all the world shall be at last
   One friendly neighborhood.[4]

          —JEANETTE PERKINS BROWN

LEADER:

Those who are close observers have noticed that nature cannot endure ugliness. Fields and forests that have been cut over will grow green again, dumps and rubbish piles will eventually be covered with vines. Nature is seldom permanently ugly.

God created beauty in the world that we might enjoy it. The perfection that we find in nature speaks of the goodness and thoughtfulness of the Creator. Seeing and appreciating beauty makes us more responsive to other manifestations of God in the world about us.

To appreciate beauty there must be an inner quality which will eventually seek some form of outward expression. Man at his best is a seeker and lover of the beautiful. He is forever creating beauty in one form or another.

To possess beauty we must become beautiful within, but we cannot do this in our own strength. God will enter our lives, help us to uproot hate, selfishness, and greed, and plant in their place love, joy, peace, and good will. We can begin now by allowing God to plan and direct our lives.

HYMN: "God, Who Touchest Earth with Beauty" or
"This Is My Father's World"

PRAYER:

O God, who hast shown thyself to mankind in various ways, we thank thee for the revelation of thyself in nature. We thank thee for the wonder of the universe, for the beauty of thy creation, for the birds, trees, flowers, and for everything thou hast made for our enjoyment. We pray that thou wilt take from us all low ambitions and selfish desires and help us to build into our lives the strength and beauty which we see in nature. As we meditate on thy plan and purpose which runs through thy creation, reveal thy purpose for our lives, and may we learn to live in harmony with thy divine will; through Jesus Christ our Lord. AMEN.

BENEDICTION:

Now may we go forth to honor thee and acknowledge thee as Lord and Master. AMEN.

SERVICE 29

FINDING GOD THROUGH FAITHFULNESS

PRELUDE: "Mood Melodie" by Wilson

CALL TO WORSHIP:
> The Lord is my light and my salvation;
>> Whom shall I fear?
> The Lord is the strength of my life;
>> Of whom shall I be afraid? . . .
> For the Lord is a great God,
>> And a great King above all gods.[1]

HYMN: "Rejoice, Ye Pure in Heart" or
"Now in the Days of Youth"

SCRIPTURE:
His lord said unto him, Well done, thou good and faithful servant: thou hast been faithful over a few things, I will make thee ruler over many things: enter thou into the joy of thy lord. . . .

He that is faithful in that which is least is faithful also in much: and he that is unjust in the least is unjust also in much. . . .

Fear none of those things which thou shalt suffer: . . . be thou faithful unto death, and I will give thee a crown of life.[2]

POEM:
> O Love divine, that stooped to share
>> Our sharpest pang, our bitterest tear!
> On thee we cast each earthborn care,
>> We smile at pain while thou art near.
>
> . . . .
>
> When drooping pleasure turns to grief,
>> And trembling faith is changed to fear,
> The murmuring wind, the quivering leaf,
>> Shall softly tell us thou art near!

185

On thee we fling our burdening woe,
　O Love divine, forever dear!
Content to suffer while we know,
　Living and dying, thou art near!
　　　　　　　—OLIVER WENDELL HOLMES

INVOCATION:

Almighty God, from whom every good prayer cometh, and who pourest out on all who desire it the spirit of grace and supplication, deliver us, when we draw night to thee, from coldness of heart and wanderings of mind: that with steadfast thoughts, and kindled affections, we may worship thee in spirit and in truth; through Jesus Christ our Lord. AMEN.

HYMN: "O for a Closer Walk with God" or
　　　　"Are Ye Able?"

LEADER:

We will hear a story of a boy who was faithful to a task that had been assigned to him.

STORY:

BRYAN UNTIEDT—A BOY HERO

Bryan started off to school that day with his little brother, just as he always did. Today it was cold, very cold, and he tied the scarf closer around his little brother's neck. It was snowing and the wind was blowing. He hoped the school bus would not be long in coming.

There it was! It stopped before his home. The two children climbed in with the other boys and girls whom the bus took every day to the school some distance away. They laughed about the wind and the snow and breathed on the windowpanes to try to make the snow melt, so that they could see through. But it was no use. If the bus had not stopped they would not have known they had reached the school.

Out they piled and ran toward the warm building where they would be all day.

All day it snowed, and by the time the bus came to take the children home, there was a real blizzard.

Bryan buttoned his little brother's coat up very tight, and helped him through the snow to the bus.

"Oh-oh! See how much it's snowed!" the children cried. Another time they would have stopped to make snowballs. But the wind drove

186

the snow in their faces today, and twenty children ran toward the bus like little goats with their heads down, as if they were going to butt something.

The bus started. The snow drove harder and harder against the windowpanes, against the windshields. The driver went slowly because he could not see through his windshield. Soon he ran off the road and into a drift.

The children inside said: "What's the matter? Why don't we go?"

The driver said: "We've run off the road. I couldn't see. The bus is stuck in the snow. I wish we were near some house." But they were far out in the country.

"I ought to go for help," said the driver, "but I don't want to leave you children alone."

It grew darker. "I must go for help," he said at last. Then he looked at Bryan.

"Bryan," he said, "I'll leave you in charge. I may be gone a long time. The nearest house is a long way off and it will be slow going."

"I'll take care of the children," Bryan said.

Then the driver said: "Make the children play. Don't let them go to sleep. If you do they will freeze."

So the driver started out to find help.

"Come on," said Bryan to the children, "let's play that game we play in school."

So they played games, games that made them exercise to keep warm. But there was no heat in the bus.

"My feet are cold," the little children wailed, and Bryan made them jump up and down. His feet were cold too, but he did not complain.

"My hands are cold," whined a child. So were Bryan's, but he took off his warm mittens to cover the child's hands. He clapped his hands over and over and made the children clap theirs, as they jumped up and down.

"I'm tired," said one after another, and stopped playing. Bryan was tired too, but he made himself go on.

"I'm so cold," sobbed his little brother, and Bryan, though he was cold too, took off his coat and gave it to his little brother.

But he must not let the children stop exercising. The driver had said they would freeze if they did.

He kept thinking of more games, and he made them keep playing until they were too tired to play any longer. What could he do? The driver was so long coming.

"I'm cold," another child and another cried. Bryan took off his scarf. He took off his sweater. My, how cold he was, but he must take care of these children! Some were acting as if they were going to sleep. They must not go to sleep. Bryan slapped them so they would fight back. Anything to keep them exercising.

At last he had thought of everything he could do. He had made himself give away most of his clothes. He had kept the children awake as long as he could. Still the driver did not come. His hands and his feet were numb, they were so cold. The children were falling asleep. He made them and made himself stay awake as long as he could. Then he fell asleep.

All night it snowed and the children slept. All night and the next morning it snowed so that in the afternoon, when a party of brave men found them, the bus was covered with snow. It was Bryan's father who found it. They wakened the sleeping children and rubbed them. They hurried them as fast as they could to hospitals. Bryan's hands and feet were frozen and he had pneumonia. But most of the children were saved and the doctors said it was only because Bryan had kept them from falling asleep as long as he had. They knew how hard it had been, and they called him brave and a hero.

The President of the United States heard about it, for the story was in all the newspapers. He said, "I want to know that boy." And he sent him an invitation to come to visit him at the White House in Washington.

When he heard about it, Bryan said to his nurse: "Won't that be great? That certainly was mighty nice of the President. I never dreamed of anything like that. I wish the rest of the kids could go along."

At last he was well enough to travel, and he went to visit the President and his wife at the White House. He slept in the bed that Lindbergh had slept in, and played with the President's little grandchildren. He was taken all around Washington to see the sights, and when he left to go back to Colorado, his mind was filled with exciting stories to share with his friends who could not take the trip.[3]

POEM:

> Teach me, my God and King,
> In all things thee to see,
> And what I do in anything,
> To do it as for thee.

To scorn the senses' away,
　While still to thee I tend;
In all I do be thou the way,
　In all be thou the end.

All may of thee partake;
　Nothing so small can be
But draws, when acted for thy sake,
　Greatness and worth from thee.

If done to obey thy laws,
　E'en servile labors shine;
Hallowed is toil, if this the cause,
　The meanest work, divine.

Thee, then, my God and King,
　In all things may I see;
And what I do, in anything,
　May it be done for thee!
　　　—GEORGE HERBERT
　　　Alt. by JOHN WESLEY

PRAYER:

Our Father, speak to us, make thyself known and reveal thy will to us. Open our eyes that we may see thee in the lives of people who have dedicated themselves to the Christian cause; open our ears that we may hear thee through thy spokesmen, through music, and all other avenues. Make us instruments in thy hands to help those who are in need, to bring cheer to those in sorrow. Help us to put selfish interests in the background, and to give ourselves in service to others. Grant that we may do our tasks faithfully each day and live in a manner that is pleasing to thee. Grant us wisdom to know what is right, and give us strength and courage to resist temptation. In Jesus' name. AMEN.

HYMN: "True-hearted, Whole-hearted, Faithful and Loyal" or
　　　"I Would Be True"

BENEDICTION:

Now unto him who is able to keep you faithful and to present you faultless before his presence, be glory and honor forever. AMEN.

FINDING GOD THROUGH PERSISTENCE

PRELUDES "Berceuse" from Jocelyn

CALL TO WORSHIP:
Know ye not that ye are the temple of God, and that the Spirit of God dwelleth in you? . . .
For as many as are led by the Spirit of God, they are the sons of God.[1]

HYMN: "Lead On, O King Eternal" or
"O Young and Fearless Prophet"

SCRIPTURE:
And they came to Jericho: and as he went out of Jericho with his disciples and a great number of people, blind Bartimeus, the son of Timeus, sat by the highway side begging. And when he heard that it was Jesus of Nazareth, he began to cry out, and say, Jesus, thou son of David, have mercy on me. And many charged him that he should hold his peace: but he cried the more a great deal, Thou son of David, have mercy on me.

And Jesus stood still, and commanded him to be called. And they call the blind man, saying unto him, Be of good comfort, rise; he calleth thee. And he, casting away his garment, rose, and came to Jesus. And Jesus answered and said unto him, What wilt thou that I should do unto thee? The blind man said unto him, Lord, that I might receive my sight. And Jesus said unto him, Go thy way; thy faith hath made thee whole. And immediately he received his sight, and followed Jesus in the way.[2]

POEM:

>He liveth long who liveth well;
>   All else is being flung away;
>He liveth longest who can tell
>   Of true things truly done each day.

Fill up each hour with what will last;
Use well the moments as they go;
The life above, when this is past,
Is the ripe fruit of life below.
—Horatius Bonar

Leader:

We will hear a story of the healing of one who was blind.

Story:

AT THE ROADSIDE

"Tell me one of the stories the wind sings to you," said Nathaniel. He was seated on the bank of a stream, around him the sheep were scattered, and beside him sat an older boy whose eyes were closed, for he was blind. Bartimeus, that was the blind lad's name, was the son of Timeus, the shepherd employed by Nathaniel's father to help care for his great flock, and like Timeus the lad was dressed in a shepherd's short tunic and striped cloak.

The boy had been blind since he was born. When he sat in the tiny hut which was his home, his face was drawn and sad and his voice sounded dull and hopeless, but out on the green fields among the sheep he was like a different lad. He would sit contentedly for hours beside a stream, listening to its ripple and murmur, and he spent whole days upon the wooded hillside with the wind blowing in his face, and such a happy smile upon his lips that no one who did not see his closed eyes would guess that he was blind. He loved to listen to the wind in the treetops and through the long grass, the rustle and flutter of falling leaves, and the swaying of the boughs. He would tell Nathaniel the songs the wind had sung, the secrets the brooks had told, and the stories of the rustling trees. In return for these tales the younger boy looked up at the blue sky with white drifting clouds, or a flock of birds flying across it, and described what he saw to the blind lad. Then while Bartimeus lay at night upon the mat on the floor of the shepherd's hut, the pictures Nathaniel had described to him floated through his mind, until instead of the blackness he seemed to see glowing skies, and flying birds, and splendid clouds.

There was another time when these bright pictures filled his mind, and made him forget his surroundings. As he could not work, and his family were very poor, he was forced to beg. Several days each week his father led him to the roadside, and there Bartimeus sat with a

191

wooden bowl outstretched for gifts. He was so used to it that he did not mind sitting there any more than being shut up in the hut. Both places were far from the sheep fields which he loved, and after all, in spite of the begging, he liked the roadside better than the house. The wind blew there occasionally, although it brought no fragrance of flowers, and sometimes a bird perched upon the wall behind him and sang a song as if to cheer him. When it was finished, he would think of the bird's flight as Nathaniel had described it, and he forgot the noise of jostling passers-by in imagining the upward sweep which the bird made when it fluttered its tiny wings.

But one twilight as the evening star began to shine softly through the silvery sky, Nathaniel sang Bartimeus the song of the new Star, the shepherd's lullaby. After that the blind lad's dreams were no longer of clouds, or birds, or sunset skies. He persuaded Nathaniel to tell him every word he knew about the Christ, the marvelous man whose grandfather had been a shepherd boy upon those very fields. Then as the blind lad lay upon his mat at night, or sat alone and helpless by the roadside, his mind was filled with glowing pictures of a gracious figure who loved children, called fishermen to be his followers, brought comfort to the saddest heart, and healed those who were sick.

"Is it possible that this wonderful Master could make a blind man see?" cried Bartimeus one day when Nathaniel had finished telling of how Jesus healed people. Nathaniel did not know, but he was almost as excited as the blind boy himself, and for days afterward they talked of what Bartimeus would do if he had his sight.

"I think I would be a shepherd and live out on the fields," he said at first, "then I could see the sun rise and set, the birds fly across the sky, and the waving of the trees when the wind sings to them."

But the next time he saw Nathaniel the blind lad had spent a day upon the roadside and had changed his mind. "I would travel everywhere," he said, "and you would go with me. We would see all kinds of men, rich and poor, soldiers and shepherds, priests and fishermen, and when we had found the finest, strongest man in the world, we would follow him."

"But first you must have your sight," said Nathaniel, "and even if the Master comes to this part of the country, we do not know that he can cure you."

But Bartimeus was full of hope. That evening as Nathaniel led him home across the fields the wind seemed to whisper that help was coming, the stream they crossed murmured comfort, and although the blind lad could not see them, the stars above his head shone brightly and Nathaniel sang,

In the hush of its coming a new Star is born,
The Star of our gladness, the Star of Christ's morn.

" 'Christ's morn,' " repeated Bartimeus. "It has dawned already in my heart and soon it may dawn before these dark eyes."

The next day Bartimeus was again led to the roadside to beg, and as the sun sank Nathaniel, instead of the shepherd father, came to bring the boy home. He took the bowl with its few tiny coins from the hands of the patient lad who sat there so forlornly, and was about to hand him his stick when an outcry arose down the street.

"He is coming," voices called, "let us hurry to meet him!" And down the street poured a crowd of men, women, and children.

"Who is it?" cried Bartimeus. "Tell me, I pray you, who is coming?" And someone called back, "It is Jesus of Nazareth."

Then above the tramping of many feet, and the pushing and ex-clamations of the crowd, rose the voice of the blind lad.

"Jesus, thou Son of David, have mercy on me," cried the pleading voice, and many around him bade him harshly to be quiet, not to disturb the Master. But again and again he cried, all the longing of his soul poured into those words, "Thou Son of David, have mercy on me."

"Can the Lord pass unheeding of that cry?" thought Nathaniel, for already the majestic, white-robed figure was opposite them. Then tears of relief and joy stood in the boy's eyes, for Jesus stood still in the center of the throng and said in a low voice to the men near him, "Call ye him."

Bartimeus had not heard those words, and a look of heartbroken disappointment was sweeping across his face when the men who had been sent reached him. "Be of good comfort," they exclaimed, "rise; he calleth thee." Throwing aside his cloak, Bartimeus sprang up and hurried, led by Nathaniel, down the path the people made, to Jesus.

Many beautiful sounds had brought delight to the sensitive ears of Bartimeus, the whisper of the wind, the songs of the birds, and the ripple of the silvery stream, but at that moment he heard a voice which was more thrilling than any music of which he had even dreamed.

"What wilt thou that I should do unto thee?" said the Christ, and the blind lad answered, "Lord, that I might receive my sight." Then Jesus said, "Go thy way; thy faith hath made thee whole."

With eyes suddenly opened, Bartimeus looked up and saw the twilight sky with one clear star shining there; around him he saw a sea of astonished faces, and before him he saw one whom he knew in a flash was the Son of God.

There was no need for him to travel the world over in search of the perfect man; he was there before the newly awakened eyes of the blind beggar. And Bartimeus thanked the Master for the great gift of his sight, not by words alone, but by following him and serving him forevermore.[3]

POEM:

> He stood before the Sanhedrim;
> The scowling rabbis gazed at him;
> He recked not of their praise or blame;
> There was no fear, there was no shame
> For one upon whose dazzled eyes
> The whole world poured its vast surprise.
> The open heaven was far too near,
> His first day's light too sweet and clear,
> To let him waste his new-gained ken
> On the hate-clouded face of men.
>
> But still they questioned, Who art thou?
> What hast thou been? What art thou now?
> Thou art not he who yesterday
> Sat here and begged beside the way,
> For he was blind.
>
> *And I am he;*
> *For I was blind, but now I see.*
>
> He told the story o'er and o'er;
> It was his full heart's only lore;
> A prophet on the Sabbath day
> Had touched his sightless eyes with clay,
> And made him see, who had been blind.
> Their words passed by him on the wind
> Which raves and howls, but cannot shock
> The hundred-fathom-rooted rock.
>
> Their threats and fury all went wide;
> They could not touch his Hebrew pride;

Their sneers at Jesus and his band,
Nameless and homeless in the land,
Their boasts of Moses and his Lord,
All could not change him by one word.

I know not what this man may be,
Sinner or saint; but as for me,
One thing I know, that I am he
Who once was blind, and now I see.

They were all doctors of renown,
The great men of a famous town,
With deep brows, wrinkled, broad and wise,
Beneath their wide phylacteries;
The wisdom of the East was theirs,
And honor crowned their silver hairs;
The man they jeered and laughed to scorn
Was unlearned, poor, and humbly born;

But he knew better far than they
What came to him that Sabbath day;
And what the Christ had done for him,
He knew, and not the Sanhedrim.[4]

—JOHN HAY

PRAYER:

Our Father, we confess to thee the lack of our faith and sympathy. Increase our faith and our concern for those in need. Help us to overcome jealousy, envy, strife, indolence, and indifference within ourselves. As we strive to serve our fellow men, may we have thy Spirit and show forth thy love. Give us wisdom and courage and make us steadfast and loyal in our devotion and faithful in thy service. Make us worthy of thy trust in us, help us to serve thee better and to follow thee more closely. Thine shall be the glory for evermore. AMEN.

HYMN: "Saviour, Like a Shepherd Lead Us" or
        "O Master, Let Me Walk with Thee"

BENEDICTION:

May God make you perfect in every good work to do his will, working in you that which is well pleasing in his sight, through Jesus Christ our Lord. AMEN.

195

SERVICE 31

FINDING GOD THROUGH PRAYER

PRELUDE: "Menuetto" from *Fantasia,* Op. 78, by Schubert

CALL TO WORSHIP:

Ask, and it shall be given you; seek, and ye shall find; knock, and it shall be opened unto you; for every one that asketh receiveth; and he that seeketh findeth; and to him that knocketh it shall be opened.[1]

HYMN: "A Charge to Keep I Have" or
"Thou Art the Way"

SCRIPTURE:

And when they were come to the multitude, there came to him a certain man, kneeling down to him, and saying, Lord, have mercy on my son; for he is a lunatic, and sore vexed: for ofttimes he falleth into the fire, and oft into the water. And I brought him to thy disciples, and they could not cure him.

Then Jesus answered and said, O faithless and perverse generation, how long shall I be with you? how long shall I suffer you? bring him hither to me. And Jesus rebuked the devil; and he departed out of him: and the child was cured that very hour.

Then came the disciples to Jesus apart, and said, Why could not we cast him out?

And Jesus said unto them, Because of your unbelief: for verily I say unto you, If ye have faith as a grain of mustard seed, ye shall say unto this mountain, Remove hence to yonder place; and it shall remove; and nothing shall be impossible unto you. Howbeit this kind goeth not out but by prayer and fasting. . . .

And all things, whatsoever ye shall ask in prayer, believing, ye shall receive. . . .

And the apostles said unto the Lord, Increase our faith.[2]

FINDING GOD THROUGH PRAYER

When the anchors that faith has cast
　Are dragging in the gale,
I am quietly holding fast
　To the things that cannot fail:

I know that right is right;
　That it is not good to lie;
That love is better than spite,
　And a neighbor than a spy;

. . . .

In the darkest night of the year,
　When the stars have all gone out,
That courage is better than fear,
　That faith is truer than doubt;

And fierce though the fiends may fight,
　And long though the angels hide,
I know that Truth and Right
　Have the universe on their side;

And that somewhere, beyond the stars,
　Is a Love that is better than fate;
When the night unlocks her bars
　I shall see Him, and I will wait.[3]
　　　　　　—WASHINGTON GLADDEN

LEADER:

We will hear a story in which some of the early Christians risked
their lives in order to carry out a divine command.

STORY:

A RISK FOR GOD

In the ancient city of Damascus a little group of people had
gathered together in much fear. They hardly dared speak out loud
after one man whispered what he had heard.

"I am sure it is the truth," he whispered. "My sister's husband heard
it in the town from someone who knows. Not one of us is safe. It's
all a trick."

"What's a trick?" asked a late-comer.

"Saul of Tarsus is in town pretending to want to join us of the Way."

"Saul of Tarsus!" exclaimed the late-comer, looking fearfully over his shoulder. "Are you sure? How do you know?"

"He came to town today. My sister's husband heard it all. He came in leaning on another man's arm. He pretends he was blinded on the road by a vision. He pretends he is now going to be a follower of the Way. It's a trick, a mean, cowardly trick. He only wants to find out where we all live."

"It's a trick worthy of Saul of Tarsus," a man said bitterly.

A woman began to wail. "Curses on Saul of Tarsus," she sobbed.

"Hush," warned the woman next her. "The walls have ears to betray us of the Way. Perhaps we can escape out of the city before morning."

"How can we go far enough away to be safe from Saul? Hasn't he come all the way from Jerusalem to Damascus, where we thought we were safe? He'd go to the end of the earth to catch one follower of Jesus."

"But we could try to find a safer place."

A quieter voice spoke. "What if Saul has had a vision? What if he does intend to follow in the Way? Would that be beyond the power of our risen Christ?"

"Ananias!" one of the men exclaimed. "You don't really believe that blackhearted deceiver? He's just trying a new trick to get more of us to take to Jerusalem to be put in prison."

"And to be stoned to death, like our dear Stephen," another added. "That was Saul's work."

"Perhaps Saul is not even in Damascus," an old man said. "Perhaps the rumor is not true. I think we ought all to go quietly to our homes, one by one, and pray God for protection."

"The kind of protection Stephen received?" a man muttered.

Ananias spoke up quickly at that. "Stephen shared the kind of protection our Lord received," he said firmly. "He knew God loved him. It is not staying alive that is most important. The important thing is to live nobly or to die nobly."

They all went to their homes and to bed. Many of them had troubled dreams of being dragged out of their beds and off to prison by Saul of Tarsus.

Ananias dreamed. In his dream, the Lord spoke to him. The Lord said: "Arise, and go into the street which is called Straight, and inquire in the house of Judas for one called Saul of Tarsus: for, behold, he prayeth."

Ananias said: "Lord, I have heard by many of this man, how much evil he hath done to thy saints at Jerusalem: and here he hath authority from the chief priests to bind all that call on thy name."

But the Lord said: "Go thy way: for he is a chosen vessel unto me, to bear my name before the Gentiles, and kings, and the children of Israel: for I will show him how great things he must suffer for my name's sake."

Ananias slipped out into the darkness and tried to walk boldly along the narrow street. He could not help feeling that somebody was waiting to spring out from the dark doorways and to carry him away to imprisonment or death.

"Was my vision truly from the Lord?" he asked himself again and again. "Am I walking into a trap? Suppose Saul is at the house of Judas. Will he take me to Jerusalem in chains? One week from tonight, shall I be dead like Stephen? Can't I serve God better by peeping into Judas' house and running away to warn my friends if Saul is really there?"

Then he remembered God's delieverance of the Israelites when they were fleeing from Pharaoh across the Red Sea. That gave him courage. Then he remembered Stephen again, and was afraid.

He was in the street called Straight. He was in front of the house of Judas. A cold chill down his back made him shiver. He could feel the hairs stand out on his neck. He asked himself, "Could I die as bravely as Stephen died?"

He remembered the story of Stephen's prayer: "Lay not this sin to their charge." That reminded him of the heroism of Jesus, and suddenly he was strong. He heard the voice of his vision again, "Go thy way."

"Yes, Lord," he said out loud. "Whether it leads me to life or to death I will go my way." And he knocked on the door of the house of Judas.

When the door was opened, he walked straight across the room without a quiver, to the dreaded and hated man, Saul. Ananias called him "Brother."

"Brother Saul, the Lord, even Jesus, who appeared unto thee in the way as thou camest, hath sent me, that thou mightest receive thy sight, and be filled with the Holy Ghost."

A sort of scale fell from Saul's eyes, and he could see again.

Ananias took a risk on faith, and to him was given the honor of baptizing that very night Saul of Tarsus, who became St. Paul of the Church Universal.[4]

POEM:

The weary one had rest, the sad had joy
   That day, and wondered how.
A plowman singing at his work had prayed,
   "Lord, help them now."

Away in foreign lands they wondered how
   Their feeble words had power.
At home the Christians, two or three had met
   To pray an hour.

Yes, we are always wondering, wondering how,
   Because we do not see
Someone unknown perhaps, and far away,
   On bended knee.

                     —AUTHOR UNKNOWN

PRAYER:

Our Father, help us to get rid of all thoughts and attitudes which are not pleasing to thee. Create within us a clean heart and renew a right spirit within us. Where there is hatred, help us to love; where there is selfishness, help us to be concerned about the welfare of others. When we are tempted to do wrong, give us courage to choose the right. May we never be satisfied with less than our best. If we have failed to give to thee our time, talents, and possessions, forgive us. When there is an opportunity to use our talents in thy service, may we answer the call willingly. Reveal thy will to us through the Scriptures, through worship, and grant us strength and courage to follow thee in every thought and action of our lives. In Jesus' name we pray. AMEN.

HYMN: "O Master, Let Me Walk with Thee" or
       "Take My Life, and Let It Be"

BENEDICTION:

May thy Spirit direct us that we may follow thee more faithfully. AMEN.

FINDING GOD THROUGH LOVE

PRELUDE: "Andante Religioso" (Fourth Sonata) by Mendelssohn

CALL TO WORSHIP:

> This is the day which the Lord hath made;
> We will rejoice and be glad in it.
> Enter into his gates with thanksgiving,
> And into his courts with praise.[1]

HYMN: "Ye Fair Green Hills of Galilee" or
"More Love to Thee, O Christ"

SCRIPTURE:

If I can speak the languages of men and even of angels, but have no love, I am only a noisy gong or a clashing cymbal. If I am inspired to preach and know all the secret truths and possess all knowledge, and if I have such perfect faith that I can move mountains, but have no love, I am nothing. Even if I give away everything I own, and give myself up, but do it in pride, not love, it does me no good. Love is patient and kind. Love is not envious or boastful. It does not put on airs. It is not rude. It does not insist on its rights. It does not become angry. It is not resentful. It is not happy over injustice, it is only happy with truth. It will bear anything, believe anything, hope for anything, endure anything. Love will never die out. . . . So faith, hope, and love endure. These are the great three, and the greatest of them is love.[2]

LEADER:

We will hear a story which will make clearer the meaning of love.

STORY:

THE WONDERFUL WORD

Once upon a time, a long while ago in a far-away land, there was a little old man who stood all day by a big gate. He could not open the gate, for there was no one who could open it. There was only one thing in the world that could make that gate swing open, and that was a word, a wonderful word. The little man knew what that word was, but he was not allowed to tell. So he stood all day by the gate, not to open it for the people who came there, but rather to tell them what they must do to get in. If anyone said the right word, and showed that he knew what the word meant, the big gate swung open, and he went inside. Many, many people came and wanted to get in.

The gate, when it opened, led into a beautiful garden, and the name of the garden was "Happy Life." Since everyone wanted to have happy life, many came and talked with the little old man, and tried to say the word that would make the gate open.

One day when the little old man was standing there, he saw a big, tall fellow coming toward him. The big, tall fellow spoke to him in a big, tall voice, and said: "I should like to get into the garden called 'Happy Life.' You will please open the gate for me."

The little old man answered: "I cannot open the gate for you. But you say the right word, and show that you know what it means, then the gate will swing open."

The big, tall fellow said: "Well, if that's the way to open the gate, I know a word which can do wonderful things. And since the gate is big and strong, I think this word ought to be spoken in a loud and mighty voice."

So the big, tall fellow lifted his big, tall voice, and standing close beside the gate, he shouted his word, "Power!"

Then he waited. But the gate never lifted its big latch by even the small part of an inch, and the hinges never creaked or groaned.

The little old man said: "You know, you have to show what the word means."

The big, tall man was angry.

"All right," he said in his big, tall voice. "I'll put some power on this gate."

So he stepped back, and he took a little run, and he rushed at the gate and kicked it just as hard as he could. The only thing that happened was that he hurt his foot, and that made him a little angrier.

Then the big, tall fellow looked around and found a big stone. He picked it up with both of his strong hands and hurled it with all his might at the gate. But the gate was not even dented or scratched.

The little old man stepped forward and said: "Mr. Big Tall Fellow, you have spoken your word, and you have shown that you know what it means, and the gate remains closed. Your word is therefore not the right one. Power will not let you into the beautiful garden called 'Happy Life.' You must go away."

So the big, tall fellow went slowly away, limping a bit painfully on the foot he had banged against the gate. And the little old man went back to his place.

Soon he saw someone else coming. This was a short fellow with a sly, scheming face, and he said to the little old man: "I should like to get into the garden called 'Happy Life.' You will please open the gate for me."

And the little old man answered: "I cannot open the gate for you. But you say the right word, and show that you know what it means, then the gate will swing open."

The short fellow with the sly, scheming face said, "All right, I know the word. It's a word that gets you ahead, and helps you to have what you want. It's a smart word, a keen word, and a wise word."

So he went up and spoke the word close before the gate, "Cleverness."

Then he waited. But the gate never lifted its big latch by even the small part of an inch, and the hinges never creaked or groaned.

The little old man said: "You know, you have to show you know what the word means."

The short fellow with the sly, scheming face said: "I know what it means. I know how to be clever and smart."

Then he went up close to the little old man and he whispered in his ear: "Listen, my friend. You are a handsome little old man. I like you very much. You know the word which will open this gate. I am just asking you to tell it to me, so that I may say it and go inside the garden which is called 'Happy Life.' "

But the little old man quietly stepped away and said: "I do indeed know the word, but I cannot tell it to you because I am on my honor."

The short fellow with the sly, scheming face answered; "But you shall tell me the word. Look! Here is gold. All this shall be yours if you tell me the word."

He showed the little old man a wallet he carried, from which he poured out many shining coins.

But the little old man answered: "No. I cannot be bought with gold. You have spoken your word, and you have shown that you know what it means; but it is not the right word. 'Cleverness' will not open the gate or let you into the beautiful garden called 'Happy Life.' "

So the short fellow with the sly, scheming face went away, hanging his head in shame because of his failure. And the little old man went back to his place.

It was a long time before anyone else came near. And then just as the big red sun was about to sink behind the mountains, a little girl with a pleasant face came to the place. She led by the hand a child even tinier than she, and the little old man guessed that he was her little brother.

And the little girl turned her pleasant face up toward the little old man and said: "I should like to get into the garden called 'Happy Life.' You will please open the gate for me."

And the little old man answered: "I cannot open the gate for you. But if you say the right word, and show that you know what it means, then the gate will swing open."

The little girl with the pleasant face did not know what to do. She looked down at the little boy that she held by the hand. Then she looked up at the little old man.

"Please," she said, "I'm just a little girl, and I don't know many words. Couldn't you help me with this one, just as my mother helps me with words in my reading lesson?"

The little old man answered, "I'm sorry, but I am not allowed to help anybody with the word."

The little girl waited several moments. Then she said slowly: "Well, I know one word that my mother says is a very wonderful word—the most wonderful word in the whole world. I'm going to say it to the big gate. I'm going to whisper it, because it may not be right."

So she stepped very quietly up to the big gate, and then very quietly she said her wonderful word, "Love."

Then she watched, and she listened, and her eyes opened wide, and her mouth began to open too. For slowly, slowly, the big, heavy latch began to lift.

"It must be the right word!" exclaimed the little girl.

"It is the right word!" exclaimed the little old man. "The latch has lifted. Now show that you know what the word means, and the gate will swing open and let you into the beautiful garden called 'Happy Life.'"

Again the little girl with the pleasant face became very sober.

"I couldn't do that," she said. "I don't know how. I don't know what to do. I—I—."

And the little girl seemed about to cry.

Just at that moment the little boy that she held by the hand really did begin to cry.

"I want to go home," he said. "I want my mother."

The little girl stooped to the frightened child and talked kindly to him.

"Don't you mind, Jimmy," she said. "I know it's been a long, hard walk, and I know you don't like this strange, big gate that won't open all the way. But you just wait a little longer, until I can think how to show that I know what 'love' means, and then I'll take you home, and I'll carry you over the rough places."

But the little boy was not satisfied and only cried more loudly.

"I want to go now. Take me home. I want my mother."

The little girl stooped again, and this time she picked up the tiny lad and held him in her arms.

"All right," she said. "Sister'll take you home. Sister'll take you home right now."

She turned and looked sadly once more at the big gate whose latch was still lifted.

"Perhaps," she said slowly, "perhaps some day when I am bigger, I can find some way to show what love means, and then the gate will open and let me in. Perhaps—."

She paused and looked again at the gate in amazement. For now the most wonderful thing of all was happening. Slowly, slowly, with a grating and creaking of hinges, the gate was opening.

"But—but I don't understand," said the little girl. "I didn't show that I know what my word, 'love,' means. I—."

"Oh, yes you did," said the little old man. "If you had not loved your little brother, you would not have been willing to take him home, or to talk so kindly to him when he cried. For love means helping people; it means being kind. It is the people who do those things who may walk in the beautiful garden called 'Happy Life.' For it is love, and only love, that can make anyone's life a happy and beautiful thing."

Then the tiny boy ceased his crying, and the little girl's face became happy and smiling again, and on a fragrant bush beyond the open gate a pleasant brown bird sang a sweet evening song.[3]

Poem:

> Love thyself last; look near, behold thy duty
> To those who walk beside thee down life's road;

Make glad their days by little acts of beauty,
　And help them bear the burden of earth's load.

Love thyself last; look far and find the stranger
　Who staggers 'neath his sin and his despair;
Go, lend a hand and lead him out of danger.
　To heights where he may see the world is fair.

. . . .

Love thyself last; and thou shalt grow in spirit
　To see, to hear, to know and understand;
The message of the stars, lo, thou shalt hear it,
　And all God's joys shall be at thy command.[4]

—ELLA WHEELER WILCOX

PRAYER:

Grant us, O Lord, to know thee and love thee and rejoice in thee. And if we cannot do these perfectly in this life, let us at least advance to higher degrees every day, till we come to do them in perfection. Let the knowledge of thee increase in us here, that it may be full hereafter. Let the love of thee grow every day more and more here, that it may be perfect hereafter; that our joy may be great in itself, and full in thee. We know, O God, that thou art a God of truth; O make good thy gracious promises to us, that our joy may be full. AMEN. —AUGUSTINE

HYMN: "My Jesus, as Thou Wilt" or
　　　"O Perfect Love"

BENEDICTION:

The spirit of Jesus and the love of God be with you all. AMEN.

SERVICE 33

FINDING GOD THROUGH JESUS

PRELUDE: "Nocturne in F" by Schumann

CALL TO WORSHIP:

> O thou great Friend to all the sons of men,
> Who once appeared in humblest guise below,
> Sin to rebuke, to break the captive's chain,
> And call thy brethren forth from want and woe.
>
> We look to thee; thy truth is still the Light
> Which guides the nations, groping on their way,
> Stumbling and falling in disastrous night,
> Yet hoping ever for the perfect day.[1]

> —THEODORE PARKER

HYMN: "O Master Workman of the Race" or
"Shepherd of Tender Youth"

SCRIPTURE:

And Jesus entered and passed through Jericho. And, behold, there was a man named Zaccheus, which was the chief among the publicans, and he was rich. And he sought to see Jesus who he was; and could not for the press, because he was little of stature. And he ran before, and climbed up into a sycamore tree to see him; for he was to pass that way. And when Jesus came to the place, he looked up, and saw him, and said unto him, Zaccheus, make haste, and come down; for to-day I must abide at thy house. And he made haste, and came down, and received him joyfully. . . .

And there were certain Greeks among them that came up to worship at the feast: the same came therefore to Philip, which was of Bethsaida of Galilee, and desired him, saying, Sir, we would see Jesus.[2]

POEM:

There was a Rabbi long ago,
  Who lived in Galilee,
And taught the truth, which but to know
  Sets human spirits free.

The people said: "Much have we heard
  From great ones in the land;
But here is One who speaks a word
  We all can understand."

He talked to them of simple things—
  Nets, lilies, greening sod.
And they perceived, as thought took wings—
  Life, universe, and God.

They crucified him on a tree
  And thought his teaching done;
But found that everlastingly
  His words go marching on.[3]

—CLARENCE EDWIN FLYNN

We will hear a story of a boy who used every opportunity to know more about Jesus.

STORY:

CURIOUS REUBEN

Reuben's curiosity would get him into trouble one day, his mother often said. Several times her words came true.

There was the time when Reuben was nearly trampled by the horses because he was so curious to know what mounted soldiers were like. He was blind, and crippled in his left leg besides, but his curiosity made him hop along feeling the legs of horses and riders, and of course he was nearly caught under the galloping hoofs.

Another time he nearly burned his coat off his back through his curiosity about fire. Someday he would wander too far away, his mother warned him. Then he would hear a wild beast growling, and be curious to know what the beast was like. He would go up to poke the beast's ribs, and there would be the end of Reuben. Now that word of his mother never did come true.

One spring afternoon Reuben was hobbling along the streets of his home town of Bethany, when he heard the boys say a band of pilgrims from Galilee was going through the town on the way to Jerusalem from the feast of the Passover. Reuben, though he could not see and had to lean his left side on a stick, was up in front of everybody as usual. He was so curious.

He hopped about among the people and learned that the very important teacher, Jesus of Nazareth, was leading the Galilean pilgrims. Reuben immediately wriggled his way through legs and skirts till he could touch the legs of the donkey on which Jesus was riding. Reuben felt flowers and clothes on the ground. He threw his own coat on the ground for the donkey to walk over. He climbed a tree and tore off a branch. Then he joined the crowd, waving his tree branch and shouting with the crowd at the top of his voice, "Hosanna! Hosanna!"

Reuben kept close to the company of Galileans all the way to Jerusalem and into the temple enclosure. The grown people had stopped singing. Perhaps they were out of breath. Reuben and the other boys and girls kept on.

Inside the temple Reuben heard Jesus' angry voice above the singing: "It is written, 'My house shall be called a house of prayer': but you make it a den of robbers."

Being curious, Reuben kept close to Jesus. Soon he heard the whistle of a whip through the air and a bleating of sheep with the loud lowing of oxen. Animals rushed by him, doves swept his face with their beating wings, an overturned table caught his lame leg. The whip lashed near him and the tip of it cut his ear lightly. At that moment a strong arm caught him up and held him close, away from the animals and the falling furniture. Reuben knew it was Jesus holding him. He could feel strong muscles playing as Jesus' right arm came down with the whip or his foot kicked over a table. "This is a house of prayer," he kept shouting. "How dare you cheat pilgrims coming here to worship?"

Finally there was quiet. Jesus spoke directly to Reuben. "How long have you been without your sight, son?"

"Since I was three years old," Reuben answered. "I can barely remember. I was sick a long time, then I couldn't see, and my left leg was twisted."

Jesus moved his hands over Reuben's eyes and down his side. And Reuben looked into Jesus' face with seeing eyes and stood straight before him. At that, other blind and lame people came near, and Jesus healed them.

You should have heard Reuben shout and sing then. "Hosanna to the son of David!" And the other boys and girls joined in.

The chief priests and scribes asked indignantly: "Do you hear these youngsters? Why don't you make them keep quiet?"

Jesus answered: "Yes, I hear them. Have you never read, 'Out of the mouth of babes thou hast perfected praise'?"

It was evening now, and Jesus went back to Bethany, Reuben still close by his side, joyfully striding along without his stick and seeing everything with his bright black eyes, and still curious.

"Are you really a king?" he asked.

Jesus answered only by quoting verses from the Prophets which Reuben had learned in the synagogue:

> Rejoice greatly, O daughter of Zion;
> Shout, O daughter of Jerusalem:
> Behold, thy King cometh unto thee;
> He is just, and having salvation;
> Lowly, and riding upon an ass,
> And upon a colt the foal of an ass.
> And I will cut off the chariot from Ephraim,
> And the horse from Jerusalem,
> And the battle bow shall be cut off;
> And he shall speak peace unto the heathen:
> And his dominion shall be from sea even to sea,
> And from the river even to the ends of the earth.[4]

POEM:

> We would see Jesus, on the mountain teaching,
> With all the listening people gathered round;
> While birds and flowers and sky above are preaching,
> The blessedness which simple trust has found.
>
> We would see Jesus, in his work of healing,
> At the eventide before the sun was set;
> Divine and human, in his deep revealing,
> Of God and man in loving service met.
>
> We would see Jesus; in the early morning
> Still as of old he calleth, "Follow me";
> Let us arise, all meaner service scorning:
> Lord, we are thine, we give ourselves to thee.[5]

—JOHN EDGAR PARK

FINDING GOD THROUGH JESUS

LEADER:

Let us recall some occasion when we felt close to God. It may have been when we heard a great musical composition, saw something beautiful, or recognized a mark of greatness in someone we admired. It may have been something altogether different that made us aware of the presence of God.

Someone said, "I searched the world over for God and then found him in my own heart." Tennyson said, "Closer is he than breathing, and nearer than hands and feet."

In the Psalms we read:

Whither shall I go from thy Spirit? or whither shall I flee from thy presence?

If I ascend into heaven, thou art there, . . .

If I take the wings of the morning, and dwell in the uttermost parts of the sea;

Even there shall thy hand lead me, and thy right hand shall hold me. . . .

How precious also are thy thoughts unto me, O God! how great is the sum of them!

If I should count them, they are more in number than the sand: when I awake, I am still with thee.

Paul said:

God that made the world and all things therein, . . . seeing he giveth to all life, and breath, and all things; . . . that they should seek the Lord, if haply they might feel after him, and find him, though he be not far from every one of us: for in him we live, and move, and have our being.

Jesus said: He that hath seen me hath seen the Father; and how sayest thou then, Show us the Father? Believest thou not that I am in the Father, and the Father in me? [6]

Through a study of the life of Jesus we can know more about God, for it is he above all others who reveals the Father to us.

The writers of the four Gospels, each from his own viewpoint, give various incidents in the life of Jesus, and record his sayings. Studying the Gospels we learn of Jesus' attitude toward people and things, and that he considered people of greater importance than things. On one occasion when some of the disciples sought places of honor for themselves, Jesus remarked, "He that is greatest among you shall be your servant."

Reuben sought every opportunity to know more about Jesus. From a study of the life of Jesus, we may know more about God, gain a proper sense of values, know what is of the greatest importance, and discover how to get along with people.

PRAYER:

Our Father, we are grateful for the revelation of thyself through the Scriptures, through thy Son, through the lives of Christian people, and through various other ways in which thou hast made thyself known. Open our eyes that we may see thee in the beauty which thou hast created, and hear thee speak to us through music and other examples of art. Help us to feel thee near at all times. Give us strength to resist temptation, guide us in the choices we make, and give us courage to stand for the right. Help us to face the loss of so-called friends, or seeming defeat, if need be in order to live by our highest standards. In Jesus' name we pray. AMEN.

HYMN: "Jesus, Thou Divine Companion" or
      "O Master, Let Me Walk with Thee"

BENEDICTION:

The Lord bless us and keep us from this day forth and even forevermore. AMEN.

SERVICE 34

LIVING AGAIN
(*Easter*)

PRELUDE: "Passion Chorale" by Bach

CALL TO WORSHIP:

> Joy dawned again on Easter Day,
> The sun shone out with fairer ray,
> When, to their longing eyes restored,
> The apostles saw their risen Lord.
>
> O Jesus, King of gentleness,
> Do thou our inmost hearts possess;
> And we to thee will ever raise
> The tribute of our grateful praise.
> —TR. JOHN MASON NEALE

HYMN: "Sing, Men and Angels, Sing" or
"Christ the Lord Is Risen Today"

SCRIPTURE:

That same day two of them were going to a village called Emmaus, about seven miles from Jerusalem, and they were talking together about all these thing that had happened. And as they were talking and discussing them, Jesus himself came up and went with them, but they were prevented from recognizing him. And he said to them,

"What is all this that you are discussing with each other on your way?"

They stopped sadly, and one of them named Cleopas said to him,

213

"Are you the only visitor to Jerusalem who does not know what has happened there lately?"

And he said,

"What is it?"

They said to him,

"About Jesus of Nazareth, who in the eyes of God and of all the people was a prophet mighty in deed and word, and how the high priests and the members of our council gave him up to be sentenced to death, and had him crucified. But we were hoping that he was to be the deliverer of Israel. Why, besides all this, it is three days since it happened. But some women of our number have astounded us. They went to the tomb early this morning and could not find his body, but came back and said that they had actually seen a vision of angels who said that he was alive. Then some of our party went to the tomb and found things just as the women had said, but they did not see him."

Then he said to them,

"How foolish you are and how slow to believe, after all that the prophets have said! Did not the Christ have to suffer thus before entering upon his glory?"

And he began with Moses and all the prophets and explained to them the passages all through the Scriptures that referred to himself. When they reached the village to which they were going, he acted as though he were going on, but they urged him not to, and said,

"Stay with us, for it is getting toward evening, and the day is nearly over."

So he went in to stay with them. And when he took his place with them at table, he took the bread and blessed it and broke it in pieces and handed it to them. Then their eyes were opened and they knew him, and he vanished from them. And they said to each other,

"Did not our hearts glow when he was talking to us on the road, and was explaining the Scriptures to us?"

And they got up immediately and went back to Jerusalem, and found the eleven and their party all together, saying that the Master had really risen and had been seen by Simon. And they told what had happened on the road, and how they had known him when he broke the bread in pieces.[1]

HYMN: "The Day of Resurrection" or
       "Joy Dawned Again on Easter Day"

THE CATERPILLAR'S JOURNEY

Once upon a time a lazy brown caterpillar started out on a journey. You would not have thought it a very long journey—just across the road and under the fence to the roots of the big maple tree, where he thought he would spin himself a hammock and hide away from the cold winds and snow which he knew would soon come. But the caterpillar thought it a long way and full of dangers. Some careless boy or girl might step on him, or an automobile or wagon might run over him. He trembled when he thought of it, but one bright day he started out. He could see a tall, white daisy on the other side of the road, and he thought he would stop and talk to her when he reached her.

It took him a long time to cross the road, and when he came to the place where he had seen the daisy there was no daisy there, only a tall brown stalk.

"Where is she?" he asked a robin who was watching him with bright eyes from a bough above.

The robin answered in a little song that said, "She is dead, she is dead."

"Oh," said the caterpillar, "I wanted to talk to her."

The robin went on singing in a soft little voice, and soon the caterpillar knew he was saying, "She shall live again, she shall live again." But the caterpillar did not understand, and he felt very sad as he went on.

Soon he began to look about him and think what he would say to the friendly green grass which had nodded to him on the other side of the road. When he looked, he saw there was no friendly green grass; everything was dry and hard. "Where is the friendly green grass?" he said to himself. "Where can it have gone?"

And then came a little whisper in his ear which he knew was the wind, "It is dead, it is dead."

The poor little caterpillar felt very lonesome, and he put his head close to the ground as he cried out, "Oh! the friendly green grass, I shall miss it so."

Then he heard the wind whisper again very softly this time, "It shall live again, it shall live again." But the little brown caterpillar did not understand, and he felt very sad as he went on.

By and by he came to the roots of the big maple tree as he looked up he saw the branches were all brown and bare and the lovely green leaves were all gone.

"Oh, dear," he said to himself, "the big maple tree is dead too."

But he heard again the soft voice of the wind as it said, "It shall live again, it shall live again."

But the caterpillar did not understand, and he felt very sad as he began to spin his silken hammock. "They are dead," he kept saying to himself, and every time he said it he heard the soft wind answer, "They shall live again, they shall live again." But the caterpillar did not understand, and he was sad.

Soon the hammock was all done, and the caterpillar was ready for his long nap. He did not hear two children who came and looked at the hammock and said to each other, "The caterpillar is dead too," but the wind heard them, and answered softly, though they did not understand, "He shall live again, he shall live again. Wait and see."

The cold wind and snow came, and stayed all winter, the birds were all away in the southland, and the wind no longer whispered in a soft voice, but whistled shrilly though the trees and shook the branches roughly.

By and by the sun grew warm and bright and the snow melted away, and spring came to all the earth. The little seeds began to grow in the warm earth and soon everything was a lovely green again. Something began to happen in the silken hammock where the caterpillar went to sleep. Slowly it came open and something moved inside. The soft wind saw it, and said, "The caterpillar is alive again." And then out of the silken hammock came a queer wet thing, not at all like the brown caterpillar. The sun shone warmly upon it, and soon it was resting there on the trunk of the big maple tree, a great beautiful butterfly, with wings of black and gold.

The butterfly did not understand, and he said to the robin who looked down at him from the branch above, "I thought I was a caterpillar." But the robin answered as before in a little song, "Now you are living again."

Then Mr. Caterpillar-Butterfly thought of his friends, the lovely white daisy, the friendly green grass, and the big maple tree, and he remembered the soft voices that said, "They shall live again." And he looked around him and there they were, every one of them, more beautiful than ever in the warm sunlight.

He did not understand, and nobody understands, but we know the soft voices were true when they said, "They shall live again, they shall live again." [2]

POEM:

> I hold you at last in my hand,
>   Exquisite child of the air.
> Can I ever understand
>   How you grew to be so fair?
>
> You came to my linden tree
>   To taste its delicious sweet,
> I sitting here in the shadow and shine
>   Playing around its feet.
>
> Now I hold you fast in my hand,
>   You marvelous butterfly,
> Till you help me to understand
>   The eternal mystery.
>
> From that creeping thing in the dust
>   To this shining bliss in the blue!
> God give me courage to trust
>   I can break my chrysalis too! [3]
>   —ALICE FREEMAN PALMER

PRAYER:
Our Father, speak to us through the Scriptures, the hymns, and the stories that we have heard today. Help us to look beyond the things of the earth that pass away to eternal things that shall always endure. May we put out of our minds all unworthy thoughts: malice, hatred, envy, jealousy, and build into our lives love, joy, peace, and good will toward all people. Give us thy spirit so that we may begin at the present time living the kind of life that is worthy to last through all ages. May we go forth to live in that faith and hope which makes eternal life real. In Jesus' name. AMEN.

HYMN: "Sing with All the Sons of Glory" or
      "Come, Ye Faithful, Raise the Strain"

BENEDICTION:
And now may the blessing of the Father be with you now and evermore. AMEN.

SERVICE 35

FOLLOWING JESUS
(*Dedication Day*)

PRELUDE: Hymn tune "Festal Song"

CALL TO WORSHIP:

The hour cometh, and now is, when the true worshippers shall worship the Father in spirit and in truth: for the Father seeketh such to worship him.

God is a Spirit: and they that worship him must worship him in spirit and in truth.[1]

HYMN: "A Charge to Keep I Have" or
      "Jesus Call Us, o'er the Tumult"

SCRIPTURE:

And Jesus, walking by the sea of Galilee, saw two brethren, Simon called Peter, and Andrew his brother, casting a net into the sea: for they were fishers. And he saith unto them, Follow me, and I will make you fishers of men. And they straightway left their nets, and followed him. And going on from thence, he saw other two brethren, James the son of Zebedee, and John his brother, in a ship with Zebedee their father, mending their nets; and he called them. And they immediately left the ship and their father, and followed him. . . .

And it came to pass, that, as they went in the way, a certain man said unto him, Lord, I will follow thee whithersoever thou goest. And Jesus said unto him, Foxes have holes, and birds of the air have nests; but the Son of man hath not where to lay his head. And he said unto another, Follow me. And he said, Lord, suffer me first to go and bury my father. Jesus said unto him, Let the dead bury their dead: but go thou and preach the kingdom of God. And another also said, Lord, I will follow thee; but let me first go bid them farewell, which are at home at my house. And Jesus said unto him, No man, having put his hand to the plow, and looking back, is fit for the kingdom of God.[2]

LEADER:

We will hear the story of Jesus calling the fishermen to follow him.

STORY:

THE LEAVING OF THE NETS

The throng of suffering people and their friends, who had poured out of the fishing village in search of the Master, returned slowly in little groups. Soon after starting they had separated, for no one knew where the great physician was, and while many searched the villages, some traveled to desert places, and others followed the bank of the river Jordan.

So it was many months before all had returned to their homes, and when they did—the deaf hearing, the blind seeing, and the lame walking—the most glorious news they brought was not of their recovery. Each one, grown person or little child, almost forgot the story of their cure in their wonder of the Master who had healed them. Their faces shone when they spoke of him, and their eyes had caught from his a light which never left them. The stories of his words, his looks, and his deeds were told again and again in the little village. The fishermen repeated them to one another as they fished at night beneath the stars, the women told them while they spun and wove, and many rocked their babies to sleep with the lullaby which the shepherd's children had sung, and which the Master knew.

The children listened entranced to every word of the stories, and often at sundown they met upon the beach and talked of times when they themselves had seen or heard the Christ. For some of the children had been healed by him, many had seen sick mothers or fathers given back their strength, and others had watched the marvelous kind things Jesus did for the people who came to him. Late one afternoon, as the fishermen launched their boats upon the waves and started out for a night's work, a lad told the listening children his story.

"For weeks I had begged my Uncle Peter to take me fishing with him," said the lad, and the children seating themselves around him upon the beach were attentive to every word. "He said I was not strong enough to pull in a net," continued the boy, "and if I went along just to watch, my weight, together with the big haul they always hoped to get, would make the boat too heavy.

"There were two boats which sailed together, my Uncle Peter's and the one belonging to his friends James and John. My uncle had a strong young fellow who went with him as a helper, for it takes two, you know, to manage a net, and every evening at sunset the boats with the four men started out. I used to stand on the beach and watch them sailing right into the heart of the sunset, and how I longed to be big enough to go too!

"Before dawn I was down again on the sands, and as the sun rose the boats came sailing back, right down the golden pathway, with the fish shining in silver heaps upon the decks.

"One evening Uncle Peter launched his boat alone and sailed around close to the beach, waiting for his helper who had not come. The fishing had been bad for several days, and unless they made a big catch that night, I had heard them say that many in the village would suffer.

"James and John had sailed far out and Uncle Peter, looking anxiously up and down the beach for the young man, caught sight of me standing there alone. He called to me to run home and tell my mother I would be back in the morning and then to come and take his helper's place. 'Even his little arms are better than none at all,' I heard him say as I rushed off. Oh, how excited I was! I ran all the way home and back to the beach, waded out to the boat and we were off, with the glow of the fading sunset around us.

"But it was not a very happy night after all. I had dreamed of lying flat on the deck looking up at the stars, the waves lapping below me, until I should feel like a bird floating between sky and sea. But the sky was dark and cloudy, and although we threw out net after net, when we drew them in there was not even a glimmer of a fish there.

"The men grew very worried, for they had counted upon the results of that night's work to feed their families. When morning came it was still cloudy, and we sailed home through a dull, dreary mist. But as we drew near the shore we saw a strange sight. Although we were in the fog the sun was shining upon the beach, blue waves were breaking upon it with showers of glittering spray, and there in the sunshine stood a glorious figure. He was the most wonderful-looking man we had ever seen. The wind blew his robes, the waves broke close to his feet, the blue sky stretched behind him, and upon his face shone the golden rays of the rising sun. We were out in the mist and the grayness, disappointed and weary, but when we saw that figure, we forgot everything but his beauty.

"The villagers heard that he was near and soon a crowd collected around him. Because of the throng we could not see him, so we anchored our boats close to the shore and dragging out the poor empty nets began to wash them. Presently we saw the Master again. So close did the people press that he could not speak to them all, and catching sight of my uncle's empty boat he stepped into it, and asked him to push out a little from the land. Then the Master sat down in the stern of the boat, and taught the eager crowd things that were more beautiful than the sea or the sunshine, and yet were simple enough for any child to understand.

"And I was there in the boat with him. I could put out my hand and touch his fluttering robes, I could hear every tone in his voice, see every glance in his eyes, and once he turned and smiled at me. I knew then that he loved me, me a poor fisher lad, and I would have died to serve him.

"The Master must have noticed the look of disappointment on the fishermen's faces when they sailed up through the fog with no fish on board. For when he had finished teaching, he said to my uncle,

" 'Launch out into the deep, and let down your nets for a draught,' and Uncle Peter answered, 'Master, we have toiled all the night, and have taken nothing: nevertheless at thy word I will let down the net.'

"So we sailed out a little and threw over the net, and when we tried to pull it in, it was so full of shining fish that the net began to break.

"Then Uncle Peter beckoned to James and John who were in the other ship, that they should come and help us. And they came, and we filled both ships so that they began to sink with the weight of the fish.

"When Uncle Peter saw it, he fell down at Jesus' knees saying, 'Depart from me, for I am a sinful man, O Lord.' For he was astonished, and so were all of us at the great draught of fishes. And Jesus said to them, 'Fear not; from henceforth thou shalt catch men.'

"I think he meant that they should draw people who needed help around them as he had done, and give them comfort and happiness. For as soon as they had brought their ships to land, Uncle Peter and James and John left their nets, and they have been with the Master ever since, following him wherever he goes.

"At first I longed to go too. But I think, as I remember his smile, I am sure that even though I must stay here and be a simple fisherman all my life, I too can be a follower of the Master." [3]

221

POEM:

O Jesus, once a Nazareth boy,
  And tempted like as we,
All inward foes help us destroy
  And spotless all to be.
We trust thee for the grace to win
  The high, victorious goal,
Where purity shall conquer sin
  In Christlike self-control.

O Jesus, Prince of life and truth,
  Beneath thy banner bright,
We dedicate our strength and youth
  To battle for the right;
We give our lives with glad intent
  To serve the world and thee,
To die, to suffer, and be spent
  To set our brothers free.

In serried ranks, with fearless tread,
  O Captain of us all,
Thy glory on our banners shed,
  We answer to thy call;
And where the fiercest battles press
  Against the hosts of sin,
To rescue those in dire distress
  We gladly enter in.
                    —AUTHOR UNKNOWN

LEADER:

The first recorded words of Jesus in the Bible are "Wist ye not that I must be about my Father's business?" and his last words on the cross were, "Father, into thy hands I commend my spirit." Throughout his ministry Jesus had one purpose—to do the will of his Father, and his entire life was lived completely within that purpose.

When the fishermen left their nets to follow Christ, a drastic change came in their lives. They left their usual occupations and went out to teach and preach the good news of the gospel and to win others to Christ.

When we choose Christ as our Master, there are certain changes that should take place in our lives and certain goals that we set for ourselves. In dedicating our lives to him we put aside selfish desires and strive to live by the will and purpose of God.

The call of Christ comes to us just as clearly as it did to the disciples. He said: "If any man will come after me, let him deny himself, and take up his cross daily, and follow me." And again: "Seek ye first the kingdom of God, and his righteousness; and all these things shall be added unto you." He calls us to put self in the background, to live by God's will, and to win others to his cause.

PRAYER:

Our Father, we have heard thy call to follow thee, but we have resisted thy Spirit. We have not loved thee as we should; our selfishness has held us back. Forgive our indifference, our lack of devotion to thee. Create in us clean hearts and renew right spirits within us. As we study the life of Jesus help us to understand more perfectly what it means to dedicate our lives to thee. Grant us courage to resist evil, to practice the golden rule in our dealings with others, to live by the teachings of Jesus, and to make the building of the kingdom of God first in our lives. As we commit our lives to thee, may we feel thy presence guiding and directing us and helping us to live in such manner that others will be drawn to thee; through Jesus Christ our Lord. AMEN.

HYMN: "Just As I Am, Thine Own to Be" or
"Hark, the Voice of Jesus Calling"

BENEDICTION:

Now unto him who is able to keep you from falling, and to present you faultless before his presence, be glory and honor, both now and evermore. AMEN.

SERVICE 36

LIVING AS BROTHERS
(*Race Relations Sunday*)

PRELUDE: Hymn tune "Ar Hyd Y Nos"

CALL TO WORSHIP:

> I sought my soul,
> But my soul I could not see.
> I sought my God,
> But my God eluded me.
> I sought my brother,
> And I found all three.

> —AUTHOR UNKNOWN

HYMN: "Jesus, Thou Divine Companion" or
"Awake, Awake to Love and Work"

SCRIPTURE:

A man that hath friends must show himself friendly: and there is a friend that sticketh closer than a brother. . . .

A friend loveth at all times, and a brother is born for adversity. . . .

This is my commandment, That ye love one another, as I have loved you. Greater love hath no man than this, that a man lay down his life for his friends. Ye are my friends, if ye do whatsoever I command you. Henceforth I call you not servants; for the servant knoweth not what his lord doeth: but I have called you friends; for all things that I have heard of my Father I have made known unto you.[1]

POEM:

> There's a comforting thought at the close of
> the day,
> When I'm weary and lonely and sad,
> That sort of grips hold of my crusty old heart

224

And bids it be merry and glad.
It gets in my soul and it drives out the blues,
And finally thrills through and through.
It is just a sweet memory that chants the refrain:
"I'm glad I touch shoulders with you!"

Did you know you were brave, did you know you
    were strong?
Did you know there was one leaning hard?
Did you know that I waited and listened and
    prayed,
And was cheered by your simplest word?
Did you know that I longed for that smile on
    your face,
For the sound of your voice ringing true?
Did you know I grew stronger and better because
I had merely touched shoulders with you?

I am glad that I live, that I battle and strive
For the place that I know I must fill;
I am thankful for sorrows; I'll meet with a grin
What fortune may send, good or ill.
I may not have wealth, I may not be great,
But I know I shall always be true,
For I have in my life that courage you gave
When once I rubbed shoulders with you.

—Author unknown

Hymn: "At Length There Dawns the Glorious Day" or
    "Where Cross the Crowded Ways of Life"

Leader:

We will hear a story of a successful businessman who was a friend
to immigrant boys.

Story:

THE NEWSBOY WHO DIDN'T FORGET

The boy was small and thin, and he stood shivering on the Boston
wharf that cold December morning in 1903. For a moment panic
swept him, and he had an impulse to turn and race back up the gang-
plank to the ocean liner that had been home to him for two long

weeks. Then he tightened his lips. No, he could not do that. It had taken all the pitiful savings of kindhearted relatives to pay his passage to the United States after his parents had died.

An agent of the Travelers' Aid Society noted the little boy with the tight, quivering lips and the foreign-looking knapsack. He came over.

"Well, my lad," he asked, "can you speak English?"

The boy's eyes brightened. "Yes, sir," he replied. "I learned—a little—at home. My father and mother—." He stopped, and his eyes filled with tears.

The agent nodded understandingly. He said: "Your home? Where is that?"

"Russia."

"Yes, thought the agent. A good many Jewish folk, like this boy, were fleeing the czarist persecution in Russia and seeking liberty and freedom in the United States. In those days America welcomed all immigrants with open arms.

"Is anyone expecting you, my boy?" he inquired.

"N-no, sir."

"A strange little boy in a strange land," said the agent. "Well, that's my job to welcome you and get you started. I'm from the Travelers' Aid."

"Oh, yes. I was told to see you. In Russia they say you're very kind."

The agent laughed. "Come along then—er—what's your name?"

"Harry Borosovsky."

"Harry—Harry Borosovsky."

At least that was the way it sounded to the agent. "Hm," he said. "Americans won't be able to pronounce that. Suppose I call you Burroughs—Harry Burroughs."

"Will that make me an American?" asked the boy eagerly.

"Not altogether," grinned the agent. "But don't you worry, Harry; you'll be an American fast enough. Let's get started."

By noon the kindly agent had found lodgings for the immigrant boy with a motherly old woman in the poorer section of Boston. By afternoon Harry had a bundle of newspapers under his arm.

"What's that for?" asked the landlady in surprise.

Harry beamed. "I'm a newsboy," he said proudly. "I'm going to sell them."

"But what's your hurry? Give yourself a chance to get acquainted with Boston."

"I can't, ma'am. I just had enough money to pay for these papers and a week's board."

"You poor child. I can wait."

"No, ma'am. My father used to tell me—never get into debt. Work hard and pay for everything."

The day was cold and there was ice on the ground. Shivering, Harry Burroughs took his stand in front of the Boston Theater where the crowds were passing. His thin voice piped in imitation of the other newsboys: "Paper! Get your evening paper! Read all about it!"

Two husky newsboys on the corner glared at the newcomer. "Hey, Pete, get a load o' the greenhorn tryin' tuh swipe our stand," said one to the other.

Pete, an older and heavier lad, grated: "Hold dese, Jim." Then he strode over to little Harry, grabbed his papers from his hands and threw them on the icy pavement.

Harry looked at his tormentor in astonishment. "What did—you—do that for?"

"Because I don't like yer mug, greenie," Pete growled. His fist shot out and caught the boy on the cheek. "Now get outa here, you foreigner. Go back where yuh came from."

The little boy staggered. Then resentment welled in him and he rushed on the bigger boy, fists flailing.

"Fight! Fight!" Newsboys and passers-by gathered in a circle. The two lads rolled in the street. Then someone yelled: "Cheese it, the cop!" and Pete broke loose and disappeared around the corner, leaving young Harry victor of the field.

There was no trouble after that. The newsboys respected Harry Burroughs as a game kid, even though he was a foreigner. He sold his papers day after day and night after night. He saved money and attracted the attention of the mayor of Boston and the governor of Massachusetts. They became his regular customers. He learned English rapidly and well, and American customs just as fast.

The newsboys were a quarrelsome lot. There were constant fights among them over the rights to certain coveted corners and to subway entrances where the most papers could be sold. After a while they began to bring their disputes to young Harry for him to decide instead of fighting it out with their fists. They formed an association with Burroughs as their head. The story got into the newspapers.

But Harry was not content to be a newsboy all his life. He went to school, and supported himself by selling papers after hours. He did so well in his studies that he won a scholarship at the Suffolk Law School. In time he became a lawyer, one of the best in Boston.

But he never forgot those cold days and nights when he stood on street corners, with no place to get warm or read good books or have a decent meal.

Harry Burroughs, when he became a famous lawyer, determined to do something about it. He started the Burroughs Newsboy Foundation to provide a building where newsboys were welcome.

Every day, after office hours, he went down to the handsome building he had erected, and talked to the boys who came in. He talked their own language—he didn't preach to them. And there were hot, nourishing meals for them, warm shower baths, a gymnasium, a library, and Burroughs himself to advise them on their problems and give them a few dollars when they were needed.

The first boys who came to scoff remained as enthusiastic members. They brought others. Finally almost every newsboy in Boston joined the club. The newspapers played it up big. Wealthy Bostonians became interested and began to contribute funds. Burroughs expanded the Foundation to include a summer camp, where boys who had never seen a cow or a green field could breathe fresh country air and put on weight. Scholarships were established and those lads who were ambitious were sent through college.

There was one thing that Harry Burroughs insisted on. Everyone was welcome to his club and his camp, regardless of what his religion, color, or race happened to be. In the beginning there was a little trouble among the boys themselves. Out on the streets and among their elders they had heard sneering remarks about other groups. The boys unconsciously absorbed these prejudices.

Once a group of Italian boys who belonged to the club received permission from Mr. Burroughs to build a reproduction of an Italian villa in the basement of the foundation. It was a beautiful thing when they were finished; with pictures, a fireplace, soft lights, and homemade furniture.

They were justly proud of their handiwork, and the other newsboys were equally enthusiastic. They were eager to play in the villa. But the Italian lads ganged up to drive the others out. "We don't want any Irish around," they yelled. "This place is for Italians only."

The directors of the foundation wanted to expel the Italians, but Mr. Burroughs said he would talk to them first. He called the sullen group to his office. He looked quietly at that. "You're Italians, aren't you?"

"And I'm a Jew, am I not?" Burroughs continued softly. "And the boys you refused to share your room with are Irish."

They shifted uneasily in their chairs.

"You've heard plenty of people say they don't want Italians, haven't you?"

"Yes, we have."

"And you didn't like it?"

"Of course not."

"Then remember the Irish don't like to be told they're not wanted, and I don't like it, either. All of us are Americans and human beings. Get to know people and you'll find those labels are not only silly but dangerous. Now what do you say?"

"I guess we never understood it that way," stammered their leader.

"Good! Remember that in the future. Remember also that in this place we share everything together."

There was no trouble after that.

The movement spread. From all over the country people came to study just how the Burroughs Newsboys Foundation worked. Then they went home and started ones just like it. Harry Burroughs, the Russian Jewish immigrant, is dead; but his work lives on. He was in fact the best friend a fellow ever had.[2]

POEM:

> Every soul that touches yours—
> Be it the slightest contact—
> Gets therefrom some good;
> Some little grace; one kindly thought;
> One aspiration yet unfelt;
> One bit of courage
> For the darkening sky;
> One gleam of faith
> To brave the thickening ills of life;
> One glimpse of brighter skies—
> To make this life worth while
> And heaven a surer heritage.
>
> —GEORGE ELIOT

PRAYER:

Our Father, who hast made us for thyself, our hearts are restless until they find rest in thee. Draw us close to thee, and may we find strength for meeting our problems. We thank thee for our friends who have brought us happiness and have encouraged us in times of temptation. If we are prone to be satisfied with a small circle of friends, forgive us. If ignorance, pride, or selfishness has kept us from making other friends, help us to learn to be friendly with people of all races, of every creed, color, and condition of life. Reveal to us the things that we can do to lead others to abundant living. Help us to be thoughtful and friendly in all our contacts. In Jesus' name we pray. AMEN.

HYMN: "God of Our Boyhood, Whom We Yield" or
        "O Thou Whose Feet Have Climbed Life's Hill"

BENEDICTION:
   May we go forth to live as brothers with people of every race and station of life. AMEN.

SERVICE 37

IN APPRECIATION OF MOTHERS
(*Mother's Day*)

PRELUDE: "The Old Refrain" by Kreisler

CALL TO WORSHIP:
> Better than gold is a peaceful home
> Where all the fireside characters come,
> The shrine of love, the heaven of life,
> Hallowed by mother, or sister, or wife.
> However humble the home may be,
> Or tried with sorrow by heaven's decree,
> The blessings that never were bought or sold,
> And center there, are better than gold.
>
> —ABRAM J. RYAN

HYMN: "Love Divine, All Loves Excelling" or
"O Perfect Love"

SCRIPTURE:
> Who can find a virtuous woman?
> > for her price is far above rubies.
> The heart of her husband doth safely trust in her,
> > so that he shall have no need of spoil.
> She will do him good and not evil
> > all the days of her life. . . .
> She stretcheth out her hand to the poor;
> > yea, she reacheth forth her hands to the needy.
> She is not afraid of the snow for her household;
> > for all her household are clothed with scarlet. . . .
> Her husband is known in the gates,
> > when he sitteth among the elders of the land. . . .

Strength and honor are her clothing;
   and she shall rejoice in time to come.
She openeth her mouth with wisdom;
   and in her tongue is the law of kindness.
She looketh well to the ways of her household,
   and eateth not the bread of idleness.
Her children arise up, and call her blessed;
   her husband also, and he praiseth her.
Many daughters have done virtuously,
   but thou excellest them all. . . .
Honor thy father and thy mother: that thy days may
   be long upon the land which the Lord thy God
   giveth thee.[1]

LEADER:

We shall hear the story of the encouragement that an artist received from his mother.

STORY:

THE MOTHER OF BENJAMIN WEST

One summer day in 1745, a seven-year-old boy living near Springfield, Pennsylvania, was asked by his mother to look after a baby relative. It is unlikely that the boy, whose name was Benjamin West, was any fonder of minding babies than other boys, and no doubt he was relieved when at last the baby fell asleep.

The mother's maiden name was Sarah Pearson. She was the daughter of a Quaker who had settled in what was at that time a backwoods country. She in turn married a Quaker, and there, amid the many hardships and dangers which the early settlers knew so well, she brought up her family of ten children, of whom Benjamin was the youngest. All through the surrounding country there were Indians, but fortunately the redskins were friendly; indeed the boast was often made that owing to the kindness and fairness of the Quakers, no drop of Quaker blood was ever shed by an Indian. Sarah West was especially fortunate in all her relations with the red sons of the forest.

That day when the infant fell asleep, young Benjamin was struck with the remarkable beauty of the sleeping child. It seems strange that this little boy of the backwoods had already learned to love the beauti-

232

ful wherever he saw it, but encouraged by his mother, he had already begun to draw and paint. On a near-by table were two bottles of ink, one red, the other blue. Benjamin took a piece of paper and soon made a drawing of the sleeping baby. Just as he finished the sketch, his mother appeared. He tried to conceal the drawing, but she saw it and examined it. Mothers are the same in every country and in every age. Sarah West looked at that picture with a fond mother's loving eyes. "Why, bless me," she exclaimed, her voice trembling with excitement, "it is a picture of little Sally." Then Benjamin's mother did something which was destined to have a great influence upon the boy's life; she threw her arms around Benjamin's neck and kissed him. Many years later when he had become one of the most famous painters, Benjamin West said: "A kiss from my mother made me a painter."

It was the encouragement he got from his mother that stimulated Benjamin's interest in painting. The Indians living near by used red and yellow paint with which to decorate their bodies, and they freely gave some to Benjamin. His mother gave him indigo; he soon found out that by mixing yellow and blue he could make green, thus he had four colors with which to paint, and he was soon fairly well launched on his career.

It was difficult for him, living in the backwoods far away from stores, to secure brushes. His mother thought of every possible plan which her ready mind suggested, but the supply could not meet the demand. One day he got the idea of making a brush from the cat's fur. The brush he made was a success, but soon he needed another, and before long the cat had big patches upon its body. "I don't know what is the matter with the cat," said Benjamin's father, "all the fur is coming out." When he found out the real reason, he hardly knew whether to chastise his painter-son or not, but eventually his amusement was so great that the boy went unpunished.

But it was his mother who, more than any other person, influenced Benjamin and encouraged him in every way. One day when he had gone to the attic, he completely forgot about school, also forgot that he had not eaten, because he was so absorbed in his painting. His father wanted to punish him, but his mother protested so much that the father forgave him. "He is a wonderful child," she said over and over again, and at last the father agreed with his wife that truant though he had been that day, he certainly was a gifted boy. When neighbors and strangers came to the home, Mrs. West fondly showed them Benjamin's paintings. The boy was quick to see that her judgment of his pictures was generally correct, and he used to say that he would rather have a compliment from his mother than from anyone else.

Benjamin was soon to need the sound advice and ecouragement which his mother knew so well how to give. It was she who was responsible for Benjamin's decision to become an artist, but now a critical situation arose. The Quakers were fine people, with high standards of living, and the best proof of this is the peaceable relations they always enjoyed with their Indian neighbors. But the Quakers did not believe in pictures; they were opposed to decorative art of any kind. They regarded pictures as indications of vanity, and so a meeting was called to discuss Benjamin's future. Here was one of their own members, not only admiring pictures, but actually devoting his life to producing that which they regarded as vanity.

The members of that Quaker meeting were disturbed, and many were most unsettled in mind. Not so the mother of Benjamin West. Her mind was made up and her decision was clear. That her boy Benjamin was unusually gifted she had no doubt, and she was equally certain that the gift was from God. She in turn doubtless influenced other members among the group, for when the meeting took place, a friend named John Williamson made a speech which turned the tide in Benjamin's favor.

Mr. Williamson reminded his hearers that the father and mother of Benjamin were people of blameless lives who had brought up their ten children in the fear of God. He proceeded to say: "It is known to you all that God is pleased from time to time to bestow on some men extraordinary gifts of mind, and you need not be told by how wonderful an inspiration Benjamin West has been led to cultivate the art of painting. God has bestowed on the youth a genius for the art, and can we believe that he bestows his gifts but for great purposes? What God has given, who shall dare to throw away? God has been pleased among us, and in this remote wilderness to endow, with the rich gifts of a peculiar spirit, this youth. May it be demonstrated by the life and works of the artist that the gift of God has not been bestowed in vain." This speech had the desired effect. Other members agreed with John Williamson, and solemnly they placed their hands upon his head and wished him God's blessings in his career as a painter. There can be no question, however, that the strongest influence in the life of Benjamin West was that of his mother.

From that day Benjamin's rise to fame was sure and steady. All the dreams that his mother had of his future were more than realized. He went to Philadelphia to study and later, when he was twenty-two, he studied in Rome. As a boy living in the backwoods, he had almost been denied educational privileges. He was quite a big boy before he saw his first painting. What he now saw in the art galleries of Rome thrilled him, and opened up a new world for his endeavors. For days he gazed in awe and admiration at the pictures he saw there.

From Rome he went to other centers of art in Italy, then on to Paris, and finally to London which he made his permanent home. In 1792 he succeeded Sir Joshua Reynolds as president of the Royal Academy of Arts, a position he held until his death in 1820. Some of his most famous pictures are familiar the world over. Among the best known are "Christ Healing the Sick," "The Death of Wolfe," "Death on the Pale Horse," and "Penn's Treaty with the Indians."

For many years previous to his death Benjamin West was greatly beloved because of the sympathy and encouragement he gave to struggling young artists. This he learned from his mother. It is safe to say that without such a mother Benjamin West never would have been heard of. It was not simply a son's devotion to a mother, but rather the sound judgment of a thoughtful man which caused Benjamin West to say: "A kiss from my mother made me a painter." [2]

POEM:

> This memory of my mother stays with me
> Throughout the years: the way she used to stand
> Framed in the door when any of her band
> Of children left . . . as long as she could see
> Their forms, she gazed, as if she seemed to be
> Trying to guard—to meet some far demand;
> And then before she turned to tasks at hand,
> She breathed a little prayer inaudibly.
>
> And now, I think, in some far Heavenly place,
> She watches still, and yet is not distressed,
> But rather as one, who after life's long race,
> Has found contentment in a well-earned rest,
> There, in a peaceful, dream-like reverie,
> She waits, from earthly cares, forever free. [3]

—MARGARET E. BRUNER

PRAYER:

Our Father, we thank thee for the heritage of our homes, for the security which has come from our parents, for the love with which they have surrounded us, and for the opportunities which have come through them. We are grateful for the unselfish giving of our mother, her nurture and training through the years. Grant us wisdom to apply her teachings and to learn to live by them. Help us to do all within our power to lessen her care and to make bright her days by loving, honoring, and respecting her, and by living worthy lives. Strengthen us, give us courage to obey thy commands, and to live as members of the family of God, in the name of thy son Jesus Christ we pray. AMEN.

HYMN: "Happy the Home When God Is There" or
"O Happy Home, Where Thou Art Loved"

BENEDICTION:

May we go forth to live as worthy members of the family of God and to honor our mothers in all the days that are ahead. AMEN.

NOTES

SERVICE 1. ATTAINING THE BEST
1. Isa. 40:31; Ps. 27:14.
2. II Pet. 1:2-7; Phil. 4:8.
3. *Idylls of the King,* "Guinevere."
4. By Katharine E. Wilkie. *Classmate,* July 27, 1952. Used by permission.

SERVICE 2. BRINGING LIGHT
1. Pss. 100:2, 4; 95:5-7.
2. Pss. 28:7-9; 36:5-10.
3. "Gradatim."
4. By Winifred Heath. *Boys Today,* July 29, 1951. Used by permission.

SERVICE 3. GIVING OPPORTUNITIES
1. Ps. 145:18-19.
2. Prov. 2:1-9; 3:13-14.
3. Georgia Harkness, *Be Still and Know,* p. 91. Copyright 1953 by Pierce and Washabaugh. Used by permission of Abingdon Press.
4. By Vincent Edwards. *Classmate,* May 7, 1944. Used by permission.

SERVICE 4. GOD'S WORKMAN
1. Deut. 31:6; Ps. 28:7; I Cor. 16:13; Isa. 12:5-6; 32:1; Luke 1:68, 79.
2. Frederick G. Gill, *John Wesley's Prayers,* p. 53. Published by Abingdon Press.
3. Leslie F. Church, *Knight of the Burning Heart,* p. 152. Used by permission of Abingdon Press.
4. By William F. McDermott. *Christian Advocate,* Oct. 6, 1949, and *Reader's Digest.* June, 1953. Used by permission.
5. "Arise, O Church of God." Reprinted by permission of *The Pulpit* from the issue of May, 1952.
6. *John Welsey's Prayers,* pp. 64, 66, 76.

SERVICE 5. A WOMAN PIONEERS IN AVIATION
1. Josh. 1:9; Ps. 27:14; Acts 28:15, 30-31; Isa. 26:4.
2. By Letha O. Lile. *Girls Today,* Feb. 17, 1952. Used by permission.
3. "Courage." From *20 Hours, 40 Minutes* by Amelia Earhart. Used by permission of G. P. Putnam's Sons, publishers.
4. "For Amelia Earhart." From *Midstream.* Used by permission of The Kaleidograph Press and the author.

SERVICE 6. MASTERING HANDICAPS
1. Pss. 122:1; 84:10.
2. Pss. 130:1-2, 5-6; 145:14, 18; Heb. 12:1-2; Rev. 3:8.
3. Frederick Brown Harris, *Spires of the Spirit,* pp. 148-51. Copyright 1952 by Pierce and Smith. Used by permission of Abingdon Press.
4. *Hamlet,* Act II, scene 2.
5. By Emmett Maum. *Boys Today,* Nov. 12, 1950. Used by permission.

SERVICE 7. GREAT, WITHOUT SEEKING TO BE GREAT
1. Ps. 95:1-2.
2. Mark 4:1-9; Matt. 14:13-14.

3. "Our Thought of Thee Is Glad with Hope."
4. Dorothy Wells Pease, *Altars Under the Sky*, p. 34. Copyright 1942 by Whitmore and Stone. Used by permission of Abingdon Press.
5. Martha E. Bonham. *Classmate*, Mar. 11, 1945. Used by permission.
6. "The Higher Good."

SERVICE 8. SHOWING KINDNESS
1. Ps. 15:1-2.
2. Gal. 6:1-10.
3. By Vincent Edwards. *Classmate*, Dec. 30, 1945. Used by permission.
4. By Vincent Edwards. *Classmate*, Jan. 18, 1948. Used by permission.
5. "Certainty." Used by permission of *The Christian-Evangelist*.
6. The Methodist Hymnal, p. 513. Used by permission of The Methodist Publishing House.

SERVICE 9. TO SET MEN FREE
1. Ps. 27:1, 3-4; Prov. 3:5-6; Phil. 4:13.
2. By Elsie McCormick. *Everybody's Weekly*, Sept. 19, 1953; *Reader's Digest*, Nov., 1953. Used by permission.
3. "Stanzas on Freedom."
4. Ernest Fremont Tittle, *A Book of Pastoral Prayer*, pp. 66-67. Used by permission of Abingdon Press.

SERVICE 10. MOUNTAIN MESSAGES
1. Hab. 2:20; Ps. 95:6-7.
2. Mark 6:30-32; Luke 9:28; Ps. 121:1.
3. By Bennie Bengtson. *Classmate*, June 13, 1948. Used by permission.
4. "Lines Composed a Few Miles Above Tintern Abbey."

SERVICE 11. SINGING OF COURAGE
1. Ps. 150:3-4, 6.
2. Pss. 66:1-2, 4; 105:1-4.
3. Georgia Harkness. *Be Still and Know*, p. 27. Copyright 1953 by Pierce and Washabaugh. Used by permission of Abingdon Press.
4. By Bennie Bengtson. *Classmate*, May 27, 1951. Used by permission.

SERVICE 12. LET ANXIOUS HEARTS GROW QUIET
1. Ps. 95:6-7.
2. Ps. 37:3-6, 11, 23-24, 37; Matt. 7:7-8; 21:22.
3. By E. Jerry Walker. *Highroad*, Aug., 1950. Used by permission.
4. "O God, in Restless Living," by Harry Emerson Fosdick. Set to music, hymn tune "Rutherford." Used by permission.
5. Ernest Fremont Tittle, *A Book of Pastoral Prayers*, pp. 35-36. Copyright 1951 by Pierce and Smith. Used by permission of Abingdon Press.

SERVICE 13. LOVE IS OF GOD
1. Ps. 103:8-14.
2. By Roy L. Smith. *The Christian Advocate*, Apr. 7, 1941. Used by permission.

SERVICE 14. IN QUIETNESS AND IN CONFIDENCE
1. Deut. 33:25, 27, 29; Ps. 62:1, 5-6, 8; Isa. 26:3-4; 30:15; Ps. 46:10; Matt. 14:23; Mark 6:31.
2. Copyright 1929 by Chester L. Bower. From *Handy*, by permission.

NOTES

SERVICE 15. VALUE OF THE INDIVIDUAL
1. "To Althea, from Prison."
2. II Cor. 3:17; Gal. 5:1, 22-23, 25; John 8:32.
3. By Induk Pahk. Copyright 1950 by Guideposts Associates, Inc. Published at Carmel, New York, and used by permission.
4. Walter Rauschenbusch, *Prayers of the Social Awakening*, pp. 144-45. The Pilgrim Press. Used by permission.

SERVICE 16. HE WHO WOULD VALIANT BE
1. Isa. 26:3-4.
2. *Julius Caesar.* Act II, scene 2.
3. Prov. 24:10; Deut. 31:6; Ps. 27:14.
4. By Paul K. McAfee. *Classmate,* Oct. 26, 1947. Used by permission.
5. Used by permission.

SERVICE 17. MESSENGERS OF GOOD NEWS
1. Mark 4:35-41; Luke 17:5.
2. "Thy Strength and My Day." Copyright. Reproduced by permission. Evangelical Publishers, Toronto, Canada.

SERVICE 18. DISPLACED PERSONS FIND A FRIEND
1. Ps. 100:4-5.
2. Ps. 1.
3. "The Meaning of Worship." Used by permission of the author and *World Call.*
4. By Robert Montgomery. *Guideposts,* Feb., 1954. Copyright 1954 by Guideposts Associates, Inc. Used by permission.

SERVICE 19. BROTHER TO THE POOR
1. Mic. 6:6, 8.
2. Matt. 26:6-11; Luke 6:20; Matt. 25:40; Mark 8:34-35.
3. By Umphrey Lee. *Cargo,* July 21, 1940. Used by permission.
4. "Christ Is Life." Used by permission of the Christian Board of Publication.
5. "Lines Composed a Few Miles Above Tintern Abbey."
6. From "Andrew Rykman's Prayer."

SERVICE 20. BUILDING A FRIENDLY WORLD
1. Ps. 24:3-5.
2. Matt. 10:1, 5-8, 16-17, 24, 33, 37-39; John 1:4; 10:10.
3. From "A Country Town."
4. By Ina Corinne Brown. *Torchbearer,* Aug. 25, 1935. Used by permission.
5. Charles M. Crowe, *Sermons on the Parables of Jesus,* pp. 9-10. Copyright 1953 by Pierce and Washabaugh. Used by permission of Abingdon Press.
6. "The Challenge," from *Poems for the Great Days.* Copyright 1948 by Stone and Pierce. Used by permission of Abingdon Press.

SERVICE 21. SERVING THE OUTPOSTS
1. Pss. 24:1; 67:3.
2. Isa. 60:3; II Cor. 4:6; John 10:16; Luke 13:29; Matt. 9:37-38; 28:18-20.
3. "Invocation." Used by permission.
4. From *Paradise Lost,* Bk. I.
5. "Christ in Introspect."
6. By Bennie Bengtson. *Classmate,* Jan. 14, 1951. Used by permission.
7. *More Hilltop Verses and Prayers,* p. 18. Copyright 1949 by Pierce and Smith. Used by permission of Abingdon Press.

SERVICE 22. MINISTERING TO THE SICK
1. Luke 8:43-48; Matt. 11:28.
2. Attributed to Elizabeth Barrett Browning, but not found in her writings.
3. By Helen G. Jefferson. *Classmate*, May 20, 1951. Used by permission.

SERVICE 23. THANKS BE TO GOD
1. Deut. 8:1, 7-11, 17-18.
2. Used by permission.
3. By Douglas MacArthur. *Guideposts*, Nov., 1953. Used by permission.
4. Georgia Harkness, *Be Still and Know*, p. 72. Copyright 1953 by Pierce and Washabaugh. Used by permission of Abingdon Press.

SERVICE 24. THE SHEPHERD SPEAKS
1. "As with Gladness Men of Old."
2. Luke 2:8-20.
3. Used by permission.

SERVICE 25. MINISTERING TO LEPERS
1. Matt. 25:34-40.
2. By E. Jerry Walker. *Highroad*, July, 1948. Used by permission.
3. Send contribution to the American Leprosy Missions, Inc., 156 Fifth Ave., New York 10, N. Y.

SERVICE 26. YE ARE MY WITNESSES
1. From A. J. William Myers, *Enriching Worship*, p. 277.
2. Luke 4:14-19; Acts 1:8; Jas. 1:17.
3. Used by permission.
4. By Margaret Slattery. *He Took It Upon Himself*, pp. 65-71. Used by permission of The Pilgrim Press.

SERVICE 27. THE LIVING WORD
1. Ps. 119:9-16, 33-34, 105; II Tim. 3:16-17.
2. "Beautiful Bible." Used by permission.
3. By Margaret Sinker. From *Every Land*. Used by permission of the British and Foreign Bible Society.
4. *The Monastery*, Bk. I, ch. xii.
5. *Be Still and Know*, p. 94. Copyright 1953 by Pierce and Washabaugh. Used by permission of Abingdon Press.

SERVICE 28. FINDING GOD THROUGH BEAUTY
1. Ps. 100:2, 5.
2. Ps. 96:1, 4; Eccl. 3:11; Ps. 96:6, 9, 11-13.
3. By Rebecca Rice. From *Exploring God's Out-of-Doors*. Copyright, The Pilgrim Press. Used by permission.
4. "The World One Neighborhood." From *As Children Worship*, by Jeanette E. Perkins. Copyright, The Pilgrim Press. Used by permission.

SERVICE 29. FINDING GOD THROUGH FAITHFULNESS
1. Pss. 27:1; 95:3.
2. Matt. 25:21; Luke 16:10; Rev. 2:10.
3. By Jeanette E. Perkins. From *Children's Worship in the Church School*. Used by permission of Harper & Bros.

SERVICE 30. FINDING GOD THROUGH PERSISTENCE
1. I Cor. 3:16; Rom. 8:14.

NOTES

2. Mark 10:46-52.
3. By Mary Stewart. From *Tell Me a Story of Jesus.* By permission of Fleming H. Revell Co.
4. "Religion and Doctrine."

SERVICE 31. FINDING GOD THROUGH PRAYER
1. Matt. 7:7-8.
2. Matt. 17:14-21; 21:22; Luke 17:5.
3. *"Ultima Veritas."*
4. By Ethel Tilley. *International Journal of Religious Education,* Mar., 1941. Used by permission.

SERVICE 32. FINDING GOD THROUGH LOVE
1. Pss. 118:24; 100:4.
2. I Cor. 13:1-8, 13. From Edgar J. Goodspeed, *The New Testament: An American Translation.* Used by permission of the University of Chicago Press.
3. By Harding W. Gaylord. From *Children's Religion.* Used by permission of The Pilgrim Press.
4. From *Poems of Power.* Used by permission of Rand, McNally & Co.

SERVICE 33. FINDING GOD THROUGH JESUS
1. "The Way, the Truth, and the Life."
2. Luke 19:1-6; John 12:20-21.
3. From *Church School,* Mar., 1941. Used by permission.
4. By Ethel Tilley. *International Journal of Religious Education,* Mar., 1941. Used by permission.
5. From *New Worship and Song,* by Winchester and Conant. Used by permission of The Pilgrim Press.
6. Ps. 139:7-10, 17-18; Acts 17:24-25, 27-28; John 14:9-10; Matt. 23:11.

SERVICE 34. LIVING AGAIN
1. Luke 24:13-35. From Edgar J. Goodspeed, *The New Testament: An American Translation.* Used by permission of the University of Chicago Press.
2. By Charlotte Brown. From *Primary Lesson Stories.* Used by permission of the Christian Board of Publication.
3. "The Butterfly."

SERVICE 35. FOLLOWING JESUS
1. John 4:23-24.
2. Matt. 4:18-22; Luke 9:57-62.
3. By Mary Stewart. From *Tell Me a Story of Jesus.* Used by permission of Fleming H. Revell Co.

SERVICE 36. LIVING AS BROTHERS
1. Prov. 18:24; 17:17; John 15:12-15.
2. By John Ladd. *Boys Today,* Nov. 16, 1947. Used by permission.

SERVICE 37. IN APPRECIATION OF MOTHERS
1. Prov. 31:10-12, 20-21, 23, 25-29; Exod. 20:12.
2. By Archer Wallace. From *Mothers of Famous Men,* published by Harper & Bros. Copyright 1931. Used by permission.
3. "Remembrance." From *Be Slow to Falter.* Used by permission of The Kaleidograph Press and the author.

SOURCES FOR HYMNS

CODE: The letter refers to the hymnal, and the number to the page on which the hymn is found in the hymnal.

A... New Hymnal for American Youth

B... Broadman Hymnal (Southern Baptist Convention)

C... Common Service Book (Lutheran)

D... Church School Hymnal for Youth (Presbyterian U.S.A.)

E... American Student Hymnal

F... Hymnal for Youth (Presbyterian U.S.A.)

G... Abingdon Song Book (Methodist)

H.. Presbyterian Hymnal (U.S.)

I... Worship and Praise

J... Hymnal for Christian Worship (Presbyterian U.S.)

M... Methodist Hymnal

N... Pilgrim Hymnal (Congregational, now United Church of Christ)

P... The Hymnal (Presbyterian U.S.A.)

R... Devotional Hymns

S Great Songs of the Church (Disciples)

T.... New Baptist Hymnal (Southern Baptist Convention)

W.. Christian Worship (Northern Baptist Convention and Disciples)

A Charge to Keep I Have
B—157; C—376; E—379; G—186; H—289; I—196; J—161; M—287; N—500; R—240; T—203; W—373

A Glory Gilds the Sacred Page
C—170; M—388; R—107; T—74

Angels, from the Realms of Glory
B—145; C—27; D—86; F—69; H—49; J—71; M—87

Are Ye Able
B—396; E—174; G—184; J—189; M—268

At Length There Dawns the Glorious Day
E—256; F—288; H—335; J—251; M-469

Awake, Awake to Love and Work
M—455; W—171

Awake, My Soul, Stretch Every Nerve
A—195; C—380; E—165; H—278; J—197; M—359; S—347

Behold a Sower! from Afar
M—391

Beneath the Cross of Jesus
A—120; B—234; D—186; E—105; F—173; G—39; H—95; I—176; J—91; M—144; N—125; P—162; R—242; S—351; T—110; W—235

Be Still, My Soul
B—479; C—181; G—121; J—215; M—73

243

Be Strong!
A—182; D—214; E—185; F—229;
M—300; N—253; P—488

Book of Books
A—69; E—337; M—390

Break Thou the Bread of Life
A—71; B—192; D—157; E—101;
F—133; G—235; H—381; I—243;
J—132; M—387; N—412; P—216;
R—199; S—354; T—81; W—461

Breathe on Me, Breath of God
A—61; B—417; D—152; E—98;
F—130; G—76; J—123; M—180;
N—201; P—213; T—146

Christ for the World We Sing
B—267; C—218; D—319; E—355;
F—250; H—404; J—266; M—481

Christ the Lord Is Risen Today
A—129; B—33; C—111; D—126;
E—331; F—104; T—118; M—154

Come, Thou Almighty King
A—38; B—32; C—164; D—24;
E—354; F—33; H—52; I—1;
J—122; M—2; P—10; S—10; T—1; W—9

Come unto Me
D—165; M—350; T—165

Come, Ye Faithful, Raise the Strain
C—108; F—108; J—101; M—151;
N—134; P—168; S—363; W—242

Come, Ye Thankful People, Come
A—322; B—136; C—484; D—360;
F—18; G—27; H—483; J—287;
M—545; S—364

Courage, Brother! Do Not Stumble
D—206; M—298

Dare to Be Brave
B—320; D—202; F—223; G—188

Dear Lord and Father of Mankind
A—152; B—401; D—236; E—80;
F—150; G—137; H—242; I—238;
J—202; M—342; N—224; P—302;
R—280; S—366; T—63; W—411

Dear Master, in Whose Life I See
M—376; N—265; P—507; W—318

Draw Thou My Soul, O Christ
A—149; D—234; E—370; F—164;
G—151; H—250; J—160; M—297;
N—232; W—299

Eternal God, Whose Power Upholds
J—276; M—476; S—225

Fairest Lord Jesus
A—137; B—211; D—136; E—58;
F—119; G—55; H—72; J—113;
M—111; S—369

Father in Heaven, Who Lovest All
A—175; D—227; E—178; M—294

Fight the Good Fight
A—207; B—270; D—212; E—158;
F—288; G—204; H—299; J—201;
M—286; N—255; P—270; R—261;
S—375; T—200; W—376

For the Beauty of the Earth
A—46; B—309; C—292; D—55;
E—357; F—42; H—71; I—100;
J—167; M—18; P—168; S—16;
T—16; W—105

From All the Dark Places
B—125; M—483

God of Grace and God of Glory
F—236; G—115; M—279; W—378

God of Our Boyhood, Whom We
Yield
D—226; E—179

God, That Madest Earth and Heaven
  A—58; C—468; D—20; E—306;
  F—24; G—21; J—30; M—43

God, Who Touchest Earth with
  Beauty
  A—223; D—222; F—178; G—152;
  J—304

Go Forth to Life
  M—296; N—474; W—319

Go, Labor On!
  F—249; H—285; J—198; M—292;
  N—330; P—376; S—381; T—206;
  W—473

Hark! the Herald Angels Sing
  A—77; B—142; C—25; D—80;
  E—361; F—68; G—28; H—59;
  J—66; M—86; S—391

Hark, the Voice of Jesus Calling
  B—407; D—162; G—185; H—283;
  M—288; S—392

Heralds of Christ
  A—258; F—235; J—264; M—482;
  T—407

He Who Would Valiant Be
  A—204; E—169; F—233; J—193;
  M—265; N—250; P—276; W—364

Holy Spirit, Truth Divine
  A—60; D—146; E—100; F—128;
  I—319; M—173; P—496; W—20

How Beauteous Were the Marks Divine
  M—116

I Know Not What the Future Hath
  A—332; M—517

In Christ There Is No East or West
  A—299; D—314; E—273; F—243;
  G—221; H—375; J—234; M—507

It Came upon the Midnight Clear
  A—78; B—141; C—29; D—76;
  E—245; F—64; H—58; J—73;
  M—92; N—73; P—127; R—56;
  S—416; T—85; W—191

I Would Be True
  A—177; D—225; I—158; J—361;
  P—469; S—119; W—184

Jesus Calls Us
  A—144; B—159; D—168; E—106;
  F—198; G—187; H—284; J—144;
  M—233; S—420

Jesus Shall Reign
  A—305; B—150; C—219; D—31;
  E—380; F—248; G—220; H—392;
  J—267; M—479; S—425

Jesus, Thou Divine Companion
  A—191; D—286; E-85; F—200;
  J—243

Jesus, Thou Joy of Loving Hearts
  C—354; F—147; G—57; H—67;
  J—206; M—345; S—427

Joy Dawned Again on Easter Day
  M—157

Joyful, Joyful, We Adore Thee
  A—43; D—48; E—49; F—6; G—3;
  H—25; J—5; M—12

Joy to the World!
  A—76; B—98; C—34; D—77;
  E—360; F—65; H—122; I—10;
  J—190; M—89; P—78; S—29;
  T—57; W—217

Just as I Am, Thine Own to Be
  A—145; B—411; D—181; E—136;
  F—171; G—143; H—280; J—310;
  S—131

Lead On, O King Eternal
  A—199; B—210; D—208; E—177;
  F—226; H—371; I—51; J—363;

M—278; P—251; S—210; T—301; W-21

Let All the World in Every Corner Sing
C—287; F—16; H—9; M—8; W—240

Lift Up Our Hearts
A—295; E—176; G—180; J—253; M—472; N—154; P—405; W—372

Lord of All Being, Throned Afar
A—33; E—1; F—56; H—87; M—62; S—18

Lord, Speak to Me
A—251; C—212; D—293; E—216; F—196; G—175; H—279; I—222; J—248; M—460; N—339; P—399; S—438; T—211; W—470

Love Divine, All Loves Excelling
A—67; B—19; C—276; D—231; E—356; F—153; G—111; H—21; I—2; J—176; M—372; N—270; P—308; R—81; S—440; T—183; W—379

Make Me a Captive, Lord
G—112; J—314; M—367

March On, O Soul, with Strength
A—184; D—220; E—110; F—234; G—192; H—300; M—264; N—247; P—273; W—359

Master, No Offering
A—252; D—277; E—229; H—277; J—246; M—464

Master, Speak! Thy Servant Heareth
G—142; M—221

'Mid All the Traffic of the Ways
A—159; F—165; G—165; H—237; J—204; M—341; P—322

More Love to Thee, O Christ
B—218; D—200; F—191; G—110; H—224; I—240; J—168; M—364; N—146; P—315; R—283; S—148; T—195; W—390

My God, I Thank Thee
A—51; B—49; D—361; E—204; F—11; H—73; I—122; M—9; P—11.

My Jesus, as Thou Wilt
B—178; C—395; F—172; H—247; J—214; M—330; N—494; P—280; S—446; T—222; W—408

My Soul, Be on Thy Guard
B—247; G—272; E—378; H—295; I—245; M—277; N—256; R—279; T—177; W—300

My Times Are in Thy Hand
H—198; M—322

Now in the Days of Youth
A—146; F—169; G—207; J—308; N—477; W—300

Now Thank We All Our God
A—325; C—283; D—358; E—303; F—17; J—289; M—7; S—560

O Brother Man, Fold to Thy Heart
A—244; B—403; D—283; E—258; F—260; J—254; M—466

O for a Closer Walk with God
T—256; M—228

O for a Heart to Praise My God
C—264; G—176; H—257; J—177; M—370; S—456

O for a Thousand Tongues to Sing
B—2; C—135; G—67; H—68; J—112; M—162; S—457

O Gracious Father of Mankind
A—66; D—72; E—34; H—85; M—305; S—163

O Jesus, I Have Promised
A—196; B—187; D—187; E—369;
F—174; H—253; I—189; J—165;
M—226; N—196; P—268; R—239;
S—462; T—193; W—308

O Jesus, Master, When Today
E—212; H—278; M—470; N—307;
W—517

O Jesus, Prince of Life and Truth
D—224; F—182; N—257

O Little Town of Bethlehem
A—82; B—144; C—31; D—78;
E—330; F—66; G—31; H—55; I—
281; J—64; M—100; N—74; P—
121; R—57; S—464; T—274; W—
306

O Lord of Heaven and Earth and Sea
A—56; C—385; G—200; H—481;
M—541; S—465

O Love that Wilt Not Let Me Go
A—154; B—231; C—343; D—196;
E—37; I—38; M—318; P—289;
S—130; T—26; W—211

O Master, Let Me Walk with Thee
A—197; B—202; D—182; E—214;
F—166; G—116; H—271; I—263;
J—245; M—259; N—291; P—364;
R—19; S—468; T—274; W—306

O Master of the Waking World
G—277; M—480

O Master Workman of the Race
A—98; D—106; E—74; F—85;
G—59; H—86; M—118; N—328;
P—140; R—62; W—210

O Perfect Love
G—415; H—484; J—296; P—484;
M—431; N—430

O Son of Man, Thou Madest Known
A—188; D—207; E—175; F—197;
G—61; M—121

O Thou Who Camest from Above
M—344

O Thou Whose Feet Have Climbed
D—272; E—342; F—263; H—329;
J—315; M—559

O Word of God Incarnate
A—68; B—75; C—169; D—155;
E—364; F—132; H—134; J—131;
M—386; N—421; P—215; T—75;
W—434

O Worship the King
A—36; B—2; C—294; D—29;
E—59; H—2; I—15; M—4; P—5;
T—7; W—7.

O Young and Fearless Prophet
M—266; S—213; W—179

O Zion, Haste, Thy Mission High
Fulfilling
A—306; B—151; C—224; D—308;
E—270; F—240; G—222; H—395;
J—257; M—475; N—372; P—382;
R—131; S—474; T—264; W—529

Rejoice, Ye Pure in Heart
A—27; B—285; D—139; E—199;
F—124; G—9; J—209; M—358;
N—476; P—297; R—181; S—483;
T—47; W—418

Rise Up, O Men of God
A—254; B—186; D—288; E—224;
F—258; G—203; H—274; J—252;
M—267; N—313; P—401; W—374

Saviour, Like a Shepherd Lead Us
B—13; C—656; H—323; I—12;
J—218; M—337; N—492; P—458;
R—157; S—490; T—377; W—401

Shepherd of Tender Youth
A—138; C—282; E—353; F—121;
H—319; M—429; S—493

Sing with All the Sons of Glory
M—150

Spirit of God, Descend upon My
Heart
A—62; E—99; F—127; G—75;
H—125; J—125; M—179

Spirit of Life, in This New Dawn
A—63; E—22; G—74; M—178

Still, Still with Thee
A—6; E—20; F—53; H—454;
J—18; M—40

Take My Life, and Let It Be
A—198; B—174; C—382; D—221;
E—142; F—175; G—131; H—268;
I—83; J—166; M—225; N—195;
P—242; R—244; S—501; T—329;
W—296

The Day of Resurrection
A—127; C—115; D—128; E—301;
F—102; H—106; J—99; M—159

The King of Love My Shepherd Is
A—50; C—345; D—59; E—35;
F—57; G—108; H—80; J—51; M—
353

The Light of God Is Falling
D—279; F—254; G—213; H—376;
J—250; M—468

The Morning Light Is Breaking
B—12; C—230; D—307; F—239;
H—406; J—260; M—487; N—364;
P—389; R—132; T—271; W—524

There's a Wideness in God's Mercy
A—55; B—182; C—256; D—63;
E—39; F—50; H—18; J—54; M—
76

The Voice of God Is Calling
D—284; E—235; F—202; G—205;
M—454; N—337; W—490

This Is My Father's World
A—39; D—52; E—51; H—70; I—
226; M—72; P—464; T—332; W—
106; S—11

Thou Art the Way
D—271; F—214; H—81; J—167;
M—332; S—516

Thou My Everlasting Portion
B—223; M—235

True-hearted, Whole-hearted, Faithful
and Loyal
F—177; M—255; I—28; R—226;
S—278; T—383

We Bear the Strain of Earthly Care
A—194; E—86; D—143; H—369;
J—119; M—471

We May Not Climb the Heavenly
Steeps
M—120; N—148; R—268; T—178

We Thank Thee, Lord, Thy Paths
A—249; B—301; D—287; E—223;
F—203; G—206; M—458; P—367;
W—495

We've a Story to Tell to the Nations
A—302; B—379; D—306; F—238;
G—215; I—146; J—261; M—501;
N—374; R—124; T—261; W—530

When I Survey the Wondrous Cross
A—123; B—191; C—97; D—118;
E—376; F—96; G—44; H—88; I—
215; J—97; M—148; N—122; P—
152; R—247; S—532; T—108;
W—228

When Morning Gilds the Skies
A—2; B—7; C—310; D—1; E—
201; F—19; G—20; H—453; J—21;
M—31; S—533

Where Cross the Crowded Ways of Life
A—265; B—405; D—268; E—60; F—253; G—214; H—330; I—230; J—268; M—465; N—140; P—410; R—24; S—536; T—276; W—519

While Shepherds Watched Their Flocks by Night
B—147; C—28; D—79; F—67; G—32; H—50; I—282; J—80; M—88; N—83; P—120; R—58; S—537; T—89; W—185

Ye Fair Green Hills of Galilee
A—102; D—100; J—83; M—124

Ye Servants of God
D—140; E—385; F—125; J—106; M—169

SELECTED BIBLIOGRAPHY

WORSHIP FOR YOUTH

Applegarth, Margaret T. *Restoring Worship*. New York: Harper & Bros., 1949.
——. *Right Here, Right Now!* New York: Harper & Bros., 1950.
Bailey, Albert Edward. *The Gospel in Art*. Boston: Pilgrim Press, 1916.
——. *The Arts and Religion*. New York: The Macmillan Co., 1944.
——. *The Gospel in Hymns*. New York: Charles Scribner's Sons, 1952.
Blackwood, Andrew W. *The Fine Art of Public Worship*. New York and Nashville: Abingdon Press, 1939.
Bowie, W. Russell. *The Story of the Bible*. New York and Nashville: Abingdon Press, 1934.
——. *The Story of Jesus*. New York: Charles Scribner's Sons, 1937.
——. *The Bible Story for Boys and Girls: New Testament*. New York and Nashville: Abingdon Press, 1951.
——. *The Bible Story for Boys and Girls: Old Testament*. New York and Nashville: Abingdon Press, 1952.
Cavert, Walter Dudley. *Remember Now*. New York and Nashville: Abingdon Press, 1944.
Cushman, Ralph S. *Practicing the Presence*. New York and Nashville: Abingdon Press, 1936.
Fisk, Margaret Palmer. *The Art of the Rhythmic Choir*. New York: Harper & Bros., 1950.
Garrett, Constance, *Think on These Things*. New York and Nashville: Abingdon Press, 1948.
Gilbert, Clark. *Devotions for Youth*. New York: Association Press, 1943.
Harkness, Georgia. *Be Still and Know*. New York and Nashville: Abingdon Press, 1953.
Harrell, Costen J. *Walking with God*. New York and Nashville: Abingdon Press, 1928.
Jones, Ilion T. *A Historical Approach to Evangelical Worship*. New York and Nashville: Abingdon Press, 1954.
Jones, E. Stanley. *Abundant Living*. New York and Nashville: Abingdon Press, 1942.
——. *The Christ of the American Road*. New York and Nashville: Abingdon Press, 1944.
——. *How to Pray*. New York and Nashville: Abingdon Press, 1951.
——. *Victorious Living*. New York and Nashville: Abingdon Press, 1936.
——. *The Way*. New York and Nashville: Abingdon Press, 1946.
——. *The Way to Power and Poise*. New York and Nashville: Abingdon Press, 1949.
Jones, Rufus M. *New Eyes for Invisibles*. New York: The Macmillan Co., 1943.
Lotz, Henry P. *The Quest for God Through Understanding*. St. Louis: Christian Board of Publication (Bethany Press), 1937.
——. *The Quest for God Through Worship*. St. Louis: Christian Board of Publication (Bethany Press), 1934.
Luccock, Halford E., and Brentano, Frances. *The Questing Spirit*. New York: Coward-McCann, 1947.
McDormand, Thomas Bruce. *The Art of Building Worship Services*. Nashville: The Broadman Press, 1942.
McIlwain, Orene. *Worship God*. Richmond: John Knox Press, 1947.
Mattoon, Laura and Bragdon, Helen. *Services for the Open*. New York: Association Press, 1947.
Myers, A. J. William, ed. *Enriching Worship*. New York: Harper & Bros., 1949.

251

Page, Kirby. *Living Creatively.* New York: Farrar & Rinehart, 1932.
———, *Living Triumphantly.* New York: Farrar & Rinehart, 1934.
Palmer, Albert W., ed. *Aids to Worship.* New York: The Macmillan Co., 1944.
Paulsen, Irwin G. *The Church School and Worship.* New York: Abingdon Press, 1940.
Pease, Dorothy Wells, ed. *Altars Under the Sky.* New York and Nashville: Abingdon Press, 1942.
Petty, Carl Wallace. *The Evening Altar.* New York and Nashville: Abingdon Press, 1940.
Phillips, D. B., Nixon, L. M., Howes, E. B., eds. *The Choice Is Always Ours.* New York: Richard R. Smith, 1948.
Porter, David. *Worship Resources for Youth.* New York: Association Press. 1948.
Quimby, Chester W. *The Jubilant Year.* New York and Nashville: Abingdon Press, 1946.
Reid, Albert C. *Resources for Worship.* New York and Nashville: Abingdon Press, 1949.
Schmitz, Charles H. *Windows Toward God.* New York and Nashville: Abingdon Press,
Smith, H. Augustine. *Lyric Religion.* New York: D. Appleton-Century Co., 1931.
Smith, Roy L. *Making a Go of Life.* New York and Nashville: Abingdon Press, 1948.
Snowden, Rita F. *While the Candle Burns.* London: Epworth Press, 1942.
Stuber, Stanley, ed. *Treasury of the Christian Faith.* New York: Association Press, 1949.
Watson, Lillian Eichler. *Light from Many Lamps.* New York: Simon & Schuster, 1951.

POEMS

Armstrong, O. V. and Helen, eds. *Prayer Poems.* New York and Nashville: Abingdon Press. 1942.
Bever, Patricia. *Stepping Stones of the Spirit.* New York: Association Press. 1951.
Bruner, Margaret E. *Be Slow to Falter.* Dallas: Kaleidograph Press, 1941.
———. *In Thoughtful Mood.* Dallas: Kaleidograph Press, 1937.
———. *Midstream.* Dallas: Kaleidograph Press, 1940.
———. *Mysteries of Earth.* Dallas: Kaleidograph Press, 1934.
———. *The Constant Heart.* Dallas: Kaleidograph Press, 1952.
———. *The Hill Road.* Dallas: Kaleidograph Press, 1932.
Clark, Thomas Curtis, ed. *Poems of Justice.* Chicago: Willett, Clark & Co., 1929.
———. *The Golden Book of Religious Verse.* New York: Garden City Publishing Co., 1941.
Clark, Thomas and Hazel, eds. *Christ in Poetry.* New York: Association Press, 1952.
Clark, Thomas Curtis and Robert Earle, eds. *Poems for the Great Days.* New York and Nashville: Abingdon Press, 1948.
Clark, Thomas Curtis and Gillespie, Esther A., eds. *1000 Quotable Poems.* Chicago: Willet, Clark & Co., 1937.
Cushman, Ralph S. *Hilltop Verses and Prayers.* New York and Nashville: Abingdon Press, 1945.
———. *Practicing the Presence.* New York and Nashville: Abingdon Press, 1936.
Cushman, Ralph S. and Robert E. *More Hilltop Verses and Prayers.* New York and Nashville: Abingdon Press, 1949.
Gibran, Kahlil. *The Prophet.* New York: Alfred A. Knopf, 1923.
Harkness, Georgia. *Be Still and Know.* New York and Nashville: Abingdon Press, 1953.
———. *The Glory of God.* New York and Nashville: Abingdon Press, 1943.
Hill, Caroline. *The World's Great Religious Poetry.* New York: The Macmillan Co., 1923.
Kagawa, Toyohiko. *Songs from the Slums.* New York and Nashville: Abingdon Press, 1935.
Kagawa, Toyohiko and Cole, Franklin. *The Willow and Bridge.* New York: Association Press, 1947.

SELECTED BIBLIOGRAPHY

Markham, Edwin. *Selected Poems.* New York: Harper & Bros., 1950.

Morgan, Angela. *Selected Poems.* New York: Dodd, Mead & Co., 1926.

Morrison, James Dalton. *Masterpieces of Religious Verse.* New York: Harper & Bros., 1948.

Mudge, James, ed. *Poems with Power to Strengthen the Soul.* New York and Nashville: Abingdon Press, 1907.

Oxenham, John. *Gentlemen—the King!* Boston: Pilgrim Press, 1928.

————. *Hearts Courageous.* New York: Methodist Book Concern, 1918.

————. *Selected Poems.* New York: Harper & Bros., 1948.

Piety, Chauncey R. *General Sam Houston.* Emory University: Banner Press, 1943.

Tagore, Rabindranath. *Collected Poems and Plays.* New York: The Macmillan Co., 1946.

van Dyke, Henry. *Collected Poems.* New York: Charles Scribner's Sons, 1920.

STORIES

Bartlett, Robert M. *They Dare to Believe.* New York: Association Press, 1952.

————. *They Dared to Live.* New York: Association Press, 1937.

————. *They Did Something About It.* New York: Association Press, 1939.

————. *They Work for Tomorrow.* New York: Association Press, 1943.

Bolton, Sarah. *Famous Men of Science.* New York: Thomas Y. Crowell Co., 1941.

————. *Lives of Girls Who Became Famous.* New York: Thomas Y. Crowell Co., 1930.

————. *Lives of Poor Boys Who Became Famous.* New York: Thomas Y. Crowell Co., 1947.

Cather, K. Dunlap. *Boyhood Stories of Famous Men.* New York: D. Appleton-Century Co., 1916.

————. *Girlhood Stories of Famous Women.* New York: D. Appleton-Century Co., 1924.

Cheley, Frank H. *Stories for Talks to Boys.* New York: Association Press, 1932.

Eddy, Sherwood. *Pathfinders of the World Missionary Crusade.* New York and Nashville: Abingdon Press, 1945.

Erdman, Mabel, ed. *Answering District Calls.* New York: Association Press, 1942.

Gill, D. M. and Pullen, A. M. *Adventures in Service.* New York: Missionary Education Movement, 1938.

————. *Victories of Peace.* London: Student Christian Movement Press.

Hume, Edward H. *Doctors Courageous.* New York: Harper & Bros., 1950.

Lantz, J. Edward, ed. *Best Religious Stories.* New York: Association Press. 1948.

————. *Stories of Christian Living.* New York: Association Press, 1950.

Lotz, Philip Henry, ed. *The Altar Hour.* St. Louis: Christian Board of Education, 1941.

————. "Creative Personalities," I-III, V-VII: *Vocations and Professions, Women Leaders, Founders of Christian Movements, Rising Above Color, Distinguished American Jews, Unused Alibis.* New York: Association Press, 1940-45.

Malone, Ted. *Ted Malone's Favorite Stories.* New York: Doubleday & Co., 1950.

Matthews, Basil. *Book of Missionary Heroes.* New York: George H. Doran Co., 1922.

Oxenham, John. *The Hidden Years.* New York: Longmans, Green & Co., 1925.

Parkman, Mary R. *Heroines of Service.* New York: D. Appleton-Century Co., 1925.

Sawyers, Mott R. *Famous Friends of God.* New York: Fleming H. Revell Co., 1933.

Slattery, Margaret. *He Took It Upon Himself.* Boston: Pilgrim Press.

Snowden, Rita F. *Safety Last.* London: Epworth Press, 1946.

————. *The Lark in the Sky.* London: Epworth Press, 1946.

————. *Never a Dull Moment.* Presbyterian Bookroom, n.d.

Stewart, Mary. *The Shepherd of Us All.* New York: Fleming H. Revell Co.

Stidger, William L. *The Human Side of Greatness.* New York: Harper & Bros., 1940.

————. *There Are Sermons in Stories.* New York and Nashville: Abingdon Press, 1942.

————. *More Sermons in Stories.* New York and Nashville: Abingdon Press, 1944.

Turnbull, Agnes S. *Far Above Rubies*. New York: Fleming H. Revell Co., 1926.
Wallace, Archer. *Overcoming Handicaps*. New York: Harper & Bros., 1927.
————. *Stories of Grit*. New York: Harper & Bros., 1930.
————. *In Spite of All*. New York and Nashville: Abingdon Press, 1944.
————. *The Field of Honor*. New York and Nashville: Abingdon Press, 1949.
————. *100 Stories for Boys*. New York and Nashville: Abingdon Press, 1947.

PRAYER

Abernethy, Jean Beaven. *Meditations for Women*. New York and Nashville: Abingdon Press, 1947.
Andrewes, Lancelot. *The Private Devotions of Lancelot Andrewes*. New York and Nashville: Abingdon Press, 1950.
Bowie, W. Russell. *Lift Up Your Hearts*. New York: The Macmillan Co., 1939.
Buttrick, George A. *Prayer*. New York and Nashville: Abingdon Press, 1942.
Campbell, Donald J. *The Adventure of Prayer*. New York and Nashville: Abingdon Press, 1949.
Clough, William A. *Father, We Thank Thee*. New York and Nashville: Abingdon Press, 1949.
Cushman, Ralph S. *Hilltop Verses and Prayers*. New York and Nashville: Abingdon Press, 1945.
Cushman, Ralph S. and Robert Earle. *More Hilltop Verses and Prayers*. New York and Nashville: Abingdon Press, 1949.
Edmonds, Henry M. *Beginning the Day*. New York and Nashville: Abingdon Press, 1951.
Finegan, Jack. *Book of Student Prayers*. New York: Association Press, 1946.
Fox, Selina F. *A Chain of Prayers Across the Ages*. New York: E. P. Dutton & Co., 1943.
Gill, Frederick C. *John Wesley's Prayers*. New York and Nashville: Abingdon Press, 1951.
Harkness, Georgia. *Be Still and Know*. New York and Nashville: Abingdon Press, 1953.
————. *The Glory of God*. New York and Nashville: Abingdon Press, 1943.
————. *Prayer and the Common Life*. New York and Nashville: Abingdon Press, 1948.
————. *Through Christ Our Lord*. New York and Nashville: Abingdon Press, 1950.
Harlow, Ralph. *Prayers for Times Like These*. New York: Association Press, 1942.
Hayward, Percy R. *Young People's Prayers*. New York: Association Press, 1945.
Hoyland, J. S. *A Book of Prayers for Youth*. New York: Association Press, 1939.
Lester, Muriel. *Ways of Praying*. London: Independent Press, 1931.
Luccock, Halford and Brentano, Frances. *The Questing Spirit*. New York: Coward-McCann, 1947.
Morton, Richard K. *A Book of Prayers for Young People*. New York and Nashville: Abingdon Press, 1935.
Murrell, Gladys C. *Channels of Devotion*. New York and Nashville: Abingdon Press, 1948.
————. *Glimpses of Grace*. New York and Nashville: Abingdon Press, 1941.
————. *Patterns for Devotion*. New York and Nashville: Abingdon Press, 1950.
Newton, Joseph Fort. *Everyday Religious Living*. New York and Nashville: Abingdon Press, 1951.
Phillips, D. B., Nixon, L. M., Howes, E. B., *et al. The Choice Is Always Ours*. New York: Richard R. Smith, 1948.
Potts, J. Manning, ed. *Prayers of the Early Church*. Nashville: Upper Room, 1954.
Rauschenbusch, Walter. *Prayers of the Social Awakening*. Boston: Pilgrim Press, 1925.
Snowden, Rita F. *Today*. London: Epworth Press, 1949.
Tittle, Ernest Fremont. *A Book of Pastoral Prayers*. New York and Nashville: Abingdon Press, 1951.
Wyon, Olive. *The School of Prayer*. Philadelphia: Westminster Press, 1944.
The Kingdom, the Power, and the Glory. New York: Oxford University Press, 1933.

INDEX OF STORIES AND SUBJECTS

#965